Beyond the Enlightenment:
Historians and Folklore in
Nineteenth Century France

INDIANA UNIVERSITY PUBLICATIONS
FOLKLORE INSTITUTE MONOGRAPH SERIES
Volume 27

Editor

Richard M. Dorson

Publications Committee

Robert J. Adams   Felix J. Oinas
Linda Dégh   W. Edson Richmond
Henry H. Glassie   Warren E. Roberts

Editorial Assistant

H. Michael Simmons

The Indiana University Folklore Series was founded in 1939 for the publication of occasional papers and monographs.

Beyond the Enlightenment

Historians and Folklore in

Nineteenth Century France

Charles Rearick

INDIANA UNIVERSITY PRESS
Bloomington and London

Published in Canada by Fitzhenry & Whiteside Limited,
Don Mills, Ontario

Manufactured in the United States of America

Library of Congress Cataloging in Publication Data

Rearick, Charles, 1942–
    Beyond the Enlightenment.

    (Indiana University publications. Folklore Institute
monograph series, v. 27)
    Bibliography: p. 171
    1. France—Historiography.   2. Folk-lore—France.
3. Historians—France.   I. Title.   II. Series: Indiana
University.   Folklore Institute.   Monograph
series, v. 27.
DC36.9.R36   944'.007'2   73–16532
ISBN 0–253–31197–7

To my parents

La notion que nous avons aujourd'hui de l'histoire des hommes a fait un grand pas en avant, au siècle dernier. Le combat des philosophes contre la superstition avait relégué au rang des choses finies et méprisables tout le poétique bagage des croyances populaires, sans paraître se douter qu'il y avait là un gros chapitre essentiel dans l'histoire de la pensée.

—GEORGE SAND,
Introduction to Laisnel de
La Salle's *Croyances et Légendes*
du Centre de la France (Paris, 1875), I, x.

Contents

Acknowledgements

I would like to thank a number of my colleagues at the University of Massachusetts—among them, Archibald R. Lewis, Howard H. Quint, and Robert H. McNeal—for their encouragement and advice. I am also grateful to the Research Council of the University of Massachusetts/Amherst for a grant partially supporting the present work. The editors of *French Historical Studies* have granted me permission to use herein material from my article, "Symbol, Legend, and History: Michelet as Folklorist-Historian," which appeared in volume 7, number 1 (Spring 1971). Professor Richard M. Dorson of Indiana University has offered valuable suggestions and support, which I greatly appreciate. Finally, I wish to acknowledge my deep gratitude to H. Stuart Hughes, who has generously given me his counsel and help from the very beginning of my work on this history.

Preface

Beyond the Enlightenment is an unusual contribution both to folklore studies and to intellectual history, two fields that rarely meet. Folklorists customarily produce collections of texts and exhaustive studies of them. Historians for the most part shy away from folkloric materials because they think them untrustworthy, and because they lack familiarity with the discipline of folklore. Yet the stuff of folklore often meshes with the stuff of history. Charles Rearick, whose field is the intellectual history of modern Europe (he trained at Harvard under Stuart Hughes), shows in the present work how a number of French historians in the first two-thirds of the nineteenth century found in folk traditions—epics, folktales, popular belief, customs, legends, popular poetry—valuable and indispensable matter for their historical writings. But the lesson from Rearick's graceful and learned study goes beyond its immediate concern, and can be applied to historians in every land who wish to write history of the people as well as of the elite.

The French historians here considered by Rearick did all, at some time, seek to write about the French common people, about serfs and peasants as well as kings and courtiers. Some of them, like Jules Michelet, author of *Satanism and Witchcraft* (*La Sorcière* in the French) and Ernest Renan, biographer of Christ, are read today in English translation; others are forgotten. Yet in common they turned to the little regarded sources of folklore, preserved in written form or extant in oral tradition, and found rewards. Thierry employed folklore to convey vivid impressions of popular character and manners and to avoid anachronistic errors. Barante perceived public opinion reflected in folklore as a historical force in the past to be reckoned with by historians. Fauriel, himself a field collector of Greek folksongs, found in Provençal epic poetry an enriching and civilizing factor in a regional culture. Ballanche detected universal historical trends in primitive epics and the representation of social crises and changes in early myths. Michelet saw in sorcery the mother of scientific thought, wrote the chronicle of France as a legend, and believed oral tradition reliable in its moral judgement and often in factual detail. Thus on checking into the nature of Revolutionary Federations, he learned that newspapers accounts calling them popular fêtes erred and popular belief was accurate in regarding them as serious organizations. And so on: Martin stressed the values of Celtic folklore in French history; Quinet searched for the French soul in epic poetry; Ozanam recognized a universal religion in all the epics; Renan understood the process of oral tradition in shaping the gospels.

Nor did folklore serve the French historians only as sources to reconstruct and interpret the past. Folklore could also point to the future. Michelet believed that legends of downtrodden peoples would hearten them for the day of revolution. Thierry conceived a history of the spiritual life of the people as forming a new tribal epic.

Many uses of folklore for the historian thus emerge from Rearick's portrayal: tradition as document, as reflector of the common folk, as expression of the national genius, the local culture, the universal man, as builder of heroes and enemy of the faith. Rearick's splendid work illustrates common concerns of historical and folklore theory.

RICHARD M. DORSON

Beyond the Enlightenment:
Historians and Folklore in
Nineteenth Century France

Introduction

When educated Europeans began to try to understand and preserve popular traditions instead of ignoring or attacking them, they opened up a vast area of man's cultural world to scholarly study. The French explorers of that long disdained area have not received the recognition due them. They are far less celebrated than France's Enlightened foes of folklore —or "popular errors." The present work is about such students of folklore. It is the story of some nineteenth-century Frenchmen who drew upon folklore theory and materials in presenting new views of history. As historians, these men revalued and reinterpreted old traditions, and they worked to shape new ones. In their way they helped to change France. While various assemblies, men on the barricades, and strong-willed rulers struck their blows against an old order, historians worked for the future by teaching a new understanding of the past. They attached new importance to the popular mind in history; they found new meanings in old symbols, legends and myths, popular poetry and songs; they popularized new symbols and traditions. Their contribution was more than one of outdoing antirevolutionaries in polemical battles of books and pamphlets. What they offered was a new mental orientation, a new historical consciousness ordered with the aid of new ideas and appropriate symbols.

Though the English word *folklore* was not coined until 1846, the countries of Europe had long possessed equivalent terms. In the eighteenth century when the Neapolitan scholar Giambattista Vico discussed "vulgar traditions," that term meant not only myths, but also such rites as marriage and burial. Today our equivalent word *folklore* has an even more comprehensive meaning: for the professionals it includes popular games, dances, agricultural methods, industrial techniques, and popular medicines as well as the many elements of folk literature. In the present study, however, *folklore* refers primarily to such traditions as myth, legend, poetry, and songs, since those were the ones that historians most often related and interpreted.

Inevitably each interpreter of popular traditions evaluated the mentality that created them, using as a point of departure the eighteenth-century idea of two contrasting mentalities—the concrete and pictorial as distinct from the abstract and rational. While the men who figure in this study were clearly more sympathetic to the first of the two—the "mythopoeic"—than the philosophes had been, they did not reject the other type. They reconsidered the value of both types. The judgment they made was not always explicit, but it was usually clear, sometimes evident in the very form and style of their writing. Their judgments, viewed against a background of eighteenth-century thought, will receive close attention, for the new views of truth, history, and the popular imagination represented an important change from those most common in the old regime. The present work focuses on the emergence of those new ideas during the Restoration, 1815–1830, and follows their development through the lifetimes of the young Restoration writers to the 1870s and 1880s.

During the first half of the nineteenth century, investigations into the popular origins of law, religion, literature, and historiography were common throughout Europe. Frenchmen were not foremost among folklore scholars, but even the heartland of the Enlightenment eventually showed an interest that would have astonished some philosophes. Historians, whose thought will be examined here, were conspicuous among the most interested.

The focus will be on the junction of two interests distinctively nineteenth-century: history and folklore. It will be on what was a kind of classical age for both disciplines: an age of the Grimms, the Grundtvigs, Geijer and Afzelius, as well as of Niebuhr, Ranke, Michelet, and Macaulay. Of note here is the often close and mutually fruitful relationship between the developing disciplines. Granted, there was no nineteenth-century Herodotus who can be claimed as a founding father by both folklorists and historians. But there were a number of men who were knowledgeable and productive in both fields. Today the working relationships are not nearly so close, and the histories of disciplines reflect this fact. Though there was only the beginning of specialization in the early nineteenth century, modern discussions project the present divisions of labor back in time so that one now finds separate histories of folklore and of historical writing, with only an occasional suggestion of the overlap between them.

For several reasons it is appropriate to study folklorist and historical thought together. Both inquiries were contemporaneous reactions against a strong Cartesian tradition. They had in common a new appreciation of the human imagination and its powers. They became vogues at the same time among men sharing many of the same interests—above all, an interest in popular life and ideas. The influence of the same foreign thought was felt in both. And the results of the two inquiries were mutually fruitful.

To be sure, not all French historians had an interest in folklore along with history. Sismondi and Tocqueville did not bring popular traditions into their histories or imitate popular traditions in style. The present effort, then, is not a study of nineteenth-century historiography, but rather a study of selected men who did show an interest in both history and folklore. Many of them were literary historians sometimes excluded from the manuals that give space to more conventional political and institutional scholars. But to draw such sharp lines is to miss the full impact of one of the important discoveries of the period: that the popular imagination was at the root of literature, law, religion, historiography, and even institutional development.

All this is not to say that there was complete harmony in the thought of the Frenchmen to be studied. For they had not broken completely with a tradition of individualism and rationalism. They believed that the entire society played a large part in the creation of literature and culture generally, yet individual genius seemed important too. They respected traditions and truths passed on from the distant past, but they had confidence in their own reason and wanted to secure freedom for change. They placed a high value on myth and legend, yet they would not accept all the fantasies of the human mind. Each "Romantic" confronted these conflicts, and each made choices and compromises as he formed his views of history and of folklore.

1

Folklore and the French

In the abandoned medieval church of Chuisnes, a visitor gazed at a statue of Saint Saintin. Noting some tokens and small coins in one of the saint's hands, he asked for an explanation, only to learn what he must have suspected: the gifts had come from persons praying to the village saint for a cure. He then approached an old woman of the village and asked to hear the tradition surrounding the place. As he later explained, "There are stories, even popular tales, which can put one on the way, if not to finding, at least to glimpsing the truth." In this cautious statement a forgotten Frenchman expressed an idea that was the point of departure for folklorist thought in the nineteenth century.

In the visitor's written account, published in 1821, he retold the tradition he had learned. It was a simple story of a wealthy woman who once made a flippant remark before the saint's tomb and then found her horses immobile—until she vowed to build a church on the spot. The noteworthy part was the conclusion, or rather the absence of one. The report ended with neither a skeptical witticism nor a pious homily. It was offered simply as interesting information, somehow valuable in itself, the fruit of a "geological and archaeological trip" through southern France one summer. The author, strictly an amateur antiquarian, was sharing some of his observations with the savants of Paris, who published them in the memoirs of the *Société royale des Antiquaires de France.*[1]

The memoirs of the Society contain other examples of a new strong interest in folklore: essays on an old Spanish romance, the traditions of the blacksmith Vélant and the legendary giant of Antwerp, notices on the popular customs and beliefs of the Deux-Sèvres and the Jura, a Flemish folk song, a report on traditional songs of Bonneval.[2] Even more evidence of this sort appears in the memoirs of the *Académie celtique*, which was the forerunner of the *Société royale.*[3] There Irminsul, an ancient Saxon idol, Graouilli the Dragon of Metz, and Belenus, god of the Gauls, receive devoted scholarly attention. The mythology of "the Northern peoples," popular beliefs about a mound of earth near Cléry, songs of the Vendée, traditions of Sologne—all found a place in the proceedings of the Academy during the years of the First Empire.

Over a decade before the founding of the Academy in 1804, the organized study of folklore had already begun. In 1790, a member of the National Assembly, Grégoire, sent out a questionnaire on the *patois* and *mœurs* of regions in France. Later as a member of the Convention, he spearheaded the effort to eliminate *patois* in order to unify the French nation, but before taking that step he had sought knowledge of the dialects and the cultures to be destroyed. The responses to his letter abound in valuable examples of regional proverbs, popular poems, songs, and fables.[4]

Under the Consulate, Lucien Bonaparte continued this kind of effort when as Minister of the Interior he ordered the prefects to gather information on popular life. His successor Chaptal put the inquiries on a more systematic basis, although the results still varied considerably according to the prefects' interest and thoroughness. During the Restoration some new "statistiques" appeared, even though the central government no longer demanded them, and in some cases they were more voluminous than those of the Empire. The *Académie des Inscriptions et Belles Lettres* joined in the research in 1818, with some aid from the government. Upon request of the Academy, the prefects asked the majors for information that was to be transmitted to a special commission of academicians. Other inquiries were ordered in 1825 and 1837.[5]

These efforts were revolutionary, yet like so much else in that category they were far from complete successes. The special commission made no final study and received relatively few documents from the provinces. The work of the *Académie celtique* had been more extensive, but it met with an equally disappointing reception. Certainly the members were enthusiastic enough, ever eager to demonstrate the grandeur and wisdom of their Druidic ancestors. But the members were few in number, the journals derisive, and the public indifferent. Finally the academicians thought it best to reorganize themselves in 1813 as the *Société des Antiquaires de France*, and the next year it became the *Société royale*. After the early years of the Restoration it investigated less and less folklore and became almost entirely devoted to menhirs and dolmens, ancient coins and inscriptions.

The so-called folklore movement, to be sure, did not sweep across France in one swift wave. A skeptical and satirical bent of the French mind still asserted itself. Even the amateur antiquarian mentioned earlier was careful to indicate that he did not actually believe the woman's story. A few years later the folklorist Desiré Monnier appeared equally defensive about studying "the light failings of a relatively unenlightened portion" of his compatriots: "everything that is in our minds and in our customs," he pleaded, "is not wholly to be condemned."[6] After all, it was the nineteenth century. "Les lumières" had made great progress. Bayle had long before demonstrated the folly of popular beliefs about comets, and Fontenelle had exposed the credulity and knavery behind the beliefs in oracles and other fabulous occurrences. Voltaire's works were pouring off the presses: 1,598,000 volumes were put into circulation in roughly the decade after 1814, declared the *Mémorial cath-*

olique in 1825, and twelve complete editions of his works appeared between 1817 and 1824.[7] A young man named Auguste Comte was soon to announce his own "philosophie positive" which would press for new scientific advance unencumbered by the dead weight of religion, tradition, and sentiment. Carrying forward the banner of the Enlightenment, he crusaded for individual judgment on the basis of clear and distinct ideas. To heed a collective judgment found in fanciful reveries was to invite ridicule. Why go back into the darkness to hear the fables of "infant" peoples when the light of reason was within sight?

If France needed a religion, she had one, not to mention the new doctrines preached by various "prophets of Paris." Why study pagan errors? In explaining why the public of 1814 would not be interested in Marchangy's *La Gaule poétique*, a reviewer in the *Journal de Paris* wrote that his contemporaries had only "scorn for this paganism of the followers of Irminsul or of the companions of Odin," for those "dogmas opposed to ours, the superstitious beliefs" of peoples outside Christianity.[8] The Church had long fought a persistent paganism among the populace, particularly in the countryside. It had no reason to look kindly on the study of non-Christian beliefs. Recently the philosophes had made the subject more than ever suspect by their practice of inserting anticlerical thrusts in discourses that ostensibly treated exotic religions. And several centuries earlier the Protestants had created a mountainous literature showing the similarity of pagan rites and Catholic ones. The deists were perhaps even less sympathetic to popular traditions than the strictly orthodox. Being more rationalist, they placed little value on any tradition, except for mankind's earliest religion, which in its undemanding simplicity bore a remarkable resemblance to the few articles of faith acceptable to a Voltaire. After this early "natural" religion, popular beliefs were unworthy of notice, for the people thenceforth had let themselves be the victims of their own fantastic imaginations or the dupes of crafty priests and rulers.

When Churchmen over the centuries did study popular traditions or pagan beliefs, the purpose was either to condemn them—sometimes as satanic superstitions—or, more sympathetically, to find in them echoes of Biblical history. Though these were the intentions behind such works as Jean-Baptiste Thiers' *Traité des superstitions* (1667) and Père Lafitau's *Mœurs des sauvages amériquains comparées aux mœurs des premiers temps* (1724), these books later became valuable sources of folklore—classical, medieval, and American Indian. In the same way manuals written for the tribunals of the Inquisition became historical sources for students of sorcery; Michelet, for example, made extensive use of Sprenger's *Malleus Maleficarum*, "intrepid fool" though the author was. The Church also gave future folklorists the collection of saints' popular legends on which a group of Belgian Jesuits, the Bollandists, labored for centuries. Although orthodox religion was not, then, an absolute hindrance to folklore study, it encouraged somewhat ritualistic conclusions.

For lovers of literature, likewise, there seemed to be little reason for gathering and revering popular traditions. France had a great body of literature created by the educated that was brilliant enough in modern times to fill every Frenchman with pride. The Russians and the Germans perhaps needed to treasure works of popular literature, but did the French? In fact, French literary talents were so abundant and productive that serious reflection and painstaking research were slighted. So it appeared to Madame de Staël,[9] and she was by no means alone in regretting the superficiality of French writing—and perhaps the French character. In a "preliminary discourse" addressed to the newly founded Celtic Academy, the academician Joseph Lavallée deplored this "French vivacity, always more creative than studious." Even if a Frenchman was studious, Lavallée lamented, he was from an early age unsympathetic to Celtic studies as a result of his Greek and Latin education. Appropriating good Enlightened phraseology for his cause, Lavallée concluded: "The Academy will thus have prejudices to combat."[10]

He could have enumerated other *préjugés*, such as literate man's faith in the written word and distrust of the human memory. This attitude worked against the study of oral traditions still living; it was less important for the classical and medieval traditions known in written versions. But joined to a low opinion of the common people, another widespread prejudice among the educated, it could indeed inhibit a respect for the study of popular traditions.

For more than a century before Lavallée's address, the practice in France had been to view traditions in the Enlightenment spirit—skeptically, critically. When men of reason did not simply dismiss or condemn an ancient "superstition," they attempted to explain everything extraordinary about it in a "reasonable" way. To account for the origin of religious myth, for example, was a pressing concern for many of Voltaire's contemporaries, if not for the great philosophe himself.[11] Was religion the creation of the fearful and ignorant? Was the primitive a potentially reasonable fellow whose myths merely depicted his social conditions and the commonplace events of a barbaric time? Or did he literally worship animals and things? Or, alternatively, did the myths have a symbolic meaning, and if so, did they refer to man's sexual life, the stars, or moral and philosophical truths? As Frank Manuel has shown in his *Eighteenth Century Confronts the Gods*, these questions were discussed with more than academic seriousness at a time when so many were so intent on judging once and for all the nature of religion and the prospects for rational progress.

Though myth was an important topic for the eighteenth century, in France it was not considered folklore as the nineteenth century understood the term. The myths were the work of either God or the Devil, priests or the individual's fantasy. Man universal in the *Urzeit* was the subject of the treatises of de Brosses, Boulanger, Fréret, and Dupuis. The French mythographers did not regard the people collectively as a creator of traditions. Nor, except for a very few, did they value the beliefs of primitive man. For a large group of French scholars, myth was worthy of notice only as a cryptic historical record of ordinary events. To the militant Enlightened ones, it was important only in the way that paganism was important for the Church—as an enemy to be taken seriously, a threat to cherished ideas. The myth-opoeic way of thinking was for them a drag on progress toward a clear and precise rational language. If modern man tried to understand it, his purpose was to expose an evil, to "unveil" deception, and then to rejoice in its defeat.[12]

Outside France, however, important challenges to the Enlightenment had been issued through the eighteenth century by men deeply sympathetic to folklore. In *The Principles of a New Science* (1725), the Neapolitan philosopher Giambattista Vico struck at the Cartesian view that the clear and distinct ideas of highly developed minds were the superior and true ones. Vico himself marveled at the powerful mentality of the first men, who "without power of ratiocination and abstraction" were "all robust sense and vigorous imagination." This capacity, he believed, enabled them to create a "poetry so sublime that the philosophies that came afterward, the arts of poetry and criticism, have produced none equal or better, and have even prevented its production."[13] During the last quarter of the century in Germany, the Lutheran preacher and teacher Johann Gottfried Herder voiced a similar appreciation of early poetic creations in reaction against the stultifying influence of French culture. Herder urged each *Volk* to remain true to its unique genius, which he found beautifully expressed in myth and folk-songs. He not only published some of those songs—his *Volks-lieder* of 1778, but also developed at length an antirationalist philosophy of history in which myth in all its sensuous imagery appeared as a precious *Volk* legacy.

Neither of these men exerted a significant influence on French thought in the eighteenth century, yet independently of them during the second half of the century some notable Frenchmen expressed discontent with reason and classicism. Rousseau and Court de Gébelin began to cast doubt on the Enlightenment scheme of progress, the scheme expounded in its classic form by Turgot and Condorcet. "How [Rousseau] inspires us with admiration for the first steps of the human mind," exclaimed Madame de Staël in 1788. Others went farther and indeed mentally plunged into the world of myth and legend. Restif de la Bretonne, Quintus Aucler, and Gleizes developed a neopolytheism in their writings, while the theosophist Saint-Martin helped to revive the idea of a primitive revelation contained in the deformed debris of later traditions.[14]

But it was not until after tumultuous years of revolution and war that doubts about individual reason and criticism became a dominant theme in French thought. By 1815 in the eyes of many, and not only conservatives, the inadequacy of rationalism had been demonstrated by the Revolution itself: could a philosophy be sound if it led to such destruction? In the Sorbonne of the early Restoration young Victor Cousin was winning applause with his philosophic criticism of Locke, Condillac, and their epigoni; he was also popularizing the new German philosophies of Kant, Hegel, and Schelling along with the Scottish school of "common sense." These he offered as antidotes to rationalism, the inadequacy of which had been formally demonstrated by Hume and Berkeley. The alternative philosophy taught by Cousin did not direct students to popular traditions, but it did limit the claims of individual reason, and it did point to other sources of truth more characteristic of the masses—sentiment, inborn categories, and "common sense."

Meanwhile outside the ranks of the academic philosophers, some men were rejecting the philosophes with one hand and embracing traditions with the other. They were the Roman Catholic apologists, who held individual reason responsible for the revolutionary cataclysm: Bonald, Maistre, and Lamennais all attacked Cartesian reason and hailed the truth of religious tradition. Bonald attacked reason per se. In the *Essai sur l'indifférence* (1817), Lamennais limited his strictures to the judgment of the individual and urged men to rely on the reason of all, a common sense preserved in tradition. Joseph de Maistre allowed individual reason at least the role of justifying faith, but he agreed with the others that tradition was the best guide. By tradition they meant all the religions of mankind and especially the Catholic, for all popular beliefs—even "superstitions"—retained some traces of the primitive revelation.[15] To find those traces and to reconstruct the original religion were reasons for a new study of all peoples' beliefs. Such an interest moved Desiré Monnier, for example, to study a local "cult of spirits" in 1834 with the hope of finding therein "the grandest thought of man, . . . the object of his first cult."[16]

This old search for man's earliest religion had received new impetus from the work of the orientalist scholars in the latter part of the eighteenth century. Following in the wake of Anquetil-Duperron and William Jones, Schlegel and other explorers of Eastern antiquity had discovered an immense old world of traditional literatures, philosophies, and religions. Where earlier Europeans had groped blindly, the modern explorers strode confidently with their new knowledge of Sanskrit, Persian, and Arabic. While the geologists Hutton, Smith, and their successors were vastly expanding the chronological framework of Bishop Ussher, the orientalists were adding new civilizations to the antiquity familiar to Europeans. Quinet voiced the enthusiasm of many in the early nineteenth century when he hailed the "Oriental Renaissance" as the equal of the classical Renaissance at the close of the Middle Ages.[17]

German scholars preceded the French in signaling the religious importance of the new discoveries. Friedrich Schlegel, for one, proclaimed in his influential *Über die Sprache und Weissheit der Indien* (1808) that Indian traditions contained magnificent remains of an original revelation. Characteristically, the Germans gave their ideas the authority and prestige of an imposing scholarly form. Friedrich Creuzer, for example, echoed Schlegel's admiration for the *Ur-religion* in his long and learned *Symbolik und Mythologie der alten Völker, besonders des Griechen* (1810–1812). This latter work was to have considerable influence in France, in part because a French scholar, Guigniaut, spent a quarter of a century translating and revising it for the benefit of the French. In so doing he helped to revive the symbolic method of interpretation so feverishly attacked by Bayle and Fontenelle a century before. There was opposition to his effort. Constant's *De la religion* (1824–1834) brought to France the refutations of Voss and Hermann, two German scholars who denied any symbolism in the myths and any preservation of divine truths by the priesthood. In addition, some classicists refused to turn from their beloved Olympus or to concede the grandeur of any peaks to the east. Yet an awe-struck respect for oriental traditions and a fondness for symbolism remained common in French intellectual life through the nineteenth century.

Strictly speaking, Schlegel, Creuzer, and their friends did not regard oriental doctrines as folklore. According to them, the people had worked only to corrupt a magnificent heritage. Their admiration went to the priestly families that had preserved the original truths from generation to generation. In their concept of the earliest revelations, however, there was the folkloric idea of a spontaneous expression of ideas and feelings. Schlegel, for example, spoke of revelation neither as a message delivered from on high, nor as the testimony of reason, but as truth received from within, through man's sentiments. This idea separated Schlegel from old orthodox as well as many deistic believers and associated him with the folklorists.

Regarded as poetry, as strictly human imaginative creations, the ancient traditions were more readily identified with folklore. Again the thinking of late eighteenth-century Germans was most influential. According to the orientalists, such works as the *Vedas* and *Ramayana* emanated from that glorious era when poetry was still mankind's natural language. These were precious gems of the "maternal language" which infant man had bequeathed to later times from the "cradle" of India. They were beautiful samples of a "natural poetry" superior to the *Kunstpoesie* of later times.[18]

Another kind of *Naturpoesie*, equally admired, was the lyric and epic poetry of barbarian or "heroic" times. Though tradition may have attached a bard's name, it was nonetheless *Volkspoesie*, a popular creation. To Herder, the Schlegels, and their associates, *Volkspoesie* and *Urpoesie* were both natural poetry too often shunted aside in favor of neoclassical mediocrities. Two centuries earlier in France Montaigne had written appreciatively of the "graces" of "popular" or "purely natural" poetry such as the rustic songs of Gascony,[19] but it was not until the end of the eighteenth century that the concept of "true poetry" was fully developed. The similarity of Homer, the Bible, Ossian, and current folk literature became a commonplace observation. Primitive, popular, spontaneous, natural—"true poetry," wherever it might be found, was becoming a vogue.

Throughout Europe this kind of poetry had begun winning admirers years before Herder was known abroad.[20] Just after the middle of the eighteenth century, a handful of those admirers independently brought out a remarkable cluster of books that signaled the new interest. In 1755, half apologizing for publishing such crude literature in a polished age, Bishop Percy gave his countrymen *Reliques of Ancient English Poetry;* a year later the Swiss-born Mallet published the runic odes of the Scandinavians; they were soon followed by Evans's Gallic bards (1764) and the work that enjoyed a success greater than any other—*The Poems of Ossian* (1760–1763), the artful deception of Macpherson. For France the most influential by far were the writings of Mallet and *Ossian*. Mallet wrote in French, and so his book went immediately to the French public and was widely read. *Ossian* was read in French as early as 1760 in a sampling translated by Turgot. Numerous other translations followed and continued to appear well into the Napoleonic period, when, it may be said, Ossian triumphed in France. His poetry was Napoleon's favorite, and it became one of twenty-two works of foreign literature on the official list of books for all the lycée libraries of France.[21]

One can conveniently observe this major change in aesthetic taste—"preromanticism"—by noting successive responses to a work such as *Ossian*. Though, as Van Tieghem points out, some of Ossian's admirers could judge the poem excellent by their beloved classical canons, most readers enjoyed it for other reasons. To men tiring of classical rigidities and artfully, or painfully, contrived effects, *Ossian* was refreshing in its simplicity and apparent naïveté. The sentiments of homeland, melancholy, and valor seemed wonderfully natural in contrast to the cold formalities of cultivated society. The setting provided a similar contrast: the bard lived in a primitive countryside of dusky heath and mist-covered hills where the winds whistled by rocky caves and groaning oaks, over rushing streams and troubled lakes.[22]

It is ironic that men with such a thirst for a draft of "natural poetry" should be fooled by a fake. Marc Bloch had reason to call the late eighteenth and early nineteenth centuries a "mythomaniac epoch": there were indeed many Macphersons. La Villemarqué's Breton songs, Mérimée's translations of Croatian songs and Illyrian stories, the medieval poems attributed to Clotilde de Surville, Moquin-Tandon's *Carya Magalonensis*—all were deceptions, in varying degrees. Yet they were generally skillful fabrications, and as such they testified no less than if they had been genuine to the growing taste for primitive literature.

Some men of letters chose to imitate openly. *Ossian* inspired dozens of emulators, but other "primitive" poems served as models too. One of the best known (in his day) of the neo-bards was Creuzé de Lesser, who endeavored to rival the Spanish romances and wrote a *Table ronde* in twenty songs, an *Amadis de Gaul*, and a *Roland*. Others took over authentic oral traditions, reworked them, and made them an individual's artistic creation. Perrault had done so in the seventeenth century with his *Contes*; to some extent so had Mme. d'Aulnoy in her *Contes de fées*; in the nineteenth cen-

tury Gérard de Nerval and Charles Nodier similarly borrowed from popular traditions, but it was perhaps George
Sand who made the most use of authentic popular legends,
incorporating them into her *Maîtres sonneurs* and other novels.

Meanwhile a number of men tried to publish the folk
literature in a form as close to the original as possible. From
the late eighteenth century, French journals and books had
diffused an abundance of songs, poems, and tales from Lapland, Germany, New Zealand, Madagascar, Finland, and
other scattered places. Here the taste for popular literature
was joined to an exoticism that had thrived since the early
explorations beyond Europe. The French maintained strong
interest in such cosmopolitan folklore longer than the Germans; well into the nineteenth century they kept alive the
spirit of the Herder who had collected the songs of all peoples, though they had no one man of Herder's stature.

Nor did they have any Grimm brothers, at least in the
first half of the century. No one put together collections of
French legends, tales, poems, and songs corresponding to
Arnim and Brentano's *Des Knaben Wunderhorn* (1805),
Görres' *Die teutschen Volksbücher* (1807), or the Grimms' great
Kinder-und Hausmärchen (1812). These works were produced
in a surge of German nationalistic spirit aroused by the
Germans' defeats at the hands of the French, but it was not
simply a matter of nationalism. The French themselves experienced little of this kind of nationalistic reaction upon
being defeated in 1814 and 1815; their special intellectual
tradition provided other sources of pride. Learned Frenchmen did not begrudge the Germans' clear leadership in folklore studies, nor did they hesitate to acknowledge it. "No
nation has surpassed the Germans," wrote the literary
scholar Xavier Marmier in 1842, "either in the study of their
own popular poetry or in that of foreign poetry."[23]

Henri Tronchon can cite appeals for French collections
of this sort even before the Revolution.[24] Right in the middle
of the eighteenth century, La Curne de Sainte-Palaye, Le-

grand d'Aussy, and others began gathering troubadour poetry.[25] Songs of Languedoc also became fashionable among a growing number. After the Revolution some influential émigrés—notably Chateaubriand and Charles Villers—returned home with an increased fondness for French songs. And at the beginning of the Restoration, Raynouard began a new era for Provençal studies with the publication of his massive books on the troubadours' literature and language. In the same period Louis-Antoine-François de Marchangy labored on the first "Dictionary of French Mythology and National Fables," unfortunately never completed or published. By 1823 the *Mémoires* of the *Société royale des Antiquaires de France* could report numerous projected or recently published editions of old Norman songs, romances, local tales and proverbs—some based on oral testimony of villagers, but most gathered from old previously neglected manuscripts.[26]

Nonetheless, the folklorists of France lagged behind those of other countries. They were clearly aware of the French backwardness in this regard. In the very first meeting of the *Académie celtique* the Secretary Eloi Johanneau exhorted his fellow researchers to follow the example set by such celebrated foreign societies as the Academy of Sciences of Saint Petersburg.[27] In 1820, similarly, the Baron de Ladoucette tried to shame his fellow academicians on to greater exertions by pointing to the foreigners, "our rivals," flocking to French archives and monuments.[28] Marchangy, impressed by the labors of such foreigners as the Grimms, deplored the fact that the French still possessed no work devoted strictly to "popular fables and French mythology." Too often, he complained, Frenchmen were blind, when not hostile, to their folklore. A respected scholar named Noël, for example, wrote a *Dictionnaire de toutes les mythologies*, yet "by an unfortunate accident," remarked Marchangy, he forgot precisely his own, the French.[29] Decades later the first issue of France's first folklore journal, *Mélusine* (1878), regretfully reminded Frenchmen that "France is almost the last country of Europe to begin the study and publication of popular poetry. For a long time we translated and admired that of other nations, without suspecting that we possess some ourselves, sometimes as beautiful, as old, as original."[30]

To find a period as important for French folklore as the period of the Napoleonic wars was for German, one would have to settle on the 1830s and the early 1840s. In the mid-thirties Souvestre and Kérardven wrote their books on the popular traditions of Brittany.[31] In 1837 Francisque Michel published the oldest and finest recension of the *Chanson de Roland*, which he had recently found in the Bodleian library at Oxford. Then in 1839 La Villemarqué offered more Breton traditions in his *Barzas-Breiz*. During the same period Leroux de Lincy presented new scholarly work of greater scope in such books as *Le livre des légendes* (1836) and his *Recueil des chants historiques* (1841–1842). However, the beginnings of this movement lay at least as far back as the eighteenth century; from *Ossian* on the story proceeds without dramatic breaks.

Many of these folklorists of nineteenth-century France made no great claims for the aesthetic qualities of the popular poetry and tales that they collected, but valued them primarily as truly natural expressions of local life—not foreign, not imitation, not the property of elites. "I have considered my efforts an act of patriotism" wrote Frédéric Rivarès referring to his book of popular songs of Béarn (1844). "[My] book is less a work of art than of patriotism," wrote Auguste Demesmay of his *Traditions populaires de Franche-Comté* in 1844. "I am trying to snatch from oblivion some of our popular traditions," he explained, "to awaken our ancient memories of religion, of glory, and of love."[32] French interest in folklore grew apace with the growth of a new regionalist and nationalist consciousness in nineteenth-century France, with the regionalist researchers being by far the most numerous and active of French folklorists. *French* culture and the French nation-state seemed reasonably well-established, but the traditions of the local *pays* or province

seemed to many to be fading or dying. Many French folklorists, then, cherished a literature that had long exercised an
influence in shaping the attitudes and ideals of the people
who had created and nurtured it. This kind of literature did
more than amuse the upper strata of society; it educated a
people; it helped civilize and unite the members of a community. It was therefore at once native, useful, and influential.

Such literature had historical value. As Thomas Percy
had explained in the introduction to his *Reliques:*

> These poems are presented . . . not as labours of art, but as effusions
> of nature, shewing the first efforts of ancient genius, and exhibiting
> the customs and opinions of remote ages. . . .
>   No active or comprehensive mind can forbear some attention to
> the reliques of antiquity; it is prompted by natural curiosity to survey
> the progress of life and manners, and to inquire by what gradations
> barbarity was civilized, grossness refined, and ignorance instructed.[33]

Ossian, too, was received as a historical document. Blair,
Turgot, Suard, Herder, and Schiller all remarked upon its
historical importance. In fact, men of every European nation looked for their own history in the Ossianic poems. For
France the bard, being a Celt, was a brother of the Gauls,
hence his poems were "a precious document on the Gauls,
true fathers of the French," as the *Gazette de Deux Ponts*
declared.[34]

The historical interest in primitive literature became
considerably stronger after the Revolution, as concern for
the past in general became more common. Whether one
looks at the new care given to monuments and documents,
or calculates the increase of history books (as Bertier de
Sauvigny does), or reads the testimony of contemporaries,
the evidence supports the accepted idea of an awakening
historical consciousness after 1815. Never before had the
French shown so much concern for preserving and treasuring their national past. The Revolution had demonstrated
how easily the old could be destroyed, and in its aftermath
it left a new and widespread respect for the relics that had

survived the destruction.[35] The feeling was not confined to political conservatives. Spurred by a growing nationalism and perhaps by guilt for past neglect and for breaking so sharply with their ancestors, Frenchmen on both left and right were ready to consider anew the value of everything that had preceded them, including folklore. Repairing a decaying gothic cathedral, measuring and sketching a crom-lech, digging for ancient coins and medals, restoring an old local tower—these became important projects during the Restoration. No more raillery for the historical-minded. As Chateaubriand observed, this was the *"sérieux siècle"*;[36] it was also the century of history par excellence.

The antiquarians of the *Académie celtique* and the *Société royale* included folklore in their researches, but like most folklorists they seldom put their bits of information into a historical context. This was the task of the historian. Already in the eighteenth century Mallet and Johannes von Müller had deliberately included myth and legend in their general histories in order to illuminate one part of popular life. In Germany the more critical and scholarly Niebuhr had drawn upon folklorist thought in fathoming the early history of Rome; his thesis arguing Livy's dependence on popular songs was the work of a man who had closely read not only Roman history, but also Herder, Wolf, *Ossian*, the Eddas, and English and Scottish ballads.[37] Folklore theory influenced French historians as well, and folklore itself—recognized as such—became a part of many histories written in nineteenth-century France, particularly as the prehistoric and medieval periods attracted more interest. But it was not merely the dearth of other sources that led the French historians to folklore. It was primarily a new conception of what history should be. Folklore became important to the historian because he had new ideas of what constituted the truth about the past. Augustin Thierry was the first of his generation to describe the new history.

2

Popular Traditions
and
Historical Truth

1. Thierry's New History

"Pharamond! Pharamond! nous avons combattu avec l'épée!" Singing this war song of the Franks, addressed to a legendary king, young Augustin Thierry marched around a vaulted study hall in the college of Blois. He had been reading Chateaubriand's *Martyrs*, and the description of the singing barbarian warriors became so real for him that he began to take part in the scene himself. Thirty years later, as a man of forty-five, he declared that this moment in 1810 was perhaps decisive for his vocation as a historian.[1]

Perhaps no other anecdote makes so clear the exciting combined appeal of folklore and history for men of Thierry's time. It conveys well the impression of an emotional reaction of which Thierry was capable, but like so much "Romantic" writing of the period it seems less reliable as a literal account of events. In any case, Thierry's actions and writing over the next several years gave no indication that his vocation had been decided: he did not plunge into a career as a historian after reliving the barbarians' excitement. The *Martyrs* was but one of the catalysts in the young man's life and the reaction was completed only after another decade had passed. Thierry still had several years of education ahead of him when he read Chateaubriand that day in 1810. He was about to begin three years of study at the Ecole Normale Supérieure, during which his historical interests did not manifest themselves. He did not take Guizot's course, nor did he make further rousing discoveries in history comparable to his encounter with the Franks.

In this period it was first Jean-Jacques Rousseau who won the devotion of the young student. Thierry read widely in Rousseau's works and reportedly learned the fourth book of *Emile* by heart.[2] Then Thierry found a new master in Henri Saint-Simon, the publicist and utopian reformer, for whom he served as secretary from 1814 to 1817.

After breaking with Saint-Simon,[3] Thierry began to write history, but he continued to write political commentary as well. In fact, his early historical essays were shots fired in a heated political battle. Yet increasingly through the years 1817 to 1820 he was becoming a historian first and foremost.[4] In contrast to Saint-Simon, he began intensive historical study. He read widely in English, Irish, and Scottish histories, along with the novels of Walter Scott. He undertook extensive research on medieval laws and institutions. In 1820 he began reading the large collection of original historians of France and the Gauls. More and more he found enjoyment in history as a fascinating story, and by 1819 he was changing his style to form a more concrete and continuous narrative.[5] Neither the old histories nor the legal documents satisfied his curiosity entirely. He supplemented them with such works as a book of Irish popular songs, which he considered an eloquent commentary on Irish history, and Walter Scott's *Ivanhoe*, which seemed to him truer than the "philosophically false" books then bearing the name of history.[6]

Finally in July of 1820, he decided to publish his manifesto. For French historiography of the nineteenth century, if not for the historian, that was a decisive moment. In a

series of letters to the *Courrier français,* Thierry issued his
famous call for historical reform and hammered away at the
glaring deficiencies of the existing histories of France. Without losing any of his original fire, he later (1834) summed it
up in these words:

> Reform in studies, reform in the manner of writing history, war on
> the writers without erudition who have not known how to paint; war
> on Mézerai, on Velly, on their continuers and on their disciples; war
> finally on the most vaunted historians of the philosophic school,
> because of their calculated dryness and their disdainful ignorance of
> national origins: such was the program of my new endeavor.[7]

Thierry's indictment of the old histories has not been
challenged, although Pierre Moreau has suggested tenta-
tively that it could be.[8] Most historians since Thierry's time
have vied with him in denouncing the compilations and bare
chronologies that then passed for history. Undeniably
Thierry had reason for more than the usual dissatisfaction
of one generation with the work of another. At the time of
Thierry's first letter, the available histories were several generations old, generally uncritical recitals of wars and the
affairs of the privileged. For the turbulent Revolutionary
and Napoleonic events had virtually brought the writing of
history to a halt. The French histories of Sismondi, Guizot,
Thiers, and Barante had not yet appeared.

Thierry was as eloquent in outlining the shape of a better
history as he was in condemning the older efforts. First of
all, he was certain that his predecessors had been mistaken
about the proper form for historical writing. It should be
narrative, he held, ever moving along a course of events,
constantly filling the senses with the sharp detail of sight
and sound. The outlines that merely listed dates and events
were simply not true histories. Nor were the stylized literary portraits or the philosophical dissertations so common
in the century of the philosophes. Here Thierry uttered one
of the common plaints of his time in its break with the
philosophes. Antipathetic to the "abstract" scholastics

though they were and critical of the Cartesian *espirit de sys-
tème*, the philosophes themselves had lost contact with realities. So had the historians who wrote in a philosophical style.
To one who, like Thierry, preferred history or literature to
philosophy, those realities were particular and sensible—the
colors, sounds, emotions, and action that would not escape
the simplest observer. The visual was particularly important
in Thierry's conception of history, ironically for a man who
was to become blind before his thirtieth year. If Voltaire had
written for the mind, Thierry wrote for the eye. While his
extraordinary imagination evoked a panorama of Gauls,
Franks, or Normans, the historian as word-painter worked
to transfer the image to paper with all possible sensory detail.

This new conception of what was historically important
meant that folklore—indeed literature of every kind—now
could offer much to the historian. It might be unreliable in
chronological exactitude; likewise for details about particular places, persons, or actions; for modern quantitative research it can hardly be taken seriously. Yet for the kind of
truth Thierry sought—colorful *impressions* of *mœurs* and
popular character—folklore was an eminently useful source.

Another consequence of Thierry's concept was that he
placed a high value upon writings contemporaneous with
the events related. Disgusted with the "false color" of later
histories, he began sweeping away all recent books and
stopped only with the oldest. There he could find the kind
of authenticity and absence of anachronism which was the
fundamental requirement of good history. Steeped in the
"true color" of the earliest writings, the historian would not
equate the Franks with the French, nor would he depict
Charlemagne with the fleur-de-lis and Philippe Augustus in
sixteenth-century steel armour. France's true history lay
"buried in the dust of the contemporary chronicles,"
Thierry declared, "whence our elegant academicians have
been careful not to draw it."[9]

When the true history finally came to light, he held, the

French people must have a central place in it. Too long the kings and courtiers had monopolized the pages of history. The French past was so much more than a genealogy of kings, so much richer than domestic annals; it was above all the actions of the nation. Too often leaders had been credited with a glory properly belonging to the people. Why? Thierry did not explain "great man" history by sneering at sycophantic writers or preaching about the insidious effects of despotic governments. In his view the problem was that historians had simply been blind to a reality, a reality perhaps less obvious in their time: the self-determined action of the masses.

> This is a very singular thing—the obstinacy of historians never to attribute any spontaneity, any conception, to the masses of men. If an entire people migrates and makes a new home for itself, it is, according to the annalists and poets, some hero who decides to found an empire to make his name famous; if new customs are established, it is some legislator who imagines them and imposes them; if a city is organized, it is some prince who gives it being; and always the people and the citizens are material for the thought of a single man.[10]

In contrast to the older historians, Thierry shared a new sense of spontaneous mass action that was one of the important insights of the age. It was as essential to the new folklore theory as to historical theory. It was as evident in Friedrich August Wolf's theory that epic develops spontaneously among the people as it was in Thierry's view of the origin of institutions. Although underestimating the contribution of leaders and overstating the spontaneity of the masses, Thierry offered a corrective to the rationalist view of isolated individuals always consciously making decisions independently of the past—to establish a social contract, to create a law code, to compose an epic.

Perhaps in those years that had known so many collective actions of crowds, armies, assemblies, and factions, the eye had become accustomed to looking for more than the single man. In Thierry's case there was another reason for noticing mass actions. He sympathized with the masses and wanted to show them their contributions to the past, thus encouraging them to make their weight felt in the present. He was not claiming a larger place in history for them simply because of their numbers. He maintained that they had been a major creative force. By emphasizing the spontaneity of this force, he was effacing the leaders and giving the people the maximum credit for their actions. For the persistent hero worshippers and the stubbornly unobservant, Thierry offered a final test: to find the real creator of an institution, he wrote, find the ones who truly needed it, and you will turn from the single leader to the often less conspicuous, but more productive, masses of men.[11]

Thierry planned to give prominence not only to the actions of the masses, but also to their ideas, sentiments, and manners. Here was obviously the place for the folklorist to introduce his findings. Although in 1820 Thierry did not explicitly call for the use of folklore in history, he did introduce such material into his narrative on the Norman conquest during the next few years (see chapter 3). The grounds for doing so were clear in 1820. He had urged historians to do their utmost to convey the richness of popular life. More forcefully than anyone before him, he had vindicated the right of all the nation, especially the part below the privileged, to receive its due from historians.

Thierry went further. Not only should the parts of the nation be represented; they should be presented as living beings, as the "heroes" of the new history. The orders, classes, cities must not appear as abstract types, but as living, feeling, desiring, struggling beings. Each "collective being" should act its part in the story, and each should impress the reader with all its particularities as a distinct individual. Only by showing the full diversity of France and by animating each part could the historian recreate the life of the nation.[12] There was more to this line of thought than a love of "local color." Thierry did have an extraordinarily high respect for differences and individualities; he was indeed in the tradition of *Historismus* in Meinecke's sense of the word. But, more to the present point, he was engaged in a larger effort to bring life into history—and to bring it home to the people.

To represent, say, a city as a living being is an ancient practice—older than Athena—and a common one in the folklore of all peoples. Only a few months before writing his letter on historical reform, Thierry had pointed out this mythopoeic device in Irish popular traditions, and he had not failed to appreciate its effectiveness:

> The Irish love to make of the fatherland a real being which one loves and which loves us; they love to speak to it without pronouncing its name, and to confound the love that they consecrate to it, this austere and perilous love, with the sweetest and happiest among the affections of the heart.[13]

The historian must adopt this device, he believed, because it alone could attach the sympathies of the people firmly to a national history. The affairs of the privileged could not evoke such sympathy, nor could an account of events in the style of the philosophers or natural scientists. The people could best identify with persons. These persons might be the masses of the past who had lived and felt as those of the present, or they might be in reality cities and groups given personal form. The analogy of a society's history and a man's life was not new, but as a working principle for the historian, it was. Moreover, no one before had advocated it with Thierry's intent—with his consciousness of its effects on the masses.

Already in the early months of 1820 Thierry had written a brief history in this manner. He called it his "Histoire véritable de Jacques Bonhomme, d'après les documents authentiques," and published it in the *Censeur européen* of May 12, 1820.[14] Around the name of the legendary peasant rebel of the fourteenth century, Thierry created his new history of the Third Estate. Perhaps "legend" is more apt. Here Thierry depicted the common people of France as a single person and gave to this "person's" biography the moral simplicity of legend: on one side, there was the good downtrodden Jacques Bonhomme, and on the other the heartless conquerors. Victim of Romans, Franks, the absolute rule of republicans and then the Empire, and finally five years of laws of exception under the Charter, Jacques Bonhomme had led a long life of servitude. In recounting these trials, Thierry made Jacques' feelings strikingly vivid: his overwhelming sadness on experiencing the Frankish invasion; his resigned fatigue as he toiled for his masters; his shame as he was himself confounded with real property; his furious outrage in the fourteenth-century rebellion. Always he loved liberty, and always he suffered under conquerors. In sum, he was that "living being," that sympathetic person through whom Thierry endeavored to give French history a greater actuality for the present reader. In Jacques Bonhomme, Thierry hoped, the French people would recognize and cherish their own ancestors.

Clearly Thierry intended the new history to reach the masses, as did many of the historians of the first half of the nineteenth century. While this aim affected subject matter and style in ways suggested above, in Thierry's opinion it did not necessarily lead to an uncritical creation of fiction. A difficult middle way was his objective: history was to be popular yet sound and true, satisfying both the experts and the lay public. By introducing the proper kind of historical truth, Thierry believed, the historian could succeed in both worlds. The era of an exclusively elite culture had passed, and a modern mass culture was not yet a full reality. Thierry was attempting to move toward the latter without abandoning old ideals of quality.

His new history, like the Homeric epics of old, was to educate a society. Thierry intended it to teach liberalism and to encourage the people in their continuing struggle for a greater freedom. It would give them a long view of the struggle, in which each conservative reaction would appear as only a temporary setback, like many before, finally overcome. In the years of the Restoration, it is clear, Thierry's historical writing had "political uses," as Stanley Mellon and Boris Réizov emphasize.[15] Although more than once Thierry expressed his weariness of political debate and claimed that he had left it behind for much needed repose in historical research, in fact his history was never divorced from current affairs. It was designed to give Frenchmen of his day an identity with temporal depth. That is, it identified them with the descendants of the conquered, of serfs, of beleaguered bourgeois, of all those who had chosen to resist oppression. In the centuries before, these groups had constituted the nation; in the period of the Restoration the liberals were their successors, burdened with the same necessity to struggle.

Though Thierry's history was to be a weapon wielded in contemporary conflict, it was also in his view a means of unifying the French people. Without question he was a champion of the Third Estate, but at the same time his conception of the nation was not so sharply limited as Siéyès' had been in 1789. Thierry was a patriot as well as a liberal. He shared the wounded pride of many Frenchmen who had seen their country divided against itself and invaded by allied armies. In these circumstances, he believed, history was especially needed. It would renew the national pride and strengthen the feelings of kinship among Frenchmen. "By turning our eyes to this long course open for so many centuries, where we follow our fathers, where we precede our children, we would detach ourselves from quarrels of the moment, from yearnings of ambition or of party, from petty fears and petty hopes."[16] This was the hope of a man who, like his erstwhile master, wanted to end a critical age and inaugurate an age of social reconstruction. The first task was to provide that society with common beliefs, an intellectual system to end the chaos of ideas and the resulting conflicts of groups. "To provide the new society with an ideological synthesis—this was the aim of thinkers of every shade of opinion, from extreme Left to equally extreme

Right," D. G. Charlton has observed of the Restoration period.[17] For Augustin Thierry the ideological synthesis would be a new history of France.

In 1827 Thierry's *Lettres sur l'histoire de France* made it clear that he himself no longer cherished the hope of being France's national historian.[18] He was to remain the one who had laid down the challenge and marked the goal. In 1820 no one could know the meanings that folklore would have for future historians of France, but clearly Thierry's ideas on history would lead those historians toward popular traditions. He had not explicitly recommended popular songs, tales, or poems to the historian, but it was evident that they offered precisely the kind of historical truth he valued. One proof is his citation of them in his history of the Norman conquest. He knew well that folklore provided a sense of popular life, particularly the mental world of the masses, and that it faithfully reflected both regional and temporal differences of custom and belief. It supplied the all-important truth of *mœurs*. In several respects it even resembled the history Thierry envisioned. Studded with concrete detail, the traditional epic or legend narrated rather than analyzed, as it appealed more to the emotions and senses than to reason. It recalled the deeds of the folk heroes, which for Thierry would be the folk themselves. And above all, it gave the people an understanding of their society's origin and development. History as Thierry described it would be the new tribal epic, a story of popular deeds and beliefs, binding together the generations and firing them with a love of country and liberalism. Without suspecting the full consequences, Thierry was bringing history into an intimate relationship with folklore.

2. *Barante's History: Public Opinion and Tradition*

Four years after Thierry's appeal for a better history, France received the first volumes of a *Histoire des ducs de*

Bourgogne et de la maison de Valois, 1364–1477, by the Baron de Barante. Without question this historian had followed the course that Thierry had marked. In 1827 Thierry himself acknowledged Barante's contributions, praising him for furthering the reform of history by the truth of his narrative.[1]

For the forty-two-year-old Barante it was a first effort as a historian in a career that was already rich and varied.[2] By training and experience he was an administrator, a *noble de robe* from a socially prominent family of Auvergne. He had served in the Napoleonic state in several capacities, and during the Restoration he served as deputy, Councillor of State, and peer (from 1817). At the same time Barante earned a reputation as a *littérateur.*[3]

Yet it is chiefly for his history of the Dukes of Burgundy that he is remembered today—not read, but remembered. In his own time the twelve-volume work was among the most popular of histories; by 1835 it was in its sixth edition. As serious historical writing, it died with its readers. Yet for at least a brief examination it deserves to be exhumed, for it offered the theory and—to a lesser degree—the practice of a new kind of history, one even more dependent on folklore than Thierry's.

Basically, Barante's approach to history was Thierry's. To know the past, he felt, one must picture it in moving images rather than abstracting ideas from it by reason or analysis. To understand another age was to perceive its individuality, through the lives not merely of kings and nobility but also of the common people. For Barante, as for Thierry, such knowledge was conveyed best by historical details of sight and sound—"true color"—combined in a narrative of events, free of the slightest intrusion of anachronism.

While Thierry had attacked primarily the careless unhistorical mentality, Barante aimed more of his criticism at falsifications due to political prejudice. After a lifetime in the stormiest period of French history, he was tired of politi-

cal contention and ideological histories. He had seen too
much of the excesses of partisan zeal, even in his family's
home, where he had witnessed the imprisonment of his father during the Terror. In his administrative career he had
excelled at reconciliation and impartiality in the most difficult of circumstances—among the conquered across the
Rhine and in the Vendée. And with a nonpolitical profes-
sionalism, he had given years of service to the Corsican he
considered a despot. Barante wanted this same absence of
politics and modern prejudice to obtain in historical writing. "People are tired of seeing history, like a docile and paid
sophist, lend itself to all the proofs that each wants to draw
from it. What people want from it is facts," wrote Barante
in the same year that Ranke called for history *wie es eigentlich
gewesen.*[4]

Thierry had already voiced a similar criticism, but
Barante's objection was not simply that such writers were
misrepresenting history. He detected a false ring in their
declamations. To him these men seemed less than completely convinced of their beliefs, despite their showy display of systems and doctrines:

> We live in a time of doubt; absolute opinions have been shaken; they
> are still producing effects more by memory than by real heat; at
> bottom, no one any longer believes in them enough to make sacrifices
> for them, and the need of composing new convictions for oneself is
> greater than the need of defending those that one appears to retain.[5]

As the biographies sketched in the present study suggest,
this sense of shaken foundations was an important precondition for the newly awakened interest in history and folklore,
a precondition sometimes obscured in discussions of positive
political, literary, and historical ideas. Barante himself was
no blatant skeptic; he had moderate beliefs as a liberal Catholic and a *doctrinaire.* But he knew well the intellectual and
spiritual uncertainties disturbing many of his contemporaries. He expected history to teach some much-needed moral

and political lessons, yet he was never contentious or dog-
matic. Careful never to overstate his own beliefs, he felt
annoyance when others did so.

Barante abhorred any kind of artificiality. In literature
he preferred the "natural" and "naive" to classical "imitation." His memoirs express his delight at hearing the popular tales of the Vendean peasants. He was equally interested
in simple eye-witness accounts of the Vendean war, and in
fact he helped write one woman's memoirs while he was
prefect in the region.[6] He felt the same pleasure in reading
the old chronicles (especially Froissart), describing them on
one occasion with such terms as "charming," "animated,"
"living, vivid, and dramatic" with a "tone at once naïve and
penetrating."[7] With much the same language and at least as
much enthusiasm, he expressed his love of Sir Walter Scott's
novels, which he considered models in the use of the historical imagination.[8] The "Romantic" Barante also admired the
classical authors Herodotus, Thucydides, Xenophon, Livy,
and Plutarch, because they wrote imaginative narrative
"with naïveté or with the inspiration of a lively and profound sentiment."[9]

Barante was indeed among the strongest advocates of the
imagination. True, he stipulated that the historian should
begin with "facts" or realities originating outside the mind
rather than the poet's impressions drawn from within.[10] His
great love of literature notwithstanding, Barante did not
wish for a revival of the poetic epic, which he considered the
ancestor of history.[11] Nor, for all his fondness for the vivid
history in Scott's novels, did he consider them historically
exact.[12] Nonetheless, to Barante the imagination was simply
neither so wild nor so unreasonable as it had seemed to the
eighteenth-century champions of reason.[13] To him it was the
means of re-experiencing the color, emotion, and movement
of history. It was an avenue by which historians could reach
and convey truth. Barante, then, was more concerned with
giving the imagination free play than with restraining or
interrupting it: if the historian paused for dissertations

about the accuracy of his details and their meaning, he broke the flow of the narrative and sacrificed the total impression being created. Likewise for discussions of political and social systems. Barante was repulsed by argument and blatant partisan opinion. Adopting Quintilian's *Scribitur ad narrandum, non ad probandum* as his motto, he decried the philosophes' penchant for denouncing past wrongs. He preferred to hear "less about errors and faults than the causes which have made those errors and faults necessary."[14] It was the progression presented with the "naïveté of narrative" that fascinated him above all.

A man of the eighteenth as well as the nineteenth century, Barante was ultimately interested in a universal history of mankind that showed the uniqueness and "spirit" of each age—"spirit" here meaning the prevalent customs and ideas of a period, in the manner of Montesquieu and Voltaire.[15] A king, for example, was of interest insofar as he represented the outlook of a majority of his contemporaries. Buttressed philosophically by Gérando, Hegel, and Cousin, this method of treating a great man as a "sign" or symbol of his epoch was Barante's way of presenting the general character of a period and breaking with the old narrow monarchical histories. Barante did not abandon the conventional recital of political and diplomatic events, but—like Thierry—he did strive to give more attention to *mœurs* and popular ideas.

His sense of historical truth differed significantly from that which seemed natural to so many of the eighteenth century. The contrast could not be more striking than in two interpretations of a fifteenth-century work of fiction, *Le Jouvencel*. In the Old Regime the historian La Curne de Sainte-Palaye had discovered facts behind the fiction: the protagonist Jouvencel was actually a nobleman named de Beuil, the count of Provenchères represented the living count of Dunois, the siege of Cax referred to the siege of Orleans, and so on. Barante could not agree. To him this was simply more of the all too ingenious detective work that had transformed Rabelais' stories, Fénelon's *Télémaque,* and La Bruyère's *Caractères* into cryptic chronicles. Barante believed instead that the *Jouvencel* represented "a situation and a class very common then":

> This is what makes the book interesting and instructive; painting a general character, circumstances proper to the whole period, it interests much more than if it tells anecdotes and particular facts.[16]

Barante, of course, was speaking of what interested himself, without considering that his predecessor had found precisely what interested *him.* The same difference in interest and perception manifested itself in interpretations of myth. It was the difference between euhemerism—the most common interpretation in the eighteenth century—and the nineteenth-century favorites, national genius and popular *mœurs.* On this question Barante stood solidly with the nineteenth century.

The problem which the historian now faced was how to know the general character of an age. Which details were unimportant pedantry and which were essential? Thierry had offered no help in this matter, but Barante had an answer: follow tradition. Contemporaries knew best what men, questions, and events were important in their time, and they had passed on this truth. Any historian who ignored it would only miss what moved and excited them.

> All these details, these petty motives, this anatomy of actions and personages that occupy us today, as disinterested spectators, remained doubtless unperceived by contemporaries, involved as they were in the whole of things; it was their happiness or unhappiness, their safety and their loss that was involved, and the details could not distract them as [they can] us. The first truth, the truest truth, as Beaumarchais says, is this total truth which is bequeathed to us by tradition, by the echo of contemporary generations.[17]

Though Barante was not ruling out the historian's responsibility for providing the long-range perspective which contemporaries lacked, he was placing an extravagant faith in tradition. Believing historical truth to be one and simple, he failed to consider that later generations might ask important questions ignored by contemporaries. In fact, he was not looking to the future at all, but only to historians of his own time whose writing fell short of his ideal. He simply felt that if they followed the oldest narratives closely, they would make their history livelier than the scholarly monograph picking over obscure minutiae, and they would avoid the worst of historical pitfalls, anachronism.

Barante believed in tradition, too, as the proper moral guide for the historian. Moral judgment was an essential part of historical truth for Barante, the descendant of several generations of Jansenists, but to impose modern standards on the past was again to falsify. His solution was once more to rely on tradition:

> Such an action passes for criminal and bloody; it spreads horror and fright. Now seek motives, explain what was necessary, that it was the condition of some great design; give it the excuse of a system of politics, of a general goal to be reached; that is very well; these are views of the more or less ingenious mind; it is not the truth.[18]

No doubt Barante here had in mind such historians of the Revolution as Mignet and Thiers who demonstrated the necessity and inevitability of the Terror. In this case he could count on the judgment of the terrorists' contemporaries. In other cases, in those periods when contemporaries condoned what he found outrageous, it seems unlikely that the morally austere Barante would stand by tradition. But whether or not he was consistent on this point, it was his readiness to depend on tradition that was remarkable. He had put forward still another argument for contemporary opinion as an ingredient of historical truth.

In fact, one may say that Barante intended it to be the chief ingredient. For the principal character of his history was to be "public opinion," presented in all its "vicissitudes, its progress, its influence."[19] This was a new kind of history, relating not only what happened but what people thought about the happening. This was the history that Voltaire had envisioned and dismissed with the statement: "There is the history of opinions, which is scarcely anything but the collection of human errors."[20] Error or not, and Barante tended to think not, opinion was a part of history, a reality to be included in a view of the past.

It was also a historical cause. Barante believed that it was the most powerful of historical causes.[21] He sensed that discussion of such general causes was becoming increasingly common in his time. Though for centuries men of letters had attached great importance to such general influences as climate, geography, and religion, the historians of France had generally not followed suit until after the Revolution. It seemed to Barante that the tumultous years of revolution and war had disposed historians to look for long-term, general causes, including public opinion. The events of his lifetime had been so immense that the old-style chain of acts and accidents—in the royal chambers or on the battlefield—now seemed disproportionate to the effects. Barante might well have added that for his own part his liberal political beliefs predisposed him to believe in the influence of public opinion. He and his fellow *doctrinaires* wanted the government to be more responsive to a broader electorate. History written as Barante proposed would present the ideal as a reality: the ideal of public opinion making its will felt in national decisions and actions.

In his history of the Burgundian dukes Barante did not succeed in bringing popular opinion into the story as the leading character. The problem of sources made it difficult enough, but there was also some question about the power actually exercised by opinion in that time. Sensing this second difficulty, Barante pointed to instances in which the rulers did show themselves answerable to opinion, as when they offered justifications, excuses, or plain lies to the people after committing acts of violence. "One remains convinced," Barante concluded, "that even in barbaric times when force reigned, when the inequality between the rights that men have to justice was a belief admitted by all, in these times when communications between citizens of the same party were so imperfect, the thought and voice of the people exercised already an immense power."[22] In a later essay, however, he observed that the fifteenth century "was ignorant of itself"; that it was only afterward that "the activity of the intelligence became at least as great as the activity of passions or of interests"; then "the history of ideas and opinions takes a larger place."[23] Barante's Burgundian history had not put public opinion in the prominent position he had claimed for it, and perhaps this later statement was an indirect acknowledgment of that failure. Nor did his subsequent histories carry out his program. His *Histoire de la Convention nationale* (1851–1853) and his *Histoire du Directoire* (1855) were political narratives as conventional as the *Histoire de ducs.*

However, at least in one brief historical essay, Barante came close to realizing his program for a history of popular opinion. The essay was his own "Jacques Bonhomme," published in 1832, twelve years after Thierry's.[24] Once more he told the story of the Third Estate represented as one person. It was a fuller story than Thierry's, presenting more facets of Jacques' life. Barante showed much more than a conquered, pitiable lover of liberty. His Jacques was conquered, but he eventually became a townsman and gained some liberties, fought with "his cousin Joan of Arc" for France against the English and Burgundians, supported Louis XI and his successors to keep the great nobles in check, acquired an immediate distaste for the Jesuits and religious persecution, and joyfully welcomed Henri IV; this Jacques soon became avid for "la gloire française" and then increasingly critical and jealous, until one day he rose to take the Bastille. He bumbled through a succession of regimes ending at last in the July days of 1830, when he became sole master. In a confused manner Barante changed the identity of Jacques from peasant to townsman to Third Estate in general, to bourgeois and worker, and finally to those humane revolutionaries of 1830, as the historian described them, but always

Jacques represented a large element of the population distinct from king, clergy, and nobility. In short, Jacques Bonhomme was the public whose opinion Barante wanted to trace through history. Attitudes and values loomed larger in this Jacques than emotions and suffering. This Jacques loved liberty, but he also loved good order, France, French literature, and the monarchy. Barante's understanding of tradition was perfectly clear here. Tradition was not a collection of stories about saints and giants, elves and ogres, but rather the attitudes and feelings of the French people toward public questions. Yet even with this limited view of tradition, Barante's history did draw on a kind of folklore insofar as it attempted to depict popular ideas over time.

Barante's search for the character of a period stopped short of popular literature, though the logic of his program would have brought him to it. He rested content with the old chronicles and memoirs, leaving to others—the Thierrys and Michelets—the exploitation of the truly popular literature of medieval France. His literary theory enabled him to satisfy his thirst for general characteristics without going beyond the writings of literate individuals. According to that theory—also expounded by Madame de Staël and Bonald—even the elite's literature was the expression not simply of an author, but of an age. Barante also knew how to glimpse what might be called the "collective consciousness" in a government document. He could deduce popular values, for example, from the sophisms chosen by officials to justify injustice.[25] Still, he did not broaden his supply of sources nearly enough to realize the kind of history he had envisioned.

In other ways as well Barante did not follow through in the direction in which he had begun. He loved the contemporary point of view and the flavor of the old chronicles, but he realized that they did not provide a full view of causes and effects.[26] His compromise was to weave together the old narratives into a comprehensive panorama, letting them suggest the general information and leaving his own work and conclusions as inconspicuous as possible. He also began with a desire to include the common people in his historical narratives, and he spoke of viewing great men as merely symbols of their epoch, but he drew back when he saw this approach undermining the idea of the individual's power and responsibility. In 1828 and again in 1829 he protested that his fellow historians had gone too far in attributing individual greatness to circumstances, and that it was wrong to strip the individual will of its power by making it "the instrument or representative of something collective." He feared that historians were suppressing the idea of liberty in history by presenting all events as the results of a necessary law or the force of general causes.[27]

Though in several respects Barante remained in a halfway position, he had gone further than anyone else toward a rapprochement of history and tradition. Despite the limited meaning he gave to tradition, he did plead for the inclusion of popular ideas and feelings in history, and not simply those of an elite. He tried to glean them from the literature of the educated and government documents, but others would soon use the same reasoning and turn to genuinely popular literature. Barante, in sum, pushed to an extreme the arguments for the importance of popular thought. To him it was the touchstone for determining historical significance and morality, and it was a major historical force. History was not only to be based on the legend that contemporaries left; it was to be the story of that legend, which was public opinion as it both judged and influenced the elites in each epoch. Moreover, to grasp the truth of the story was the work of the imagination, not of analysis. The proper approach was empathy, not scholarly detachment. The more naïve the narrative sounded and the more authentically foreign to the present, so much the better. Barante may have taken modern literature and classical history for models, but in fact his history touched upon legend at many points.

3. Ballanche: The Truth of Primitive Traditions

Dans les temps d'affaiblissement des croyances particulières et trans-
formées, il y a des esprits très élevés qui resistent à l'incrédulité et qui
cherchent un appui dans les croyances générales et primitives.
　　Les voix des traditions primitives se font entendre de nouveau dans
les époques palingénésiques.

—Ballanche,
Essais de palingénésie sociale

"The old Europe, which has traditions, memories, ancestors, wants to regenerate itself without renouncing its traditions, without trampling underfoot its memories, without
denying its ancestors."[1] According to Pierre-Simon Ballanche, this was the problem facing Europe in the period of
the Restoration. He knew the dilemma well, for he had
experienced it personally. A self-styled Janus—one face to
the past, one to the future—he loved the old Europe but he
also wanted to see a new one emerge. How could the two be
reconciled? How could the partisans of the old Europe and
those of the new be induced to respect each other's claim to
history? Ballanche's answer was that a reconciliation could
take place when men gained a proper understanding of social change. For that, he urged them to search in the ancient
myths. To explain and to justify the modern social upheaval,
Ballanche knew of no better guide than some of the oldest
traditions of mankind.

　　Ballanche's texts were primarily Biblical and classical
mythology. Even more than Barante, he was a man firmly
rooted in the old Europe, a Europe in which the gods and
demigods of Greece and Rome left little room for Breton
fairies and legendary French peasants. Though he did most
of his writing during the Restoration, Ballanche was born
well before the Revolution, in 1776, nineteen years before
Thierry, six years before Barante. His well-to-do parents,
good bourgeois of Lyons, had instilled in him their devoted

love of the Church, free of any philosophical reservations. When the Jacobins' Revolution came to Lyons in 1793 and triumphed after two months of siege, Ballanche felt unmitigated revulsion. With the cult of the Supreme Being installed in the churches, much of the city burned and demolished, the guillotine bloody for months, his father imprisoned as a suspect, and the family printing house confiscated, Ballanche felt no calling to be a reconciler. He welcomed Napoleon's rule for its promise of internal order, but after Waterloo he rejoiced at the restoration of a Bourbon king. Though he had come to dislike Bonaparte's despotism, in 1815 he was as much opposed to the ideas of a social contract, universal suffrage, and equality as he had been two decades earlier.[2]

But there were some new ideas that he accepted. His ideas on literature, for example, were wholly "Romantic." In his very earliest published work, *Du sentiment considéré dans ses rapports avec la littérature et les arts* (1801), Ballanche attacked the old "artificial" rules and in their stead called for genius inspired by nature. From his youth on, he dreamed of writing new epics in accordance with this theory. His first attempt, never published, was a plaintive poem on Lyons' revolutionary martyrdom. Through the rest of his life, he continued to write epics, many of which remained in fragmentary form or unpublished. Under the Empire he worked on, but did not publish, "La foi promise aux Gentils," a "Jeanne d'Arc" an "Inès de Castro," and later he published his *Antigone* (1814), *Le vieillard et le jeune homme* (1819), *L'homme sans nom* (1820), *Orphée* (1829), *La vision d'Hébal* (1831), and *La ville des expiations* (1832–1835). As a writer of romantic epic, Ballanche was in the vanguard.[3]

As he left the old Europe behind him in literary theory and practice, so he did in politics, though more gradually and less completely. During the early Restoration the sharp conflict between Ultras and Liberals deeply distressed him. From 1817 on he saw the battle first-hand in Paris, after selling his Lyons printing business and moving to the capital to be near his friends—André-Marie Ampère, Dugas-Mont-bel, Camille Jordan—and his love, Madame Récamier. In Paris in 1818 his *Essai sur les institutions sociales dans leur rapport avec les idées nouvelles* first announced his mellowed political views and his desire to be a social mediator. To Maistre and Bonald he responded that France had had enough blood-letting and sacrifice; the executioners had already done all too much. From the liberals he asked for more respect for institutions, especially for the Church, and a willingness to wait for gradual change. He was still a firm supporter of the Bourbons, though Louis XVIII's performance had disappointed him. He was still defending inequality, and he still saw no need for any doctrinal change in religion. But he was now insisting that social and institutional change was necessary. Specifically he asserted that the Church should sever all ties with the state, and he appealed for a number of important changes in his society, changes he believed consonant with the new level reached by the progressing human spirit. Among them were the abolition of capital punishment, an end to duelling and war, liberation of colonies, the suppression of exclusive nationalist sentiments, and aid for the poor, including health and old-age benefits and housing improvements.[4] Nine years later in his *Essais de Palingénésie sociale*, he asserted not only that the people should participate in power, but that power should come from them. The divine missions of great men had ended, he declared, and the people were now entering into their own.[5]

Reflecting on his writing, scattered as it was over several decades, Ballanche always stressed its continuity and relatedness. For example, he called his *Essai sur les institutions sociales* an introduction to his *Palingénésie sociale*, and the germ of the later work.[6] It is true that in the earlier one he had at least adumbrated the major ideas of the *Palingénésie*. For the most part, the formative period of his intellectual life *was* behind him, and it was a rich one. From an early age he had been introduced to a wide range of literature and scholarly works, readily accessible in the printing concern of his father and in the family's large library. Weak and ill during his early manhood, he had spent much of his time alone, reading. In the last years of the eighteenth century, he had joined a circle of learned men united by serious religious, philosophical, and literary interests, and there he had become acquainted with Dugas-Montbel, future translator of Homer; André-Marie Ampère, scientist but also student of literature and philosophy; Camille Jordan, publicist; and the baron de Gérando, philosopher. From his *Essai sur les institutions* of 1818 it is clear that he had carefully read Burke, Ancillon, and Maistre and had learned well their arguments for following experience rather than rationalist theory. And in his discussion of language and its origins, he showed a familiarity with a broad range of theorists of his own time and the preceding century—notably, Rousseau, William Jones, Gérando, Wilhelm Schlegel, Humbolt, and Maistre and Bonald.

Yet his book of 1818 was only the germ of his major work of 1827 and nothing more. In the interval, his thought developed as he later recalled, "with events and with my own meditations":

> Several years of historical studies, observations of every kind, the extraordinary circumstances that since 1814 have matured at once all the populations of our Europe, until then in different ages of society, circumstances which have so prodigiously accelerated the march of the human mind; without doubt also a trip that I just made to Italy: all has reacted on me.[7]

In the course of that journey to Italy in 1823, he had visited Rome and Naples with Dugas-Montbel, and about that time he became familiar with the writings of Vico.

The imprint of Vico is clear in much of the *Palingénésie sociale*. Ballanche's new eagerness to grasp the laws of universal history and his use of Roman history as the model of a universal pattern were undoubtedly inspired by the Neapolitan philosopher. In the following discussion of Ballanche's thought, other instances of borrowing will be ap-

parent, yet not all of them were direct echoes of Vico. As
Max Harold Fisch's introduction to Vico's autobiography
shows in detail,[8] Vichian thought had been percolating
through Europe for over a century. The maze of indirect
links between Ballanche and Vico poses difficult problems
which have not yet been fully explored, but undoubtedly
Joseph de Maistre would emerge as one important link. In
any case, the *direct* contact was established in 1823. Ballanche was then working on his *Essais de Palingénésie,* and it
was in this major work of a few years later that he set forth
his fully developed theories of myth and history.

Ballanche was a poet, a seer, a prophet, a social and literary theorist, but above all in his later years he was a philosopher of history. Like Thierry and Barante, he wanted to give
his age an understanding of history, and he agreed with
them that neither reason nor recent historical writing could
provide that understanding. Ballanche relied instead on
primitive traditions. To him they promised a historical truth
that was not merely a vivid image of folkways and actions,
but rather an insight into the meaning of universal history.
In the shadow of Bossuet, Vico, Herder, and Hegel, Ballanche was groping for his own "philosophy" of history.

Ballanche's case against reason was the common one
among conservatives after the Revolution: reason leads its
devotees astray because it ignores past experience. Instead of
seeking all possible assistance from the previous experience
of mankind, instead of searching through the past for wisdom already acquired, reason strikes out alone, with only the
scanty resources of the present moment. Without deigning
to parry with the philosophes, Ballanche went straight for
"the Titan of doubt," the "Prometheus of modern philosophy," the arch despiser of tradition—Descartes. If this man
could have confronted the sages of the Academy and of the
Lyceum, of the sanctuaries of Egypt and the East, and the
Church fathers as well, Ballanche asked, would he have
dared to say that each man is self-sufficient and "has nothing

to learn from the human race or from what the human race has done?" Descartes' reason was not enough. Socrates' was not enough. "The more man separates himself from tradition," Ballanche concluded, "the more he finds himself alone, directly in the presence of mystery."[9]

Deeply impressed with the limitations of the individual's intellect, Ballanche believed in the conservative's assumption that there is a good reason for what is and what has been. "No prejudice, no superstition, exists without a reason."[10] Man must seek that reason before judging and destroying. As Ballanche had once used this argument against the revolutionaries, now he used it against those who scorned ancient traditions:

> The human spirit is obliged to search always, to inquire, even at present, with Pythagoras, Socrates, Parmenides, Timeus, Plato, Zeno, Democritus, Epicurus; with Olympiodorus, Sallust, Procius; with the fathers and the doctors; it is obliged to interrogate the centuries, the fables, the traditions. Everything has a voice to instruct, both the earth, and the firmament, and the peoples, and the sages of all times and places, and the emblems and symbols which were the diverse veils of the one truth.[11]

By "interrogating the centuries," Ballanche believed, man was not restricting himself to human wisdom, for within religious traditions there was a spark of the divine revelation. Thus Ballanche espoused the old doctrine of a primitive revelation, an idea recently refurbished by the orientalist scholars and Joseph de Maistre. With Lamennais, he maintained that the true traditions were those that were found among all societies in all centuries: universality and "perpetuity" were the signs of truth. However, Ballanche did not rigorously look for these criteria before he declared a tradition true. Ignoring the travel literature of recent centuries, he did not test his interpretations by a study of, say, Lapland or Aztec mythology. He restricted his search to classical sources and, even there, all too readily found a slightly disguised Genesis at every turn. His confidence on the matter was like an act of faith, not requiring rational demonstration or a mass of evidence.

The obverse of his belief seemed equally certain to him: no error could hold sway over many peoples for long periods of time. For Ballanche truth and error were simply not so sharply distinguishable as they were for those of a philosophic cast of mind. An error that lasted, he maintained, always had a truth as its root. He did not attribute that truth to a past revelation in every case, nor did he take the pragmatic view that an idea that "worked" was ipso facto true. Sometimes he suggested that the errors of an earlier age led to the truth of a later one: as Newton arrived at his general law of physics by way of Descartes' vortices, so false religions teaching love prepared the way for Christianity.[12] At other times, in an even more relativist vein, Ballanche spoke of popular beliefs as being true because they represented one stage of thought reached by the progressing human mind; they were true for their time.[13] This was the view that became most important for folklorist researches. A belief, even though erroneous by present standards, was worthy of study, because it represented a reality for one society in one stage of its development. This idea of Ballanche's was a consequence not only of a historical interest in the development of the human mind, but of a deep sense of the unyielding mystery in the world, a refusal to laugh at other people's beliefs or to scoff in Voltaire's manner, and a reverence for every human society, no matter how unsound its foundations might seem to one outside it.

In the *Palingénésie sociale*, Ballanche stressed particularly the truth of the primitive beliefs that constituted a cosmogony of prehistory. Both revealed to man and experienced by man at the beginning of time, those truths were eternally true, in and beyond history. To Ballanche they were of paramount interest because they were the key to history. Generally traditions such as the common origin of all races and the original fall of man recounted primitive events that shaped the course of all later history. Comparing the history of mankind to a biography of an individual, and tirelessly repeating that the two were identical, Ballanche chided those who studied only the old age of humanity and neglected its all-important childhood. As the events of childhood were crucial for the life of a man, so the early cosmogonic acts were crucial for the history of mankind. Likewise the genius of a people resulted from a primitive event.[14] At a time when the historical mode of thought was becoming dominant, Ballanche merely carried this kind of explanation to its logical end. To understand the contemporary social turmoil, he held, one should seek its primitive origin, not by reconstructing it rationally as the philosophes did with their state of nature, but rather by looking for it in the traditions that had been passed down from the beginning. "I always take tradition as my point of departure," declared Ballanche.[15] Above all, he took traditions concerning the beginnings of the world and of men.

Quite apart from their truth or lasting consequences, primitive traditions were revered by Ballanche because in them he glimpsed an awesome language, of which only the slightest traces remained in modern French. From his predecessors he took the old idea that the earliest language was poetic, but he rejected the theory that language was a human invention, developed from rude exclamations or imitations of natural sounds. Agreeing with Maistre and Bonald, Ballanche contended that language had been divinely revealed to man in the beginning. To believe that it was invented was to fall into the same error that yielded the idea of a social contract and deism. Man was not a rational creature who could invent institutions and language. Man could not have reason—or any other attribute of humanity—without first developing his humanity in society, with the aid of a God-given language.[16] The revelation of language was for Ballanche's primitive what the lightning and thunderclap were for Vico's.

Ballanche's admiration for this earliest language was

boundless. Its rhythm, he held, was spontaneous and natural, not the contrived, artificial construction of modern poetry. Its images were so intimately bound to its meaning that
the effect was incomparably direct and powerful. It was far
different from modern prose, debilitated by ever more
analytical circumlocutions. Whereas language now copied
the empirical world with descriptive terms, formerly it
evoked the speaker's sentiments in the minds of listeners
without translation into precise empirical concepts. Purely
a spoken language, primitive poetry lived always on the lips
of men instead of being buried in books as dead writing
intended only to be read.[17]

Ballanche himself wrote books and wrote in prose, but
clearly he was far from believing that writing and the printing press were unmixed blessings. Not only did oral literature have a greater impact than written, he held, but also it
was more responsible and prudent. The poet who spoke to
his contemporaries in person did not scoff and mock as Voltaire (always Voltaire) had done when writing alone in his
study, isolated from his fellows, his judgment uncorrected
by a general spirit of traditions and society.

> Isolated men can obey a thousand bad penchants; united, a *reverential*
> sense of shame, as Montaigne said, grips them, so true is it that God
> has placed a moral instinct in society.[18]

A darling of the eighteenth-century salons, Voltaire was not
the closeted writer that Ballanche's contrast implied, yet he
was also not immediately subject to the social pressure of the
whole society, as Ballanche would have him.

The symbolic nature of primitive language also made it
more serious and moral than its modern counterpart, according to Ballanche. Symbol had always performed lofty
missions. One of them was to communicate cosmogonic
truths not confined to a particular segment of time. Since
man was a creature of historical time, his mind com-
prehended only successively what the divine mind saw at

once. Symbol enabled him to approach and to glimpse divine truth. In the symbolic language of Genesis, for example, the creation was effected in days; to the nontemporal mind those days might signify simultaneity or eternity. Or symbol might communicate directly and immediately the general sentiment of a period, or a principle; it might represent an entire people, or a long social evolution. In each case, the truths it conveyed were those most worthy of man's consideration, since they were universals, "poetic characters" as Vico called them. Ballanche thus reaffirmed Aristotle's contention that poetry was philosophic by nature and assimilated the idea into his description of the primitive language. Poetic, symbolic, philosophic, this ideal language combined the best of philosophy and history: it expressed universal truths clothed in concrete images, and it presented them successively.[19]

In sum, the supposed primitive language had an energy and a power of which modern prose retained barely a trace. Only such a language, Ballanche maintained, could have civilized mankind. Civilization did not spring forth when reason took command, taming a wild, savage imagination and leading men to make a contract. Rather it was the language of the imagination, divinely bestowed, that had the power to "refine morals, to elevate sentiments, to enlarge the faculties."

> The miracles of Orpheus and Amphion are not at all vain fables. Without this lyre of gold, the peoples of Thrace would have remained savage, and the walls of Thebes would never have been raised. Try, if you will, by means of arid codes, to make the benefits of civilization penetrate to the barbarian hordes which have not lived under the yoke and under the protection of laws.[20]

In Ballanche's appreciation of primitive language, there was some regret for the loss of a pristine linguistic power, but there was no desire to retreat to a primitive society. He praised the lyre of Orpheus for its role in *civilizing* a people. Regrettably the people lost the precious lyre after it had played all too well, but they should not try to preserve it for all times by silencing it. On balance, Ballanche believed that civilization was progress, and he valued the primitive traditions and language which had contributed to that progress.

He also believed that the primitive traditions and language could still be of service, more particularly to France of the Restoration. For those traditions provided an insight into the origins and destinies of human society, and that was exactly what the French needed after the upheaval of the Revolution. The old certainties had been shaken, and belief was weakening. France was in the midst of a palingenesis, a death from which new life was emerging. But what kind of life would France have, and how could she know the right course to take during the confusion and conflict? Self-knowledge was the first need of a society caught in the dislocations of palingenesis—that is, regeneration. "Know thyself"—the oracle of Delphi spoke not only to individuals but also to societies, thought Ballanche. To gain the self-knowledge, men should consult the primitive traditions both of mankind and of their particular society. Each people had a mission to perform and a particular individuality to realize, both of which were expressed in the earliest national traditions. But these were merely variations on a theme common to all mankind. When Ballanche pleaded for more historical research into early epochs, with special attention to languages, law, and poetry, he did not mean Thierry's kind of national history, but rather universal history, and particularly man's most ancient history, which was expressed in primitive traditions.[21]

Those traditions might lead not only to self-knowledge, but also to a new world-view. Never, Ballanche believed, had there been a greater need for one. At a time when an overpowering prose was stifling the imagination, when old beliefs were dying, and when intellectual chaos was threatening, primitive traditions offered a religious and historical synthesis *sub specie aeternitatis*. With their symbols and universals, they provided a unified world-view that could never be attained by analysis and abstract modern prose. By the power of their example, they could reawaken the intuitive sense of moderns, so that the emerging new beliefs might be more penetrating and comprehensive.[22]

Ballanche was well suited for the study of traditions, granted that they were as he described them. He lacked the philological and historical erudition of some of his contemporaries—as he readily admitted—but he considered his own extraordinary intuition to be more than adequate compensation. In fact, he believed that "scientific" studies might have made him less fit for understanding his subject.[23] Ballanche had grown up in a city famous for its mystical and illuminist circles—followers of Saint-Martin, Fabre-d'Olivet, Swedenborg—and from a young age he had absorbed their ideas. Throughout his life he had visions, or what he called "second sight." Living alone in his adult years, painfully self-conscious because of his face badly scarred by surgery, hurt and depressed by failure to win either of the two women he had loved, Ballanche found consolation in religious and occult books. He prided himself on his empathy with the spirit of traditions. In introducing his *Orphée*, for example, he boasted:

> Permit me to affirm that the inspiration which I obey is closer to primitive inspiration than that of Virgil; yes, I have more than Virgil, incomparably more, the sentiment of things that I dare call divine. . . .[24]

No one, he believed, was better qualified to understand primitive poetic traditions than the sympathetic, inspired seeker that he was.

Much of the difficulty in Ballanche's writing was a result of his belief in his special inspiration. When he wrote his *L'homme sans nom* or his *Vision d'Hébal*—his epics—his rapport with the ancient epics was perhaps an asset. While his literary writing did not approach the heights of the dynamic poetry he had described, it was clear and direct. But in his prolegomena to the *Palingénésie sociale*, the results were not so satisfactory. Even in this expository prose, he adhered to some of the stylistic practices he believed to be those of the primitive poets. Prizing the spontaneity of his thought, he left it disorderly, discontinuous, and repetitious. Avoiding analytical comment or precision, he remained content with obscurity. The total impression was what mattered to him and he thought that it would emerge from the whole of his writing. His ideal was always the "spontaneous poem like those of Homer, like the Ramayana or the Eddas" and not the "arranged poem like those of the Alexandrians."

> It is not at all by borrowings made with discernment, coordinated with elegance, that one can establish an exact and complete system of ideas; it is by a view which hovers over the whole, by the collective impression received at a common center, by the assimilation of the divine or human thought with one's own thought.[25]

This quotation can serve as a description of Ballanche's method, but unfortunately the result was never an "exact and complete system of ideas."

Ballanche felt not only that he personally was well suited for the task, but also that his century was. Great political storms, like the early geological catastrophes, stimulated the imagination. The Revolution had been a new "cosmogonic chaos," and as such it gave moderns a better idea of the titanic changes that had occurred in the earliest periods of the earth and of society.[26] Writers of the early nineteenth century commonly expressed the confident belief that they had an unprecedented advantage for understanding the past: they had lived through such a full range of momentous events compressed into less than thirty years—revolution, war, conquest, chaos and change of every kind. Sharing this feeling, Ballanche was eager to use the insights of recent experience to illuminate ancient traditions, and perhaps even more eager to illuminate the modern *palingénésie* by principles abstracted from the ancient traditions.

So Ballanche peered back into the darkness of antiquity

with the torch of the revolutionary experience. One of his major discoveries was that the old myths did not record particular deeds of this or that Lydian ruler, nor did they relate to astronomical phenomena such as the sun and stars. Rather they represented social crises and changes. When Hercules took the sky off Atlas' shoulders and held it himself, a new people had made its appearance with a new royal dynasty. When Jupiter usurped Saturn's throne and was in turn replaced by Bacchus, a similar social revolution on earth had taken place.[27] Collective man—society—was the subject of myth, and not the individual historical figures singled out by the euhemerist mythographers of the eighteenth century. Here Ballanche was in agreement with Vico, as were many of the nineteenth-century mythographers. Not that Vico converted Ballanche to a social interpretation of myth. The latter arrived at this view himself, though Vico probably reinforced it.[28] In retrospect such a view of myth seems the natural one for a man like Ballanche to have held, engrossed as he was in the problems of society and wedded as he was to the German "philosophy of identity," according to which society was an organism, a "collective man" whose life was that of the individual writ large.

On occasion he conceded that the primitive imagination often did make an allegorical type of a historical individual, that there were great men who became the heroes of myth and legend. But the particular historical or biographical details did not interest him at all; the hero's mission and the tradition itself were everything to him. What mattered was simply that societies in the past had been led by men on divine missions, men who had intuitively sensed the future and conducted their society forward through a palingenesic period. What mattered about heroes since the advent of Christianity was even more definitely not the heroes themselves. Ballanche attributed the deeds of a man like Bonaparte and the resulting legend to a general sentiment of which the individual was only the symbol.[29]

A second of Ballanche's major conclusions was that the

earliest traditions contained religious dogmas, and not merely a vague, confused history. Every ancient people preserved the memory of the common origin of all mankind and a subsequent dispersal, a primeval fault resulting in human suffering and toil, and the promise of a *réparateur*, one who makes right and restores. But these were more than memories; they were truths—dogmas—applying to man's condition through all later history. Such dogmas not only constituted the essential content of tradition; they also helped explain the very process of myth formation: when people created a mythical hero by personification, they were striving to overcome a primeval division and to recreate an original solidarity, seeking to "remake collective man" in myth as in history.[30] Myth, then, like history, could not be understood apart from the primitive dogmas. After a century in which one French mythographer after another had unveiled primitive religion to disclose the worship of fetishes, stars, or something equally foolish to the Enlightened, Ballanche asserted that religious truth was there after all. The myths contained dogmas, indeed the eternal truths still taught by the Church.

With this emphasis on dogma Ballanche's views resembled not those of the folklorist, interested in popular literature per se, but those of the theosophist, who looked through the fantastic fables of the people only for secret true dogmas preserved in pure form by priests or scholars. Ballanche's belief in revelation, too, seemingly separated him from the folklorist, who saw beliefs and literature welling up from the people autonomously and spontaneously. However, he did have much in common with the folklorist. He believed that the study of the various forms of folkloric themes was an important way of grasping each society's individuality, since each people put its own particular stamp on the original traditions. Moreover, he was eager to follow the life of the tradition itself, not merely the dogmas it might convey. Believing with Vico that human thought created the world as it was for man, Ballanche endeavored to recreate for himself the mental world of the past in an effort to understand the development of man and society. So he was attentive to the collective condition of man and the intellectual horizons reflected in myth. If epic poetry had been steadily continued from antiquity to the present, he held, it would have been the best history of mankind, because it presented the universals, the most important ideas, of each period.[31] To Ballanche, then, traditions were much more than vehicles for dogma. In large measure his perspective was indeed that of a folklorist as well as a historian.

While disapproving of the superstition and error in popular traditions, he did not for that reason condemn them nor jeer at them. Because in his view he could not know the full design of Providence nor understand all its mysterious ways, he was hesitant to judge. His first impulse was to believe that an idea had a rightful place in history. Successive religions, for example, had been impregnated with some truth, of which Christianity was the full expression; Ballanche looked at the truth rather than the error. If there were errors along the way, they were errors only by later standards. On the question of historical judgment Ballanche was far closer to Ranke and Döllinger than to Lord Acton.

As Ballanche sifted through traditions to discover those beliefs that were universal, hence true, he found not only confirmation of his religion, but also a key to history. For the beliefs that in one sense were religious dogmas were at the same time universal historical formulae. History not only began with the fall of man, consequent division, expiatory suffering, and struggle against nature, but it continually repeated the original pattern. The primitive myth became history in every society. Myth and history, then, formed a continuum. On both ends of history, into the distant past and into the future, lay the realm of myth, while through the middle segment the universal myth was at work in human history. In Ballanche's words: "Mythology is condensed and, so to speak, algebraic history."[32] The whole continuum became clear to one who grasped the "formula" or myth working throughout. To "divine the past" was to foresee the future. The historian of tradition was therefore also a prophet.

Ballanche planned to demonstrate the validity of his scheme in detail by a specific historical example: Roman history. In no other part of his writing was he more indebted to Vico than in his *"Formule générale de l'histoire de tous les peuples, appliquée à l'histoire du peuple romain."* But his interpretation or "general formula" was his own. To him the conflict of patricians and plebeians was a struggle of initiators against "initiables," a struggle common to all societies. Humanity had been divided into these two groups after the fall in order to prepare mankind for expiation. When divided, the wrong weighing on man was less burdensome, and the process of rehabilitation could be worked out by man himself in society. The process took the form of social struggle. After establishing laws of marriage and property and other rights for themselves, the patricians refused to carry out their initiating role and obstinately resisted the plebeians. But they could not succeed indefinitely against the forces of movement working according to the providential plan.[33] The latter struggled again and again, and step by step assumed responsibility and won rights through a long series of trials. Thus the old story of expiation through suffering was equated in Ballanche's mind with emancipation through social conflict.

Ballanche's view of history was a common eighteenth- and nineteenth-century scheme of progress, a movement toward greater consciousness and liberty, and, as with Saint-Simon and Marx, toward a new society emerging from social conflict. But for Ballanche happiness was not a part of progress. He did not expect it in history any more than in his personal life. As the myth taught, happiness had been forfeited by man for the sake of greater consciousness—first of all, consciousness of good and evil. The level of human intelligence and morality would rise, Ballanche predicted, but the necessary cost would be pain, sacrifice, and conflict.

Without them, man would rest and there would be no change, no rehabilitation or emancipation, no education of mankind, no history.

For Ballanche, the universal myth of suffering and progress was equally true in a particular history like that of the Romans, in the life of an individual, and in universal history. In world history, Ballanche saw an opposition between the "immobile Orient" and the mobile West, but the details of this conflict, unfortunately, he did not spell out. Nor did he apply the universal myth specifically to French history. In this case, however, the message was clear.

French history fell under the ægis of Christianity, which was the greatest initiation of all time, originating with the greatest expiation. With the advent of Christianity, all men were brought together into a common moral life under one dispensation. Though the patricians had not recognized it, the era of castes was closed; all men had now received the word and had become fully responsible for their own expiations. While marking this great divide in human history, Ballanche—characteristically—expected its consequences to be worked out gradually. He did not criticize the monarchy or aristocracy of the preceding centuries, but he did admonish their present representatives to recognize and to accept the great initiation in France of the nineteenth century. The palingenesis—regeneration—of the Revolution had fulfilled the promise of Christianity. No more tutelage of the people. No more avant-gardes on divine missions to lead the people ahead, through a trial and a new conquest of freedom and responsibility. Now all men were moving ahead individually but at roughly the same pace, and the leaders were only representatives of the emerging destiny, not makers of it. Individuality was replacing the old solidarity. All men were beginning to participate in the moral and intellectual life of the epoch, and they were also beginning to share in the political power. The barriers of castes, classes, and orders were being lowered. Property, too, would cease to divide. "The abolition of classes and the liberation of property are

the result of evolutionary [*évolutif*] Christianity," declared
Ballanche, a man sometimes classed with Maistre and Bonald.[34] In moving toward the reunification of mankind, history was returning to its mythical beginning: after the long
division, the original unity of mankind was reemerging.

In the new society, traditions would once more live
among the whole population, but they would be mobile and
responsive to the general sentiment of the time. They would
take the form of a continuous flux of opinion rather than
rigid beliefs like those of the past, transmitted with little
change from one generation to another. Ballanche thus
agreed with Barante that public opinion was the modern
equivalent of tradition.[35] In the present and future, he held,
popular beliefs would reign no less than in the past, but in
the new and supple form of public opinion.

In reconciling the past, present, and future, Ballanche
wanted to demonstrate the agreement of religious traditions
and modern science. Impressed with recent advances in linguistic and geological knowledge, he repeatedly called for
more study of traditions, particularly those of the Orient,
and expressed confidence that science would confirm the
myth of Genesis. It would be difficult to find a mind more
alien to scientific method than Ballanche's, or to the exacting
work of the philologists, yet he was eager to welcome the
respected young sciences to the side of tradition. In his insis-
tence on the harmony of religious myth and science, there
may have been an inkling of future conflict. But surely he
had no presentiment of how completely the traditions he
loved and the historical method he used were to be rejected,
later in his century, in the very name of science.

Another of Ballanche's hopes went equally unrealized.
He wanted to speak for his age, and he wanted his age to hear
his message. Among the literary elite he was well-known as
a writer and member of the Académie Française. He exerted
direct influence on—among others—Frédéric Ozanam, Edgar Quinet, and Jean Reynaud, to be discussed later. The
first two were indeed his good friends, and they paid tribute

to him warmly. Ballanche enjoyed their company, but wanted his thought to reach beyond a cultivated minority. Through the Restoration he kept alive some hope, buoyed by occasional experiences like the one when he could joyfully report, after explaining his ideas to a laborer, "I felt myself understood!" This experience, however, was not a common one. Ballanche's shyness and introversion kept him from winning many followers through personal communication, and the obscurity and incompleteness of his writing restricted the influence of his books. His friend Fernand Denis was correct when he remarked: "It is necessary to be a poet and a historian to understand you and to have a feeling for you."[36] There was doubtless a dearth of poet-historians among the general reading public, but the fault did not lie entirely with the readers. Ballanche fell far short of being the Orpheus of the Restoration.

Yet, partly by his influence and perhaps more by the independent movement of minds in the same channels, a number of Ballanche's ideas on myth appeared again and again in writing on the subject in the first half of the nineteenth century. The search through all the traditions of the world continued, and—as we shall see—Ballanche's successors continued to seek a universal history in primitive epic poetry, and dogma and historical law in myth. Ballanche, then, stated one kind of truth that men of his age sought in folklore and history. Add to his views the truth that Thierry found there—*mœurs* and national character—and that which Barante found—public opinion as a historical force and a guide for later judgment of history—and the range of Restoration thought on folklore is well represented. Others, however, went on to take a closer look at a greater variety of popular traditions, and to give further thought to their origins, their transmission over time, and their effects on society.

3

Historians of France—
Friends of Folklore

1. Fauriel and Thierry: The Folklore of the Vanquished

Dans l'interprétation et l'intelligence historique des poésies et chants nationaux, des romances ou épopées populaires, . . . [Fauriel] a été un maître sagace, incomparable, et le premier qui ait donné l'éveil chez nous.

—SAINTE-BEUVE, *Portraits contemporains* (New ed.; Paris, 1870), IV, 230.

In the same year that Barante's history began to appear, Claude Fauriel made the most original, scholarly, and lasting of any contribution to folklore studies during the Restoration. It was a collection of modern Greek folksongs, gathered directly from Greeks, translated into French, and accompanied by ample notes as well as a learned preliminary discourse of over 150 pages.[1] For France it was the first collection of popular songs carefully and methodically gathered by a Frenchman. For all of Europe it was the first published anthology of modern Greek songs.

Probably no one in France was better prepared for such an undertaking. Thoroughly familiar with the latest philological and literary work of his time, Fauriel was even personally acquainted with many of the writers responsible for the new thought; he maintained particularly close friendships with Madame de Staël, Friedrich Schlegel, Manzoni, Guizot, and Thierry. As early as the year VIII (1799), he was studying Vico's *Scienza nuova* and taking notes that were directly relevant to much of his later literary and historical work;[2] in the notes were Vico's major axioms, his important methodological comments, and key points, most of them from the book on the poetic wisdom of humanity's earliest age. Fauriel, moreover, was one of the first in France to adopt the "song" or "cantilène" theory of epic, the theory of Wolf, the Grimms, and Lachmann; that theory was implicit in his book of 1824, in which he spoke of the Greek songs as the germs of a new epic. Finally, few could match his linguistic expertise, which enabled him to study popular literature on the broadest comparative basis—to move with ease from the Eddas to Provençal romances, from the *Iliad* to the *Mahabharata*. Greek, Latin, English, and Italian he had learned as a collegian from his Oratorian teachers in Tournon and Lyons. Sanskrit he learned from the famed William Hamilton in the early years of the Empire, becoming one of the first in France to know it. By the year of the first Restoration he had studied Persian, Armenian, Hebrew, and Manchu, and more thoroughly he had taught himself Arabic and almost all the Indo-European tongues except the Slavic.[3]

Along with his erudition, he had a strong predilection for primitive literature. As a young man during the Revolution, he read Ossian zealously and translated one of the poems for himself. Homer also won his devotion. In the year of Thermidor, Fauriel often fled "persecuting" men and sought solitude to read, indeed to devour (*dévorer*), the Homeric epics and to translate his favorite part of the *Iliad*.[4] For the rest of his life he continued to love most of all the simple poetry that he believed "natural," spontaneous, naïve—in short, refreshingly different from most contemporary poetry, which seemed forced and false, imitative rather than original. Primitive poetry pleased by its very deficiency of art: the "contrast or disproportion between the simplicity of means and the plenitude of effect" constituted its "principal charm." To contemplate the uncultivated genius, he declared, was a pleasure comparable to viewing a "picturesque mass of rocks" or "an old forest."[5] Turning from the classical poem and garden alike, Fauriel shared the Romantics' delight in less refined works.

With such an outlook and background, Fauriel was ideally suited for the study to which he devoted most of his life, the study of the history and literature of the early stages of civilization. No man figuring in the present work deserves the double appellation of historian and folklorist more than Fauriel, for he made outstanding contributions to both fields, as well as to literature. His earliest major works were in poetry: translations of Baggeson's *Parthenaïs* in 1810, Berchet's *I profughi di Parga* in 1823, and of course the Greek folk songs in 1824–25. He also translated two of Manzoni's tragedies: *Il conte di Carmagnola* and *Adelchi* (1823). Intensive historical research occupied him especially in his last twenty-five years. Fauriel's career thus roughly followed the pattern which he believed characteristic of the development of civilization: poetry in youth and historical prose in maturity.

During those last twenty-five years he planned to write a monumental history of Southern Gaul from the migrations of the earliest inhabitants through the decline and fall of Provençal civilization in the thirteenth century. He completed only one-third of the projected work before his death in 1844, but the three published volumes[6] were impressive enough to win him recognition as the authority of his time on the Midi. After the Revolution of 1830, his friends Guizot and Cousin used their influence to create, for the first time in France and in the faculty of Paris, a chair of foreign literature to which Fauriel was named. In this position he continued to concern himself with the literature and history of "heroic ages," lecturing over the next fourteen years on the Homeric poems, Serbian and Greek songs, the origins of the Italian language and Dante, Spanish literature, and Provençal poetry.

In the praise that two notable Frenchmen of the last century lavished on the deceased Fauriel, there is agreement that he exerted an enormous influence on the intellectual life of his time and that his greatness lay in the freshness and range of his thought. Sainte-Beuve called him "the precursor, the secret but direct initiator, the inoculator of most of the distinguished minds of that time in history, in literary method, in criticism."[7] Renan spoke of him in superlatives: "M. Fauriel is questionably the man of our century who has put into circulation the most ideas, inaugurated the most branches of study, perceived the most new results in the realm of historical works."[8] Of the historians, Augustin Thierry acknowledged the greatest debt to Fauriel. Graciously, Thierry even passed to Fauriel the title of "father of the historical reform," designating him as the "first who conceived and wanted to do what has been carried out for some years, . . . who has given the impetus and, I can say it, lent ideas to me. . . ."[9]

Today it is difficult to reassess Fauriel's contribution because he was, as Sainte-Beuve remarked, a "secret initiator." He published relatively little and transmitted much of his thought through lectures and conversation with friends. Consequently, his reputation has not been widespread in either his own time or ours, and it would probably be even slighter if men like Sainte-Beuve and Renan had not left glowing eulogies. As in the subsequent case of Lord Acton, Fauriel never came close to realizing his potential in his publications. He set his ideal so high that he often despaired of reaching it. Disdaining the feverish efforts of lesser men, he was inclined to hold himself aloof from their activity, to study, to reflect, and—as a writer—to procrastinate. In a revealing letter written in 1801, he remarked that he was letting his thought lie fallow because literary fame was too cheap at the present time; "it has too numerous and especially too vulgar lovers to tempt certain minds which have more pride than vanity."[10] This attitude seems to have reasserted itself often throughout Fauriel's life. Fame continued to have vulgar lovers, and Fauriel was ever anxious to distinguish himself from them, yet ever melancholic about the worth of his efforts.[11] His friends repeatedly tried to prod him to produce more. In 1817 Guizot urged him to write an article on Vico for the *Archives philosophiques;*[12] Fauriel failed to do so and thus forfeited the honor of introducing Vico to France. Thierry also tried to spur his friend on: *"Avancez, pour Dieu! avancez!"* he wrote in 1821. "I have almost as great a desire to see you publish as to see myself."[13] His friends' concern for his work did not cease even with his death in 1846, for they published several courses of lectures and manuscripts posthumously: a three-volume *Histoire de la poésie provençale* (1846), a memoir on life under the Consulate with the title *Les derniers jours du Consulat* (1886), two volumes entitled *Dante et les origines de la langue et la littérature italiennes* (1854), and a number of articles in the *Histoire littéraire de la France.*[14]

Fauriel tended to withdraw as much from the heated politics of the age as from the demands of publication. He occupied various posts in the Revolutionary government of his hometown, Saint-Etienne, and served as secretary to a general in the South of France, but his general political attitude was one of pessimistic reserve. Without opposing the Revolution, he had little hope that it would improve man or society. Antipathetic to conscription and war, he found a model in William Penn and, as he remarked to a friend, saw in himself the makings of a Quaker. Under the Empire he turned to the Stoics and began writing a book on their thought. In the same period he planned a book on the life of Jesus, emphasizing humane ethics while playing down miracles and dogma.[15] During the Restoration he shared the liberal opinions of his friends, but he did not engage in politics or propound political views in his writings. In the anthology of Greek songs, it was apparent that his sympathies lay with the revolutionaries in their struggle against the Turks, and his book has been credited with winning friends in Western Europe for the Greeks. But he subdued his partisanship severely and offered the songs to the public ostensibly because he believed them to be beautiful, enlightening commentaries on the Greek people—both ancient and modern —and useful to anyone studying modern Greek.[16]

Fauriel's writing was in fact generally austere and judicious. He admired primitive literature as much as anyone, but for him it was a gem from the past to be treasured, yet never to be duplicated or imitated. His was an age of prose, history, and science, and he partook of his age fully. He was more familiar with the philological and natural sciences than were Thierry, Barante, or Ballanche. In the early years of the Empire, he had been a member of Madame Helvétius's circle at Auteuil, at that time dominated by the *Idéologues,* and one of them, the physiologist Cabanis, was his closest friend; Fauriel himself became an avid student of botany.[17] His model for style in historical writing seems to have been the scientific or philological monograph rather than the old chronicle, epic, or novel. In his writing there was lengthy critical discussion of evidence with little of the evocative imagery advocated by some of his fellow historians.

Fauriel, then, devoted his energies to studying and discussing popular traditions without emulating them. If the collection of Greek songs was his most important study of contemporary folklore, his most original work on the folklore of the past was his history of Provençal poetry, presented first as lectures in the early 1830s. Though most of the poems and chronicles discussed there could not be classed as folklore, Fauriel was always alert to passages that seemed to bear that stamp. In chronicles, for example, he detected paraphrases of popular songs and fictional incidents borrowed from popular traditions.[18] In court poetry, too, he rediscovered popular contributions. As Vico and Wolf had unveiled popular oral traditions long hidden behind the name *Homer,* now Fauriel pointed to the popular sources of Provençal poetry. Literature, he believed, drew its life from the common people, and it found in them its most faithful guardian through the centuries. In his commentary on the

Greek songs, he had pointed out ancient mythological figures—Charon, the Fates, the Furies, and the Satyrs—that still lived in the songs of modern Greeks, though sometimes altered and disguised. In his history of Provençal poetry again he showed ancient pagan traditions long enduring in popular literature: genres such as love poems as well as episodes such as the adventures of Odysseus, which Fauriel found surviving as the legendary adventures of Raimond de Bosquet. Added to these popular memories of paganism were "original and spontaneous" expressions of medieval religious and historical life: for example, the pious legends and the "romanesque" stories of Christian lords in combat with Saracens. And added to the latter was the influence of the manners and morals of the Arabs in Spain, where the future knightly ideals of love, honor, and courage were already highly esteemed.[19]

In Fauriel's view such were the sources of Provençal poetry; they were less ecclesiastical and aristocratic than popular. While conceding that the poetry of the troubadours had tended to become confined to courts and châteaux, he held that it had never completely lost contact with the people. The poetry that originated with the people eventually returned to them. Weary of their efforts to amuse with the increasingly refined literature of the châteaux, many troubadours descended to the streets and countryside to sing a more popular poetry. Fauriel did not neglect to note that the romances of the Round Table owed less to the popular milieu than the Carolingian romances. Nonetheless, in both cases he attributed to the people a part in creating what appeared to be simply the literature of the educated and of the social elite.[20] Similarly, in his lectures on Dante, he called attention to the poet's debts to popular poetry, including mythical figures such as the guardians of the circle of hell and themes such as the fantastic journey beyond this world. Scholarly, dispassionate, detached from politics though he was, Fauriel was taking part in a democratic revolution in literary history.

Fauriel's most startling discovery was that epic poetry had flowered in the Provençal civilization. Some earlier students of Provençal literature—Dietz, Raynouard, Galvani—had signaled the beauty of the region's lyric poetry, but had not suspected the presence of epics as well. While lamenting the loss of most of this literature, Fauriel cited references to it in extant chronicles and poems, and he argued that the surviving *Chansons de gestes*, the written romances of knighthood, had originated as oral epic poetry. First he had to discredit the idea that the romances were abruptly conceived and written in their present prose form. Noting discrepancies and stylistic differences in the manner of the Homeric philologists, Fauriel found the romances to be composed of heterogeneous parts, based on old, once separate oral traditions. He then gave short shrift to the idea that the earliest version of the romances had been prose. His main arguments were that this belief was contrary to the evidence of all other epics and indeed contrary to "the general march of the human mind"—echoes of Vico—and that before the use of writing, verse had been a necessary aid for the memory. To describe the actual formation of the Provençal epics, he combined Vico's views on the Homeric epics with the *cantilène* theory of the Germans: simple, short popular songs spontaneously emerging from the people had been gradually joined together and elaborated to form a lengthy poem of epic proportions. The romances of Charlemagne, for example, had received their final prose form in the twelfth and thirteenth centuries, but the germs had been present in the popular songs of Charlemagne's own day.[21]

Fauriel's discovery of epic poems was welcome to the French ego at a time when even the Bohemians were discovering their own native Homer. If Hugo and Lamartine were working to belie the old dictum that "the French do not have a head for epic," Fauriel was doing no less, through historical research. But Fauriel's intent went far beyond theirs. He claimed not merely that France had heroic epic poetry, too; he asserted that Provençal poetry was *the* source from which almost all European epics derived. Ariosto's *Orlando furioso* was an obvious example; others were rather startling: the Germans' song of the Nibelungen and the Scandinavian Wilkina sagas, for example, Fauriel traced to a Provençal oral tradition, which Walther of Aquitaine had recast and passed on to French posterity. The Breton folklorists' beloved romances of the Round Table, too, Fauriel linked to Southern Gaul, arguing that the romances had taken on the trappings of chivalry and assumed their most familiar form in the Provençal milieu and in the hands of Provençal poets.[22]

Fauriel maintained a clear distinction between Provençal and French. He was not an ardent nationalist, nor was his historical study designed to flatter the French ego. At heart he was a regionalist, one of the fathers of the reawakening Provençal consciousness in the nineteenth century.[23] He identified in sympathies more with the vanquished Provençal civilization than with the victors—the French crusaders, the destroyers from the North. His contemporaries did not fail to see the regionalist favoritism in his work; his most severe critics were folklore and literary scholars from other regions who leaped to the defence of their own. From Brittany La Villemarqué hastened to reclaim the Round Table even in its finished form for the Celts, and Paulin Paris in behalf of northern or French literature protested against the new arrogant pretensions of the Provençal champion. "It was France of the North which marched, ensigns unfurled, against France of the South," declared H. Fortoul in recalling the conflict.[24]

The part that Fauriel assigned to the popular imagination was not seriously disputed. The *cantilène* theory, in particular, won widespread acceptance and held sway in France until the major revisionary work of Joseph Bédier in the early decades of this century. Following Fauriel, other French scholars such as Amaury Duval, Jean-Jacques Ampère, Charles d'Héricault, Léon Gautier, and Gaston Paris applied the *cantilène* theory to medieval literature. Even Paulin Paris, at first Fauriel's most outspoken critic, eventually followed suit. By the 1860s Paris was a complete convert and ungrudgingly paid homage to Fauriel for first introducing the theory to France.[25] Through this theory Fauriel had given to the people a share in the honor accruing to the nobility's finest literature—without provoking an aristocratic reaction.

Literature so closely linked to the people seemed to Fauriel excellent evidence of popular life for several reasons. First, because primitive poetry was spontaneous and "naïve," it revealed "national" character more faithfully than the meditated works of an individual: with the individual's reflection came guile, concealment, deceit. Secondly, he felt certain that the popular poetry portrayed the folkways of the people accurately because otherwise it would not have become popular; the people did not cherish literature alien to their folkways. Finally, imaginative literature inevitably reflected its historical milieu. Hence folklore could provide truth about popular ideas and manners over long periods of time. If his collection of Greek songs were complete, Fauriel declared, it "would be at once both the true national history of modern Greece, and the most faithful tableau of the folkways of its inhabitants."[26] But some traditions were more historical than others; some, such as the klephts' songs, were clearly based on the memory of historical events and persons. Fauriel took special note of such traditions; having served as a history for an untutored people, they could yield sound historical information to the modern historian if they were critically interpreted. In his history of Southern Gaul, he discussed a number of these traditions critically, both in text and in the appendix, where he placed his "observations on the fabulous narrative of the marriage of Clovis and Clothilde," and comments on a fragment of an old "Basque national song." He tried to separate the fiction from the history, but he avoided the euhemerists' mistake of drawing historical particulars from popular narratives.

The truths that Fauriel most often discerned in historical traditions were popular emotions. The people clothed a skeleton of history—an event, a man—with poetic detail and infused into it their feelings. National pride and hatred, resentment and defiance—they were the truths in tradition for Fauriel. When encountering the legend of a hero, he passed over details about the man's character and actions and dwelled on the national pride and desire for independence that moved the people to develop the legend. As the Greek songs had celebrated the rebel chieftains, so the legends of Southern Gaul celebrated local potentates leading the struggle against the encroaching royal authority. Fauriel looked into the fictional difficulties that Clovis had to overcome to win Clothilde, and he saw the deep-seated enmity of Franks and Burgundians. Fauriel examined the stories about Guiomat, the German who restored Chilpéric to his people, and he found the popular desire for a Frankish leader and antipathy for a Roman usurper.[27] A large part of folklore, then, documented what Fauriel considered the most important part of any national history—the struggle for independence. As he surveyed the traditions of the Greek, Serbian, Czech, and Provençal peoples, Fauriel found one dominant theme: a love of independence, and conversely, a hatred for any foreign conqueror.

A melancholy man, himself often cheered by literature, Fauriel was sensitive to the consolation and encouragement that popular traditions provided to defeated peoples. He had no doubt that the songs celebrating national heroes strengthened the popular will to resist the conquerors and kept the identity of the people intact even when, as with the Greeks, the nation was reduced to bands of rebels in the mountains.[28] Folklore, then, was an important source of social cohesion. Though filled with superstitions and fictions abhorrent to the mentality of a philosophe, popular traditions did not enslave but rather helped a people to maintain their individuality, even when defeated, and encouraged them to regain their independence.

Folklore, particularly popular poetry, also helped to civilize a people. While Chateaubriand and other ardent Catholics were rehabilitating the Church by lauding its role in elevating the morals, learning, and art of Europe, Fauriel focused instead on the civilizing role of popular poetry, continuing from Greek and Roman antiquity through the Middle Ages and even into recent times in places like Greece. Most of all, he hailed the civilizing power of Provençal poetry. That power began to be exerted, he held, in the ninth century, when the centers of classical learning shifted to the North, allowing local and popular literature to blossom in Southern Gaul. The ancient love songs, transformed under the influence of Christian and Arabic morality, evolved into beautiful Provençal poems that expressed the best of medieval ideals: reverence for women, love, social grace, elegance, honor, courage, humane behavior. With the aid of the troubadours, those ideals became a force in the society. For the members of the elite began to rival each other by excelling in these virtues, in order to be celebrated in the troubadours' songs and thereby gain fame and prestige. The clergy recognized the hold that the old pagan traditions in their modern form had over the people and tried to Christianize this literature, but the clergy's own influence was comparatively ineffective. Consequently the frustrated ecclesiastics hated Provençal, and after the Albigensian war, they encouraged the Pope to prohibit the use of the language. But the ancient traditions had already done their work: the ideal of knighthood, the finest offspring of Provençal poetry, became a part of the European heritage. Through the far-ranging influence of Provençal literature, the ideals of the Midi spread over Europe.[29] For Fauriel, then, Provençal civilization, before being so brutally destroyed, had ushered in the modern age and had endowed it with modernity's finest ideals as well as a brilliant literature. Again, despite his sympathy for barbarism, he was primarily concerned with the means by which civilization advanced.

While Fauriel worked to correct an excessively rationalist view of the civilizing process, he did not neglect the limitations of popular poetry. He recognized that it sometimes lost contact with everyday reality and wandered aimlessly in the mists of fantasy. While this "romanesque" poetry provided glimpses of the popular mind to the historian, it did not elevate a society or inspire a people to establish its autonomy and Fauriel therefore valued it less than the domestic and heroic songs.[30] He further believed that primitive literature did not owe its happiest form to the masses of people alone, spontaneously creating, but rather to the special talents of an individual genius. Although—to take the classic case of Homer—Fauriel did not accept the traditions about a blind bard as historically reliable, he did believe that an extraordinarily gifted rhapsode had intervened to stitch together the century-old oral traditions, in this way composing the masterpiece known to later times. Arguing that the spontaneous action of the ordinary people did not yield such results, Fauriel pointed to evidence that in any community the more talented singers, often the blind and old with specially developed memories, were the ones who carried the traditions to the sublime heights of art.[31] Even after the popular poetry had passed into their hands, unfortunately, it was sometimes lost or obliterated in a disaster like the Albigensian crusade. Ironically, the best means of preserving poetic traditions was also their death stroke: the introduction of writing removed the need for memorization of the poetry and thus made the metric form unnecessary and increasingly artificial. Poetry soon lost its grace, vitality, and naturalness, and at the same time prose attracted by its freer form and by its novelty. Eventually the chronicles that were once poetic history, intimately related to popular tradition, became abstract formulæ, and the abstract thought of science and philosophy came to play an ever larger part in the life of the society. For Fauriel, then, the advent of writing and prose inevitably marked the end of a poetic epoch and the beginning of a scientific one.

Folklore, in sum, played an important but not all-sufficient role in civilization, according to Fauriel. Inevitably one day it gave way to science. Fauriel accepted this as fact; there was little "romantic" escapism in his love of folklore. As he wrote to a friend who had become intoxicated with the common spirits of Romanticism:

> . . . we will have great quarrels, not precisely about Walter Scott, not even about your enthusiasm for fairies, for sorcerers, for legends; I love life everywhere, and that of ignorant and barbaric times has things which please me and charm me perhaps as much as anyone. But I would not want you to have an exclusive and absolute enthusiasm for these things; . . . it is necessary to comprehend the past and to love it, but not at the expense of either the present, or the future.[32]

The present and future were ages of science, he believed, yet even then folklore was deserving of appreciation, not only for its beauty but also for what it revealed about particular peoples and for what it had done in the past.

We have already noted some of Fauriel's friends and some estimates of his far-reaching influence. To the names mentioned earlier, one may add the literary and folklore scholar Jean-Jacques Ampère and two men who loom large in the present study: Quinet and Ozanam. But the one who was closest to Fauriel has already been mentioned and discussed—Augustin Thierry.

It is not known when Thierry and Fauriel first met. The earliest letters from one to the other date from 1821, but the contents indicate that their friendship was already well established.[33] In any event, when Thierry was writing his history of the Norman conquest in the early 1820s, the two men were often together discussing history and folklore. In 1834 Thierry reminisced about those years with his "intimate confidant":

> . . . this friend, this sure and faithful counselor . . . was the scholarly, the ingenious M. Fauriel, in whom sagacity, justness of mind and grace of language seem to have been personified. His judgments, shrewd and sound, were my rule in doubt; and the sympathy with which he followed my works stimulated me to move ahead. Rarely

did I come from our long conversations without my thought having been advanced, without it having gained something in clarity or in firmness. After thirteen years, I still recall our evening walks, which extended in the summer over a great part of the outer boulevards, and during which I retold with an endless abundance the most minute details of chronicles and legends, all of which made my conquerors and conquered of the eleventh century living for me. . . .[34]

From late 1823 to 1825 Fauriel was in Italy, collecting folk songs from Greek refugees, but upon his return to France the two men were together again, this time in the Midi. They traveled together through the Southern provinces, as Fauriel gathered material for his history of Southern Gaul, and Thierry, now losing his sight, studied historical monuments.[35]

Undoubtedly in the early 1820s Fauriel encouraged Thierry to probe the past through popular traditions. Certainly Fauriel broadened his friend's knowledge of them. The evidence is in the *Histoire de la conquête de l'Angleterre par les Normands*, which appeared one year after the collection of Greek songs. Citing those songs and Fauriel's "historical discourse," Thierry acknowledged that they had already shown the importance of folklore in the history of the vanquished and that his own investigation into Anglo-Saxon traditions led to the same conclusions.[36] But Fauriel was not the only one who suggested to Thierry the testimony of folklore. About 1820 the latter began studying the English history of Sharon Turner and was strongly impressed with the author's effective use of folklore:

> The prodigious quantity of details that this work contains on the folkways and the social state of the German conquerors of Great Britain and on the indigenous Britains, the numerous citations of original poems, by Celtic Bards or Northern scalds, gripped me with a kind of interest that I had not yet felt in my historical research.[37]

Thierry's favorite novelist, Walter Scott, also set an example by introducing ballads and other popular poetry into his historical novels.

Wholeheartedly Thierry adopted this practice himself. Into his *Histoire de la conquête de l'Angleterre* he incorporated an abundance of folklore, deliberately inserted into the text as historical evidence about popular life. "The national traditions of the least known populations, and old popular poems," he declared, "have furnished me many indications of the mode of existence, the sentiments and the ideas of men, in the times and diverse places where I transport the reader."[38] The popular traditions he cited were as diverse as legends about the death of Robin Hood and Ethelred's son Alfred, Scandinavian songs concerning the death of native kings, "patriotic superstitions" of the English, and popular poems celebrating Anglo-Saxon outlaws. And added to the history were numerous "pièces justificatives," including a "national song of the Anglo-Saxons on the victory of Brunanburg," "poetic narratives of the battle of Hastings," popular ballads—one about a supposed meeting of King Richard and Robin Hood and another about the birth of Robin Hood, a Scottish ballad on the battle of Bothwel bridge, popular ballads on the captivity and marriage of Gilbert Becket, and a poetic narrative about King William's enquiry as to the probable future of his sons. In view of Sharon Turner's earlier work, it appears that Thierry was in error when he said that he had gathered Anglo-Saxon history "where no one had sought it, in legends, traditions, and popular poems."[39] But his assertion is admissible if one limits it to French historians: as a wholly sympathetic and assiduous explorer of popular traditions, he led the way in the historiography of his compatriots.

For him folklore had virtually the same meaning that it had for Fauriel. It most often testified to the undying patriotism of distinct peoples. Even when the masses of people were subjugated, they continued their traditions. Undaunted, they expressed their desire for independence and hatred of the conqueror in songs and legends celebrating the bold few who continued to fight the oppressor. Their heroes in modern Greece were the rebels in the mountains; in En-

gland after the Norman conquest, they were outlaws like
Robin Hood. In the largely conquered France of the
fifteenth century, they were the combatants led by Joan of
Arc. In Western Britain, they were the legendary leaders of
the vanquished Celtic people, a people that expressed its
hope in the songs of Arthur: the Celtic bards sang "a mysterious eternity" reserved for their people's name and language, and the people themselves eagerly believed.[40]

Thierry's great gift as a folklorist was his sensitivity to
the emotions that had fed the popular traditions. As in his
portrait of Jacques Bonhomme, so in his other histories he
felt most keenly the sadness of the defeated and their indomitable love of freedom. With clear insight he described
the process by which baseless hope fed on itself, among the
Welsh, for example: "The wishes of the bards passed for
promises; their expectation was prophecy; even silence
affirmed; if they did not sing the death of Arthur, it was
proof that Arthur lived still."[41] Thierry recognized the folly,
but with him empathy precluded ridicule. And it was not
only nationalist folklore that he understood in this way but
also the religious stories of the people. In his *Récits des temps
mérovingiens,* for example, he retold the medieval tale of a
miracle: on the tomb of an abandoned and murdered queen
hung a lamp that mysteriously unhooked itself one day and
fell to the marble base without breaking or going out. Ignoring the question of plausibility, he commented only on the
effect of the oral tradition on the listeners of centuries ago:

> Similar narratives can make us smile, we who read them in the old
> books written for men of another age; but, in the sixth century, when
> these legends passed from mouth to mouth as the living and poetic
> expression of popular sentiments and faith, people became pensive
> and wept upon hearing them told.[42]

Through this emotional involvement with the past and the
people, foreshadowing Michelet, Thierry came to his understanding of folklore.

In his history of the Norman conquest, the popular emotions that played the greatest role were nationalist ones, with which Thierry sympathized completely. His nationalism was that of a liberal in Metternich's Europe, where the forces of reaction where thwarting the nationalist aspirations of Greeks, Italians, Germans, Belgians. Far closer in spirit to Herder than to Treitschke, Thierry as well as Fauriel sympathized with the defeated, the oppressed, the small nationalities. Nothing was more alien to him than the belief that the larger nations had a destiny to fulfill for which smaller nations or groups should be sacrificed. Impressed by contemporary physiological theories of race, he insisted that "races" or "nationalities" (synonymous for Thierry) even within old established states were distinct, basic units not easily effaced or assimilated into a large and foreign group. For Thierry, then, folklore revealed the abiding strength of such a nationality's identity and its hatred for a conqueror, even centuries after the conquest. In fact, he attached so much importance to the determinant of "race" that often he seemed to regard folklore as merely part of a superstructure, an expression of something more basic, something material or rather biological.

But at times Thierry commented on folklore's effects on the society, presenting folklore as a strong social force that kept alive hope and preserved national identity. He noted, for example, how the Celtic people of Britain embellished their life of poverty in a harsh land with memories and hopes, which enabled them to accept present distress as only temporary and always to look forward to the restoration of their power in Britain. Along with the emphasis on "race," then, Thierry recognized the power that ideas—in this case, folklore—could have within a society.

He understood this kind of power well. As we have already seen, he believed that a properly written history of France could have the same power for strengthening French liberalism. And he tried to make his own historical writing more effective by consciously incorporating into it some of the characteristics of folklore. "The naïveté of color of legends" was one of the ingredients in his formula for historical writing, he declared in 1834.[43] Moreover, in writing the history of the Norman conquest, as in the essay on Jacques Bonhomme, Thierry tried to "give a kind of historical life to the masses of men" like that of individual persons in order to lend more human interest to the history of nations, and he called his story an epic.[44] He also conceived of his *Récits des temps mérovingiens* (1833–36) as an epic,[45] and not merely in the sense that a history today may be called such. The conception of the *Récits* derived entirely from current folk-lore theory on the origins of epic; it was probably the first history so conceived. Thierry, that is, saw himself perform-ing the function of the epic poet in the manner described by the *cantilène* theory of the Germans and Fauriel. For the materials of his epic, he used the narratives of Gregory of Tours, which were in Thierry's view "old national songs."[46] Like popular songs, they were merely episodic and short, but they could be ordered and arranged to form a long epic. So Augustin Thierry, the man whom Chateaubriand had called a new Homer, played the part of the rhapsode and wove together Gregory's "songs" to form a new epic for his nineteenth-century readers.

But Thierry did not continue long in this role. For he harbored a polemical and critical spirit that would not long allow him merely to narrate, paint, or sing. True, a love of historical authenticity had induced him to keep his opinions inconscpicuous in the *Récits*, and the same love had moved him and Mignet to plan in 1826 a history of France com-posed solely of the words of the chronicles themselves, pre-sented in chronological order. They soon abandoned this project, however, discovering that a "work where art played no part was antipathetic to us."[47] It was not only art that was lacking, but criticism. The latter became more important to Thierry after the first edition of his *Histoire de la Conquête*. His 1834 formula for historical writing included "the severe reason of modern historians" as well as the legend-tellers' naïveté.[48] And he himself followed that formula. In 1827, he published a collection of his critical articles and letters on French history; in 1834 he reprinted more of them in his *Dix ans d'études historiques*, and six years later he attached to his *Récits des temps mérovingiens* a long critical review of French historiography, "Considérations sur l'histoire de France."

He also responded to Michelet's histories in the 1830s with criticism and a call for reason. Rather than announcing them the fulfillment of his program of 1820—though in many ways it was fulfilled in Michelet's history—Thierry attacked the symbolism and bold interpretations of the young historian, condemning the "use of methods borrowed from metaphysics, that of Vico, by which all histories are created in the image of a single one, Roman history, and this method imported from Germany which sees in each fact the sign of an idea, and in the course of human events a perpetual psychomachy." Calling history "a science which has for its object real facts and positive testimonies," Thierry asserted that the proper method for historians was "analysis and exact observation."[49]

Joined to this new mood was Thierry's diminishing sympathy for the common people. Brother-in-arms to Guizot and ardent admirer of La Fayette, Thierry became a staunch Orleanist. His old loyalties to the people, to the neglected masses, were increasingly limited to the middle class. Beginning in 1834, he collaborated in the collecting of town and communal charters, and in 1853 he summed up his work in an *Essai sur l'histoire des tiers états*. This history of the Third Estate was far from the legend of Jacques Bonhomme; it was rather the history of the bourgeoisie, the Estates-General, and a tableau of municipal France, all presented in the kind of language that the younger Thierry had denounced as abstract and philosophical. After the *Récits des temps mérovingiens*, then, Thierry did not write history that depicted popular *mœurs* and color and popular life, and so he no longer had the old reasons for studying folklore. He left folklore, and Jacques Bonhomme, behind him.

2. *Michelet: Between History and Legend*

In the last years of the Restoration, a young professor named Jules Michelet recorded his ideas and projects for studies in folklore. In March of 1828 he conceived an "Encyclopédie des chants populaires" and urged himself to "introduce into it some systematic order."[1] There is no doubt about his model for this project: "See Herder: Voice of the People in Songs," he noted. In June he read the *Nibelungenlied* and the next month Walter Scott's *Minstrelsy of the Scottish Border*, translated by Artaud.[2] From mid-August to mid-September he was in Germany reading German history and folk literature—including works by Ludwig Tieck, Jacob Grimm, Joseph von Görres (the *Volksbücher*), and Achim von Arnim. He also met there such scholars as Görres, folklorist and orientalist, and Friedrich Creuzer, the leading exponent of the symbolic interpretation of myth.[3] During the next six months, as Michelet read the *Volsünga Saga*, Arnim and Brentano's *Des Knaben Wunderhorn*, and Grimm's *Über den altdeutschen Meistergesang*,[4] the idea of translations was uppermost in his mind. In June of 1829 he jotted down his "idea of a translation of great epic monuments," and later in the month he began translating Grimm's *Meistergesang*. He thought of doing the same for the *Wunderhorn*. In the same month he also perused Görres' *Altteutsche Volks-und Meisterlieder* and the *Volksbücher*, along with the Grimms' *Altdeutsche Wälder*, perhaps with translation in mind. In any case, he was still mulling over the idea of translation in October of 1829, when he wrote in his journal: "Works carried out in common, under my direction, for example a translation of the *Nibelungenlied* by several students of the Ecole Préparatoire."[5]

Michelet did not carry out these projects. In August of 1829 he was relieved of teaching philosophy and put in charge of history alone, and in the next several decades his lecturing and writing in history occupied him completely. In late June 1829, moreover, he recorded second thoughts about translating Grimm's *Meistergesang*, commenting that the book was not very interesting in itself, but was "good to incorporate into an essay on the old German nationality."[6] This thought soon prevailed with him generally, as he turned from his translation projects to historical writing alone.

In view of Michelet's personal background, it is in some ways remarkable that he even made plans for folklore studies. Unlike many folklorists rooted in rural and small-town life changing little over the generations, Michelet knew only the bustle of Paris, where life was anything but traditional in his youth during the years of the Directory, Consulate, and First Empire. Until he was thirty years old, he had traveled outside the city only once, and then only briefly. His parents did not have deep roots even in Paris, having migrated there from separate provincial towns, and they did not maintain a tradition of religious belief and practice: Herder and the Grimm brothers came from strongly devout families; Michelet's father was a Voltairean.[7]

Of course, Michelet broadened his horizons beyond Paris through reading from an early age at home. Included in his early reading were such works as *Ossian* and the *Dictionnaire de la fable* by Chompré. But far more important, it seems, was the condition in which his family found itself during the years of the First Empire. Working in his father's printing shop, Michelet led an austere and impoverished life that later, of course, he associated with the life of the *peuple*.[8] Identifying himself with the people and nurturing an almost obsessive love for them, the young historian was disposed to look sympathetically upon their thought—their folklore— and even to attribute to them what hitherto had been considered the work of great individuals, priests, or God.

During those difficult early years, too, Michelet's famous imagination came into its own, compensating for his drab and lonely situation by creating a brilliant world of fantasy:

"The more the life of a young man has been uniform and solitary, the more the imagination is struck," he concluded.[9] Later as a historian he brought to his subject a poetic mentality that Vico had considered characteristic of primitive man and child, giving "sense and passion to insensate things,"[10] animating the inanimate and personifying the nonpersonal —France, the Revolution, cities, armies, even buildings such as the Bastille. When he looked over his life upon completion of his history of France (1869), he distinguished his own work by saying that he was the first historian to treat France "as a soul and a person."[11] This fundamental bent of Michelet's mind was conducive to the sympathetic study of folklore.

His philosophical education, which was inseparable from his historical education, provided a reasoned basis for such a sympathy. The philosophies of history by Vico, Condorcet, Kant, Lessing, Herder, and others that Michelet read in the decisive year 1824 all offered speculations on the development of the world of men in contrast to the world of nature. But it was Vico who fully revealed to Michelet the important role of folklore in the early stages of civilization. Eager to contemplate the wisdom of the past, Michelet welcomed Vico's protest against the arrogance of Cartesian philosophers who scorned the changing world of history, language, and poetry in their preference for the timeless truths attainable through individual reason. Imbued with democratic sentiments, Michelet readily received the demonstration that the people had made themselves through their institutions, founded by a spontaneous "common sense" in ages before reflective, analytical thought. In Vico, that is, he found elaborated the idea that the wisdom of the past was embodied in religion, poetry, and institutions created by "humanity" rather than a few great men or divine intervention: he learned that "vulgar wisdom" was the mother of philosophic wisdom, that the "true Homer" was the Greek people themselves, and that other founding fathers were also poetic characters representing an entire society. Vico's symbolic interpretations of the founding fathers and his rehabilitation of "vulgar wisdom" thus transformed all early ideas and traditions into a kind of folklore, a creation of the popular mind. Michelet adopted this view and carried it further, attaching great importance to vulgar wisdom and popular accounts of history even in periods far beyond the early times treated by Vico.

For his detailed historical studies, Michelet looked to folklore for evidence of popular *mœurs* and character. He had first considered the use of popular vocabulary and general literature for this purpose.[12] Then in 1828, the year when Quinet's first work on Herder appeared, he read the *Nibelungenlied* and other works of folk literature in preparation for a study of the "old German nationality," and he made his first German trip to gather other materials of this sort.[13] To Vico's ideas that primitive literature was a collective creation and that it was spontaneous rather than reflective, Michelet added the idea—more German than Vichian —that a distinct national character was reflected in popular traditions. He concluded that folklore was therefore a true history, even though erroneous in historical minutiae:

> The myths and the poetry of barbarian peoples present the traditions of this [barbaric] time; they are ordinarily the true national history of a people, such as its genius has made it. The story of William Tell has for centuries aroused the enthusiasm of the Swiss. . . . This narrative may well not be real, but it is eminently true, that is to say, perfectly conformable to the character of the people which has taken it for history. The history of Roland, nephew of Charlemagne, is false in its details. Einhard says only one word; he reports that at Roncevaux *Rolandus praefectus Britannici limitis* perished. People have built on so light a foundation a true history, that is to say conformable to the genius and to the situation of those who have invented it.[14]

Interest in national genius, common in that era of increasing national consciousness, naturally had appeal for the passionately patriotic Michelet.

But he looked for regional as well as national character in folklore, as one would expect of a man intent upon resur-

recting the French past in all its diversity. Besides familiariz-
ing himself with the literary legends of France—Roland,
Mélusine, Renard, Merlin, the Four Sons Aymon—he was
careful to note local folklore in the course of his travels and
to record his observations in his journal. As he went through
Dauphiné in 1830, for example, he noted the satiric songs
popular with young villagers, copied down several titles of
popular poems sold at Grenoble, and recorded such local
customs as the practice of planting a weeping willow at the
door of a forsaken lover. A few years later he studied Breton
songs at Morlaix. Traveling through Wales in 1834, he was
eager to question a fellow passenger, a peasant, on popular
songs of the region, and in Aquitaine the next year he noted
the motifs of a Poitevin song he had heard in the original
dialect.[15] In no other section of his history did he concen-
trate more of such local folklore than in his famous "Tableau
de la France."[16] There he noted such expressions of popular
character as the violent wild dances of Provence and the
ironic, witty fabliaux of Champagne. There, too, he introduced folklore into his geographical descriptions: Breton
lore on the nearby islands and rough coast of Brittany, the
popular belief that the Rhône was a living and often angry
monster, stories of the miraculous stag and Saint Hubert in
the Ardennes forest. And as he made observations on social
structure, popular beliefs came to mind: in discussing the
small social distance between the Breton nobleman and the
peasant, for example, he considered noteworthy not only the
poverty of the Breton nobles, but also the belief of many
peasants that they were descended from Arthur or the fairy
Morgan.

First, then, Michelet acquired a philosophical understanding of folklore—folklore regarded as a spontaneous,
instinctive wisdom and an expression of character—and
then looked for specific examples to be included in his historical writing. In his *Introduction à l'histoire universelle* (1831),
for the first time he set forth his own philosophy of history
and attempted to elucidate the personality or genius of

France by contrasting it with that of the surrounding states. His conviction, like Augustin Thierry's and others' in that time of sharp social and political conflict, was that the nation needed to cut through the fog of contemporary confusion and to sight once more its historical character and mission.

For Michelet national character was expressed in popular traditions, language, heroic figures such as Joan of Arc, and particular historical events. In his universal history of 1831, however, he neglected French folklore and devoted most of his remarks on France to these other expressions. He commented on examples of German and Italian folklore, but he pointedly dissociated the French genius from this kind of thought. Caught up in the enthusiasm of the 1830 revolution and eager for the French to lead Europe into the future, Michelet urged his compatriots to arm themselves with reason and to assert their will for liberty, casting off such encumbrances of the past as poetry, symbol, and material and concrete images. In developing his theme of the age-old struggle between liberty and fatalism, Michelet restated the Vichian progression of human history from mute symbol through poetry to prose, but he omitted any *ricorsi*, relegated symbol and poetry exclusively to the distant past, and hailed prose as the way of progress. Freedom's vanguard, France, was the land of prose, he insisted, and prose was the most advanced form of language. For prose was the least materialized form, the least concrete and figurative, the most abstract and therefore the freest of matter and nature, the form that was most common to all men, and therefore the most egalitarian. In the progression of language it was the last form, the one beyond which there was only action, and therefore it was the one befitting a people who by acting led Europe to freedom. In glorifying the "Three Glorious Days" of 1830, Michelet thus revived the spirit of the Enlightenment, praising the dissolving power of reason and revolution. "March, then, child of Providence," he cried, meaning march in the course that he believed natural to the French: analysis, the dialectic, criticism, action.[17] In the present and future life of France, Michelet in 1831 saw no place for folklore.

But subsequently, as he wrote his Roman history and the first volumes of the history of France, his desire to "resurrect" the integral life of the past led him to include folklore in his purview. He was willing to do justice to folklore, as to the Church, in the past even though he considered it retrogressive in the present. The Michelet of the 1830s was after all a scholar, bold in his interpretations yet energetic in his researches, chief of the historical section of the Archives Nationales, professor of history at the Ecole Normale Supérieure, and prolific writer of history.

It was in those years that he offered one of his outstanding contributions to the study of popular traditions, his *Origines du droit français cherchées dans les symboles et formules du droit universel* (1837). As he proudly acknowledged, it was inspired by Jacob Grimm's study of early German law, the *Deutsche Rechtsalterthümer* (1828), which Quinet had sent from Germany to his friend in 1829. When Michelet was planning to translate Grimm's *Meistergesang* in 1829, he entered into correspondence with the author and continued it in the 1830s on the subject of early German law. Grimm offered him encouragement and helped him to translate some of the more obscure texts.[18]

Michelet's subject was French law in its early poetic forms, which according to Vico's scheme were first material rather than verbal symbols, and then spoken formulæ. Law in this stage was popular, a kind of folklore living among the people. In a book like Grimm's, Michelet declared, one could hear "not the hypotheses of a man, but the living voice of antiquity itself."[19] To Michelet such a law revealed the people's most intimate beliefs and morals. These he arranged and presented in the form of a "juridical biography" of man in the poetic age, beginning with the laws relating to birth and then moving to those concerning childhood, manhood, marriage, property, and so on through death. For Michelet this law was "an enchanted forest" that held him spellbound regardless of his will. "I wandered there in all directions; every instant I found new scenes there, clearings, shadows, half-light, full of mystery. . . ." It was a "kingdom of dreams" that he left only with great reluctance. "Men and peoples, we have difficulty detaching our eyes from it. We leave this fairyland of youth only with regret. We resume our march, but we turn our heads away; we sigh, old children."[20] In no other work did he reveal so clearly his fascination for symbol, in this case the symbols of German law.

Michelet also revealed great delight in discovering the similarity of symbols in the laws of many peoples. Never an exclusive nationalist, he welcomed the support that the new comparative studies of law, language, mythology, and religion were lending to the idea of the common origin and brotherhood of all mankind. He felt a kind of religious awe in contemplating the "fraternity of peoples, fraternity of ideas, in ancient law."

> It filled me with great emotion when I heard this universal choir for the first time.
>
> From my little existence of a moment, I saw, I touched, unworthy, the eternal communion of mankind.[21]

But he sensed that many others would not be so moved by ancient law. Those accustomed to the austerity of modern French law could only smile and scorn "the gravely puerile forms of ancient jurisprudence."[22] As a historian he defended its symbols and formulæ from such prideful moderns. He knew well the power of symbol to imprint itself firmly on the memory of a man in a nascent civilization, a power that he ascribed to an elegant simplicity and a close association of moral law with nature. Solemnly preserved over generations, such legal forms were strong safeguards against setbacks to civilization: law so fixed in traditional form often necessitated lengthy interpretation, but it was in little danger of being lost or destroyed.

At the same time, however, such cumbersome and

equivocal poetic forms eventually hampered the progress of the critical mind. Though enchanted by popular symbols, Michelet was as certain now as in 1831 that they were childish things which should be given up in maturity. He hailed the advance of the human mind beyond symbol and formula as a liberation from the "tyranny of forms." The mind became freer when it broke with the mute symbol and expressed itself in the spoken symbol, the formula; it further freed itself when it cast off the bonds of rhyme and rhythm. For Michelet, again, prose was the form of the wholly free intellect; only with prose could the mind dispel the ambiguity of symbol, make distinctions, define, and thereby create the world of man. And once more he affirmed that prose was the form most congenial to the French genius. To "ultrasymbolic" Germany he opposed "antisymbolic" France.[23]

In strictly French law Michelet could find little remaining evidence of poetic symbols. Over half the texts in his book actually came from German sources, even though Michelet had not limited his research to law books but had searched through chronicles, tales, and fabliaux as well. The problem was not simply that the evidence had disappeared, he concluded, but that France had had but a brief period of symbolic law. The French genius was antipathetic to symbol: "France is the true continuer of Rome. It pursues the work of interpretation. Logical, prosaic, antisymbolic work."[24] French history to the Michelet of 1837 appeared, appropriately, a work of reason:

> To generalize, to centralize is to suppress originality of detail, to strip it of its individuality in order to dissolve it in a great unity. In all forms France has rigorously followed this procedure of reasoning in its history. Its history is a living logic, a syllogism of which royalty was the middle term.[25]

Thus characterizing the French genius as antisymbolic and rational, and French history as a "living logic," Michelet dissociated the French identity from symbolic folklore.

Michelet himself, of course, was not entirely antisymbolic. In his Roman history and his history of France not only mythical figures like Hercules, or men like Charles VI and Luther, but even buildings like the contrasting Parisian churches of Saint-Jacques-de-la-Boucherie and Saint-Jean served to symbolize ideas or the people. As a method of historical interpretation, Michelet obviously approved of symbol, though with reservations. It was useful for generalizing, he thought, but an antisymbolic exposition was equally useful and indeed necessary for bringing out details and distinctions. Michelet's point was that, in order to progress, a people had to move beyond the stage in which there was only symbolic and poetic thought. Once thought had freed itself of the concrete, material form, it could be master of what before had been its prison; moderns writing in prose and capable of critical reason did well to exploit occasionally the literary advantages of symbol. When Michelet denigrated symbol, he did so out of a belief that it had served its purpose and served it well, but that criticism and prose in the present situation promised the greatest progress for the human mind.

In the decade after he published the *Origines du droit*, Michelet significantly altered his views of the primitive mind, history, and folklore. The change was apparent in his intensely personal book, *Le peuple*, published in 1846 and often viewed in retrospect as a harbinger of the Revolution two years later. Having thrown himself into vigorous opposition to the July Monarchy and the Jesuits, Michelet came to believe more strongly than ever that troubled France needed to know itself through its history:

> In order to regain faith in France, to hope in its future, it is necessary to go back to its past, to study thoroughly its natural genius.[26]

While the governments and conservatives had blackened the memory of the Revolutionary years, the devotees of the Revolutionary faith had blackened the memory of the centuries before 1789. As a result, the common people were ignorant of themselves and cultivated Frenchmen were ignorant of the people.

To correct what he considered a profound misunderstanding dividing the educated from the *peuple*, Michelet devoted considerable attention in *Le peuple* to expounding the nature of the popular mind. In the interval since the *Origines du droit* Michelet clearly had had second thoughts about the primitive poetic mentality. He now exalted it, not only as a worthy part of the past but as a valuable force for the present and the future. Whereas before he had seen progress in the movement away from instinct toward reflection, from the concrete to the abstract, and from the synthesis of symbol to analysis and criticism, now he sang the praises of the less advanced form of thought. He now lamented that his own thought had become excessively abstract. Finally, he now depreciated scholarly writing about the primitive mind and heartily commended direct observation of the child and the peasant:

> Your son, like the peasant of Brittany and the Pyrenees, continually speaks the language of the Bible or of the *Iliad*. The boldest criticism of the Vicos, of the Wolfs, of the Niebuhrs, is nothing in comparison with the luminous and profound flashes of light that certain words of the child will suddenly cast for you into the night of antiquity. While observing the historic and *narrative* form that he gives even to abstract ideas, how often will you feel how the infant peoples have had to *narrate* their dogmas in legends and to make a story [*histoire*] of each moral truth.[27]

But Michelet was now interested in the mind of those whom he called the *simples* for much more than an understanding of history. Tired of the self-satisfaction and immobility of the government of Guizot and Louis Philippe, he longed for an assertion of heroic will, a renewal of the revolutionary tradition. The abstract prose that he once had thought bordered on action now seemed to lead only to endless, sterile discussion and writing, while the young mind of the *simple* seemed to divine the truth at once and to act by instinct.

Yet Michelet was not a thoroughgoing primitivist. His ideal was the genius who combined both instinct and reflection. One cannot help thinking that he was painting a self-portrait as he described his ideal. Certainly he made it clear that he combined both kinds of mentality within himself and that he personally faced the same problem of reconciling the two that society faced: "The general battle of the world [between instinct and reflection] is less discordant still than the one that I carry in me, the dispute of me with myself, the combat of the homo-duplex."[28] Michelet as conciliator tried to explain to the *simples* the value of reflection, and to the educated he tried to impart an appreciation of the *simples*. Yet it is clear that he labored more to defend the *simples*, not only because he now favored them, but also because their type of mind seemed to him the one in greatest need of an apology: increasing mechanization and the dry abstract education forced upon children were stifling the instincts and imagination, while the widespread failure to appreciate the primitive genius, along with the Church's doctrine of original sin, was resulting in the slaughter of the "infant peoples" around the world.[29] The book *Le peuple*, Michelet hoped, would help protect the infant peoples which remained by convincing men of the goodness of the people and the blessings of the primitive mind.

A threat to the doctrines of *Le peuple* lay in the dark history of superstitions, popular beliefs in demons and witchcraft. Unlike many folklorists who brought to light only the happier traditions of the people, Michelet faced the challenge squarely. In the early volumes of his history of France, he had discussed the medieval practice of sorcery, and in *La sorcière* of 1862 he fully developed the story and his conclusions. More than ever alienated from the Church and the government, now the Second Empire, Michelet in the village of Hyères clung to his wife and to his faith in the people.

Michelet's *Sorcière*, one of the most penetrating studies of witchcraft written in nineteenth-century France, resurrected a part of the past long condemned to ignominious death—the thousand-year life of the sorceress in Western Europe. Telling the story from the viewpoint of the popular mind, recreating its ideas and emotions, he sought to show that the folklore about Satan and the sorceress was a consequence of popular despair, and not simply of "human flightiness," the "inconstancy of fallen nature," or the "fortuitous temptations of concupiscence."[30]

Never doubting the good heart of the people, Michelet easily found support for his faith in medieval folklore other than witchcraft: the legends of saints, in which he found the dreams and values of the people, and popular tales, in which he saw the pitiable wishes of the abject peasants, their desire for a treasure to end poverty or for a sleeping beauty to love. It was especially the woman who poured into such tales her compassion, compassion for the child beaten by the stepmother, for the scorned and abused younger sons, and for the beasts which she endowed with souls and feelings. But it was also the woman who took up the practice of sorcery. Not without help, however. Michelet savored the irony of the Church's role in arming its enemy. By preaching against demons and a corporeal Satan, the Church testified to their existence and power. By fearfully trying to stop the popular creation of legends about miracles and saints, the Church helped turn the popular imagination back to the local pagan spirits, fairies, elves, and deities that had lived on in the shadow of Christianity.[31]

Still, something more was necessary. Michelet maintained that for the people to accept hell as they did in the company of Satan and the sorceress, they had to be fleeing another hell on earth—a feudal society in which the common people suffered from economic deprivation, social tyrannies, and a harsh repressive Church doctrine that held man and nature to be evil. In the beliefs and practices of sorcery, the people found relief from their toilsome life and release for natural appetites and emotions denied by the Church. Instead of docilely accepting the sexual abstinence or monogamy dictated by economic necessity and the Church, the people found fulfillment in the nocturnal *sabbat,* using the sorceress' arts of birth control and abortion; instead of fasting, there they feasted; instead of resigning themselves to death and accepting all the ills of life as trivia and preparation for the hereafter, they came to the sorceress and received medicine, treatment, sympathy, and the consolation of contact with deceased loved ones. Michelet thus explained the folklore of the sorceress by recreating medieval popular life, a life in which the imagination was heightened by desperate circumstances, irrepressible hopes, and the sorceress' drugs. The folklore of the sorceress, he contended, was not the product of malevolence, simple fantasy, or the design of evil men. It was a popular dream of liberty and joy on earth and a surreptitious effort to realize them.

Michelet did not hide the worst of witchcraft. His story unfolded as a tragedy which ended in the cruel persecution of pitiful half-mad old women. But out of the tradition of sorcery, he argued, came the natural sciences which the Church had condemned. Michelet's Satan was

> this dangerous magician who, while some argued over the sex of angels and other sublime questions, worked unceasingly with realities, created chemistry, physics, mathematics.
> Medicine, especially, is the true satanism, a revolt against illness, the deserved scourge of God. [It was] manifest sin to stop the soul on [its] way toward heaven, to plunge it again into life.[32]

Michelet here executed an extraordinary coup for folklore. To credit the people with epic poems such as the Homeric masterpieces had been a bold move. But to proclaim folklore the mother of science, the idol of the age, was to bestow on it the most prized laurel. While not regretting the ultimate destruction of sorcery by the sciences, Michelet wanted the victorious new spirit, science, to know its humble, barbaric beginnings among the people.

Though Michelet now added his voice to the chorus of those who exalted science, he did not by the same token relegate folklore to the past. From at least as early as the 1840s he believed that there was a future for folklore, a future to which he wanted to contribute himself. Michelet came to reconsider the potential role of folklore in the present because he became eager to mold popular opinion and to win it for his cause. As a youth he had written in his journal of an ambition to write popular books: "If I have the talent for it, I would love to write for the people books that would be sold at a very low price."[33] In the latter half of his life his ambition bore fruit—not only in the 1850s, when he wrote popular books for his meager living, but also in the 1840s, when he wanted more than ever to exert an influence on the course of national life. Having resigned from the Ecole Normale Supérieure in 1837, he now lectured at the Collège de France to a more popular audience, and he began to reflect at length on the question of truly popular education, particularly as he became more politically engaged in the early 1840s. This question became most urgent perhaps during the Second Republic, but over the decades his books and journals reflected his continuing concern for the education of the people.[34]

His basic conviction was that such an education should be simple and direct so that it could reach even the most untutored of Frenchmen. Specifically he proposed schools for adults, newspapers, circulating libraries, and short bulletins for the literate; an illustrated press, songs sung in different dialects across France, posters, clubs for public readings, popular dramas, and concerts for the illiterate.[35] But in the end he devoted his energies to writing books. Reexamining his style of writing during the 1840s, he found it wanting and yearned to satisfy more popular tastes. In *Le peuple* he lamented that his thought and language were too abstract, too far removed from the mentality of the *simples;* he had not attained the ideal of "grandiose simplicity" he had once envisioned. There was too much art in his writing, he observed several years later, sighing "O sancta simplicitas."[36]

In 1854, again:

How I would like to speak in *prose!* The oratorical rhythm pursues me and makes of me a kind of aborted poet. I escape it only at times, in rare moments of passionate simplicity.[37]

Michelet had already looked for new models; he had searched for the characteristics of books that had exerted a strong influence over the people. In his journal (Dec. 3, 1847), he summarized his investigation, grouping popular books into three categories:

1. Examination of great popular books, for and by the people: their formation, their influence. Here Vico [has put it aptly]: *The people has made the people.*
2. Examination of semi-popular books which, although aristocratic, have been adopted by peoples. Example: Virgil, Dante, Tasso.
3. Examination of books made for a class, at first didactic, then popularized. Example: the manuals that prepared for the *Imitation.*[38]

Michelet hoped to write books like those in the first category, popular creations. Of the various forms, legend seemed the most promising to him. As he pondered the problem of educating the people in the religion of *la patrie*, the efficacy of medieval legend came to mind:

See, in the Middle Ages, how the popular or pacific legend of the saints, the popular and noble legend of the gallant knights led to the noble and chivalric ideal. Reciprocal education which re-descended and ennobled all the people.[39]

He now hoped and believed that the legend of France could have the same civilizing, educating effects. He wanted to be more than a historian of such folklore; he wanted to be the propagator of legend, a legend that would educate the French people in the present.

Michelet pinned his hopes on legend because he felt that it could reach the largest audience and have the greatest appeal, conveying ideas as it did in a simple, imaginative form. The bases of his belief were Vico's theories of understanding and of folklore. According to the first, one understood not by rational analysis or external observation, but by *making*, proceeding anew mentally through the steps in the formation of man's intellectual or institutional world. And since—according to the folklore theory—the people made legend, they could therefore best understand legend.

In the 1840s one legend, above all, occupied Michelet's mind: the legend of France. The history he once called "living logic" was now legend: the story of the people, made by the people, and much of it still told by the people. The ambition of an individual to write folklore apparently contradicted the current theory that held folklore to be collective, spontaneous, and oral, but for Michelet there was no contradiction. The people had made the legend and still cherished it, though they now knew it only inadequately; *he* merely recorded it. For that matter, he was one with the people—no intellectual was ever more convinced of that— and so he was merely continuing the work of popular creation. Moreover, in writing the legend of France, particularly the recent part, he relied directly on oral tradition, as he proudly announced. On the subject of small property before the Revolution, for example, he reported having learned much from conversation with peasants and deplored the infrequency of such research *sur le vif*.[40] It was for his *Histoire de la Révolution*, more than for any other work, that he practiced this method. While not neglecting books and manuscripts, he supplemented them with oral tradition, which he recommended to future historians with the highest praise:

> The base which deceives the least, we are happy to say to those who will come after us, is that which young scholars distrust the most, and which a persevering science ends by finding as true as it is strong, indestructible: it is popular belief.[41]

Though in details it was often mistaken, he conceded, on the whole it was true. Michelet meant first that legend was true as the "history of the heart of the people and of its imagination."[42] But he also maintained that it was a reliable guide to the history of observable events. When historical "science" conflicted with popular belief, he had found that additional research proved the people to be correct. He noted, for example, that the newspapers had presented the Revolutionary Federations simply as popular fêtes; finding these accounts in conflict with the effusive reminiscences of the people, Michelet investigated further into minutes and reports and found that the Federations were large armed gatherings in towns and villages throughout France, comprising all elements of the population and thus capable of demonstrating the immense strength of the revolutionary nation to a quickly dispirited aristocracy.

Oral tradition he found particularly reliable in its moral judgment, which appeared to him almost unanimous. Regarding things, he conceded, the people were sometimes mistaken, though most often silent; but regarding men, the people were rarely mistaken. The popular acclaim accorded the two Napoleons was obviously evidence to the contrary. Michelet explained this mistake on the part of the people by simply remarking that "gloire" and misfortune, Austerlitz and Saint-Helena, had led popular judgment astray, and, apparently unperturbed, he continued his apologia for the popular mind. Using arguments that resembled Prosper de Barante's ideas on tradition and Rousseau's concept of the general will, he maintained that oral tradition was the best moral guide because it carried the judgment of the entire population rather than the special pleading of parties which one found in newspapers. His supreme argument, however, was inspired by Vico: the people knew history best because they had made it. Therefore the conscientious historian must begin by noting the traditions preserved in the hearts and mouths of the people.[43]

Michelet wanted not only to teach French history as legend,[44] but also to convince the people that the legend of France was as complete, as uplifting as any legend ever conceived by man. One of the chief rivals of the legend and

religion of France was, of course, Christianity. To counter
its attractions, Michelet felt obliged to show that none of
them was lacking in the legend of France, and he did so in
Le peuple. For saints, France had Saint Louis, the Virgin of
Orleans, and the efficacious young generals of the Revolution. Miracles? What else was the military victory of 1792?
Redemptions? There were two: one by Saint Joan, the other
by the Revolution. "Finally," he concluded, "for the supreme lesson, the immense faculty of devotion, of sacrifice,
that our fathers have shown, and how so many times France
has given its life for the world."[45]

But there were rivals besides Christianity—other national legends. Michelet felt obliged to show the French
legend superior to them too. Declaring the French tradition
the most universal, he asserted that it best continued the
"great human movement" from India through Greece to
Rome; that it carried forward the ideals of all humanity
through such Frenchmen as Charlemagne, Saint Louis,
Louis XIV, and Napoleon; and that it was also the one that
had captured the imagination of all peoples and had become
the "talk of the world." In contrast, the German legends of
Siegfried, Frederick Barbarossa, Goetz with the iron hand,
and others were "poetic dreams which turn life toward the
past, toward the impossible and vain regrets." The historic
legends of England—the victories of Edward III and Eliza-
beth—were not moral models, and in any case their tradition
was broken and incomplete:

> The ballads of Robin Hood and others which the Middle Ages cher-
> ished ended with Shakespeare; Shakespeare was killed by the Bible,
> by Cromwell and by Milton, which were effaced by industrialism and
> the half-great men of recent times.[46]

Michelet's arguments for the superiority of the French legend (now in his mind indistinguishable from history) contained something of the familiar idea that France is a mi-
crocosm of Europe or of mankind, but they were less

arguments than scattered illustrations of his assertions. A faith like Michelet's did not admit of closely reasoned demonstrations.

In the 1850s, with France firmly under the control of Napoleon III, Michelet concentrated on one episode in the legend: the Revolution and its heroes—the people, women, and soldiers. But he also took a growing interest in the current legends of other nations, particularly the small oppressed nationalities. By writing their legends he hoped to encourage the democratic sentiments not only of the people of France but also of other European nationalities not yet enjoying national autonomy. Soon after his dismissal from the Collège de France following the coup d'état of Napoleon III, Michelet began planning a *Légende d'or de la démocratie*. In 1854 he realized his plan, in part at least, by publishing the *Légendes democratiques du Nord*, stories of the heroic efforts of democratic leaders in Poland, Russia, and Rumania. Indeed, all the elements of legend were there: martyrs, heroes, saints—the new saints of democracy—even an *"homme-fée"* in the person of the astonishing Polish general Benn. These stories were legends, like the legend of France, because they were on the lips of the people across Europe, and because the people were making the stories through their actions and through their representatives, the heroic leaders. Michelet gave such peoples their own legend in written, literary form and he also encouraged them to treasure other forms of their folklore such as Rumanian popular songs and Polish popular poems.[47] His hope was that folklore in his time would have the same effects that his contemporaries Augustin Thierry and Claude Fauriel had described in their histories: it would hearten the defeated, unite them, and steel them for the struggle for independence.

Michelet's last effort to educate by folklore was his *Bible de l'humanité*, published in 1864. Again he considered himself merely the recorder of traditions created by the masses of men: "All was so well prepared that the weakest hand has sufficed to write it, but the author is mankind itself."[48] What mankind had created was nothing less than its own Bible. Through the centuries from ancient India on, Michelet showed, the people had created the finest religious traditions, the highest ideals known to man. From humanity itself came all the values that Michelet held most dear: love, justice, liberty, reverence for nature, family, and work. Repeating his summary of Vico of some thirty years earlier, and the conclusion of Renan one year before in the *Vie de Jésus*, he asserted that there were no divine men. Nor was there a great primitive revelation or a priesthood that had preserved truth and educated the people, contrary to the beliefs of Creuzer and the orientalists. A precept such as "Love thy neighbor as thyself" could be found in Confucius, the Stoic philosophers, and Leviticus as well as in the New Testament, but in each case the popular master echoed the thought of the people. The people made themselves. Hence, their Bible contained nothing miraculous or supernatural. The gods were "sons of the human soul," "effects" of a particular national genius, and in turn they were "causes," shaping the history of that national genius.

In this final survey of traditions Michelet set forth his vision of the reconciliation of all men, holding that the traditions of humanity were harmonious. Despite such retrogressive religions as the Near Eastern cults of Grace and medieval Catholicism, man's traditions had on balance progressed from oldest India through the French Revolution. One brilliant light streamed through the corridor of time, illuminating a procession of men joined together in a common fraternity and in common hope. They constituted one humanity creating one continuous tradition. Michelet, among the most nationalist of French historians, ended by writing one of the most cosmopolitan essays on folklore in his century.

Judging by the number of editions of Michelet's books, the sheer quantity of writing devoted to him and the estimates of historiographers, one may conclude that he was probably the most widely-read historian and legend-maker of the nineteenth-century France.[49] His influence has appeared regrettable to some. Out of a concern for individual freedom and international harmony, Hans Kohn and Pieter Geyl have pointed to the dangers of the "messianic" nationalism and the cult of the Revolution found in *Le peuple* and the *Histoire de la Révolution française.*[50] Edmund Wilson and Lucien Febvre, on the other hand, have reminded our age of the Michelet who championed liberty against fatalism.[51] Hans Kohn, too, has noted that part of Michelet's legacy; Oscar Haac, Jeanlouis Cornuz, and Paul Viallaneix have treated it at greater length.[52] Michelet's idea of education by folklore was conceived, I think, in the liberal spirit stressed by these historians. In his view, all folklore—including the legend of France—welled up from the people in a ceaseless, free act of creation; it was not a set doctrine imposed from above once and for all, but a continuing process of self-definition; not indoctrination, but self-creation. To combat the readiness of the French masses to submit to kings, priests, and Napoleons, it was perhaps useful to emphasize, even to over-emphasize, the people's capability to decide their own fortunes, to formulate and to realize their own ideals. And to convey a sense of its newly emerging historical identity to this divided people not yet cut off from folklore of centuries past, it was perhaps fitting that the historian should look to a traditional folkloric form—legend—for a model to guide his own efforts. It was, in any case, consciously and purposefully as folklorist-historian that Michelet worked to present to the people their legends, their Bible, and their history.

3. Henri Martin and Druidic Wisdom

Working somewhat in the shadow cast by the prominent Michelet was France's other national historian of the mid–nineteenth century, Henri Martin. Though twelve years younger than Michelet, he wrote his multi-volume history of France during the same years in which Michelet wrote his, from the 1830s to the 1860s. And like his older friend, Martin believed that modern France had much to learn from the folklore of the past.

Today Martin is more overshadowed by Michelet than he was a century ago; Michelet's works are still being reprinted; Martin's are not. For our time Martin's writing may serve as a convenient sourcebook of nineteenth-century republican ideology and nationalist history in a popularized form, but that is all. His style had little of the poetic power of Michelet's, and his interpretative ability was inferior as well. As Martin's over-appreciative biographer has remarked, Martin was not a great writer, but he was incontestably a writer.[1] In this fatuous statement there is a bit of truth: Martin wrote rapidly, and he wrote much. After spending several years writing novels, poetry, and plays in the late 1820s and early 1830s, he turned to history, and in a few months in 1833 wrote his first volume of a history of France.[2]

History was then selling well; Martin was interested in it; newly married, he was unemployed; and so when approached by an enterprising bookseller with the idea of a popular national history, he did not hesitate to abandon literature and begin at twenty-three what became his life work. Like the work Thierry and Mignet had once projected, it was to be a history of France "by the principal historians" of many centuries.[3] His name did not even appear on the first volume. The prospectus promised the readers that by spending fifteen minutes a day for two years with the new work they would gain a thorough knowledge of French history.[4] For his part, Martin promised to seek "always the dramatic and picturesque side of history, the one that interests the greatest number."[5] Unabashedly Martin began as a self-proclaimed popularizer.

Like Thierry, he became dissatisfied with following the original histories so closely and began to write his own work later in 1833. Within three years he had completed the first edition of fifteen volumes, covering French history from the earliest times to the Revolution of 1789. For the nineteen-volume second edition, he did more scholarly work, and he won official recognition for parts of it: prizes from the Académie des Inscriptions et Belles-Lettres, the Académie Française, and the Institut.[6] For the third and fourth editions he further revised the history and introduced into it new material from his reading, which was largely in secondary sources. He tried to keep abreast of anthropological, archaeological, and folklore scholarship as well as historical research, and, as a result, he gained respectability and membership in the Académie des Sciences Morales et Politiques (1871) and the Académie Française (1878). Yet he was never an archival researcher or an original scholar.

I intend here neither to attack nor to rehabilitate Martin as a historian of France. The dust on his volumes in the libraries implies a judgment that is not disputed here. What is of interest is the part that folklore had in his conception of France, its character and history. Not that his views were particularly original. Among interpreters of folklore there was no one more eclectic than he, although he was a critic of eclecticism in philosophy. In his thought one finds ideas already expounded by Thierry, Ballanche, and Michelet, and nothing new in his method or working presuppositions. However, his conclusions were different from theirs. More than any other historian of his age, he argued the importance of Celtic folklore in French history. The Celtic, particularly the Breton, folklorists were probably the most active of the folklorists of nineteenth-century France. Though Martin had no personal or family ties to the Bretons—he was born in Saint-Quentin—he became "an incorrigible Celt," as he once described himself, and through his historical and folklorist studies he contributed to the Celtic folklore movement.[7]

In his history, as I have already suggested, Martin echoed themes familiar to the reader of the 1830s and 1840s, themes readily identified with the historians mentioned above and with the Saint-Simonian Jean Reynaud, who was Martin's spiritual and philosophical tutor and friend. Martin was one of many writers and academics who expressed increasing concern over the divisions and weakness of French society, particularly in the 1840s, when Guizot's opponents were growing much stronger and a bitter clash seemed to be approaching. Martin's answer to the social and political problem was the familiar one of recalling to Frenchmen their history—reawakening their interest in "the primitive traditions of their country and race," as he stated in his introduction to the second edition of his history.[8] Like Michelet, he interrupted his work on French history not long before the Revolution of 1848 to write a relatively short tract, *De la France, de son génie, et de ses destinées* (1847), which was intended to give his troubled country the sure sense of its identity and mission that his history of France offered in longer form. On the title page appeared the dictum that had been a recurring motif in Ballanche's writing: *know thyself.*

Like Ballanche, Martin believed that the best way to gain self-knowledge was to study primitive traditions. Born in 1813, he was a child of a post-revolutionary France whose new distrust of reason was accompanied by a new readiness to trust tradition and sentiment. Regarding reason, he accepted the verdict of the conservatives: it only led a people to lack respect for the past and for their institutions. Though a liberal and a partisan of the Revolution, Martin further agreed with the conservatives that society should adhere to tradition, but of course he did not revere the same traditions that they did, nor did he go so far as to rely on tradition alone. Strongly anticlerical, Martin refused to follow Lamennais in accepting all purportedly universal—hence divinely inspired—traditions, but rather reserved the right to test them by his individual reason and sentiment before granting them the status of truth. He trusted sentiment in particular: "sentiment seizes the true and the good intuitively." In the long French dialogue between the followers of Descartes and those of Pascal, Martin and other students of folklore agreed that the heart indeed has its reasons unknown to the mind. Appropriately he quoted this classical text and, enlarging upon it, set forth the romantic doctrine that sentiment was a spontaneous intuitive reason, less distracted, less subject to error than reflective reason. Sentiment seemed to him a good guide for societies as well as individuals, and collective sentiment, or "common sense," seemed particularly reliable for France, the French being the people most bountifully endowed with sentiment.[9] With its special gifts the Gallic mind had naturally produced some especially important traditions. Unfortunately, many of them had been obscured and forgotten, so that his contemporaries, Martin believed, lacked a sense of historical purpose, a sense of their nation's individuality, meaning France's liberal mission in Europe. It was to convey to France its purpose that Martin wrote at length about those distinctively French traditions, the ones antedating Roman and German accretions: Druidic doctrines and the ideas, legends, and songs that had emerged from them after the decline of Druidism.

At the beginning of Martin's first history of France was a picture of a bearded Druid in white robes cutting the sacred *gui*, while a crowd of Gauls looked on intently.[10] Martin intended the picture not merely to illustrate an early Gallic custom but to call attention at the outset to a tradition that had shaped all subsequent French history: offspring of the national genius, Druidic sentiments and ideas had never ceased to make themselves felt through the many centuries of French history. It was not mere coincidence that Martin's idea of a primitive doctrine working throughout all later history resembled Ballanche's: between the two men there was a direct intellectual link in Jean Reynaud, the man who introduced Martin to Druidism and to whom Martin dedicated *De la France*. Reynaud had assimilated Ballanche's thought in the 1820s and then had shifted the emphasis from universal primordial myths to Druidic traditions. He met Martin in 1833, when the latter was just beginning to write history, and quickly converted his new friend to Druidism. During the next three decades the two men were the closest of friends and associates in the exploration of Druidic antiquity. Martin added to Reynaud's teachings through his own study and placed them in a more detailed historical context, but Reynaud had supplied the basic interpretations from which his friend never departed.

In Druidic myth and the philosophic triads of the Celtic bards, Martin—following Reynaud—discerned the best preserved remnants of the much discussed primitive religion stemming from Asia. To show just how well they were preserved, Martin compared Druidic beliefs to those of other peoples, always taking as his standard of comparison the same Judaeo-Christian tradition exploited by the most orthodox Catholic students of mythology. He found, for example, that the Druids had kept the primitive dogmas prohibiting divine images and idols, while the Greeks and Romans had gone astray. Similarly the Druids had clung to the belief in one supreme God, Esus, the other deities of Celtic folklore being merely angels and spirits and symbolic heroes such as *Gwyon*, the Gallic Prometheus, and *Hu le Puissant*, the Gallic Moses. In addition, Martin contended, the Druids regarded creation as a free act of divine will and not a fated natural event; they treasured the doctrine of man's immortal soul; they preserved the tradition of universal renewals of the earth by water and fire, renewals which Martin identified as early geological upheavals, volcanic activity, and floods; and long before the advent of Christianity, they held in honor the belief in a trinity, composed of God-in-himself, God-Liberty, and God-Truth. To the Druidic doctrines, moreover, the people added the belief that the heroes of their society would someday return to save their brothers and to avenge their country's misfortunes, and the people went to the dolmens and tombs to listen for voices and other signs of resurrection. No other people, he concluded, had anticipated Christianity so fully, and no other had been so well prepared to receive it.[11]

Thus joining the old hunt for the primitive religion and the pagan antecedents of Christianity, Martin endeavored to carry off the prize for his own cause—republican, anticlerical, and nationalist. He did so by finding his ideals in Druidism and by tracing the Druids back to the Asiatic "cradle." Since the beginning, he agreed with the orthodox scholars, priests had preserved the primitive religion, but the Druidic priests he sharply distinguished from their later Catholic counterparts. Martin's priests were intellectuals, *national* leaders, chosen according to ability alone; they performed functions that made them the prototypes of modern scientists, historians, and philosophers rather than modern priests.[12] They resembled also the well-trained administrative elite that he advocated for the French government of his own time. Martin, son of an upper bourgeois family, attributed to this elite of talent an important part in creating and preserving Druidic traditions; he did not speak of Gallic beliefs as being spontaneously created by the *people*. Yet he did consider those beliefs to be emanations of the Gallic genius, and he believed that the people had preserved the spirit of Druidism long after the disappearance of the priests and had enlarged their inheritance by adding to dogma popular legend and song.[13] Hence the Celtic beliefs were both folklore and the property of a respectably democratic elite; they were as old as any Near Eastern religion, yet they were distinctively French. The deists had undercut the importance of the Church by preaching the sufficiency of reason and "natural religion"; Martin and Reynaud did so in the new manner—by finding a suitable tradition and expounding it as an alternative to the Church.

Like the Catholic scholars who traced their own beliefs to a primordial Asiatic religion, Martin had more than a strictly historical interest in the Druidic beliefs, for they seemed to him in the main still tenable. He was one of the many liberal Frenchmen of his century who were outside the Church yet still imbued with a strong moral and religious spirit. In his religious testament of 1883, he asked to be buried by a liberal Protestant clergyman, explaining that he had beliefs not practiced by any organized body.[14] Undoubtedly among them were the Druidic doctrines he had long studied. Indeed he was always more interested in the clear and precise doctrine of the Druids than in the enveloping symbols or the naïve poetic expressions of that doctrine. Behind the symbols on the dolmens and in Celtic mythology, he eagerly searched for metaphysical and moral truths. The two truths to which he attached the greatest importance were the allegedly Druidic doctrines of God's existence and the immortal soul, possessed of a distinctive individuality and free will—the minimal religion to which many a French republican limited himself. Tracing these beliefs to a pre-Christian and Celtic antiquity, Martin rooted his adopted religion in the oldest traditions of man and thereby bypassed the Church that was opposed to his nationalist and democratic hopes.

Martin—patriotic, indeed chauvinistic, anticlerical and democratic—found his political and social ideals as well as his religious beliefs in Druidic traditions and society. That society, he held, was a federative democracy with the annual election of leaders and a proper division of power; an open nonhereditary aristocracy; a priesthood of savants, always open to talent, national rather than cosmopolitan; and a ready body of able warriors, celebrated for their courage in battle.[15]

Yet Druidism and early Celtic society had their defects, Martin admitted, and none more notorious than the practice of human sacrifice. Without excusing the practice, Martin tried to mollify the sensibilities of moderns by arguing that the victims were often volunteers wanting to cleanse themselves of wrongdoing or to appease divine anger; at other times they were criminals, captured enemies, or slaves of a deceased master. Another serious fault he recognized was the lack of discipline that made Gallic society weak and anarchic and Gallic men violent, turbulent, excessively individualistic, and given to wine and women. Still another

Gallic fault was the absence of a sentiment and precept of love. As a result, the warriors were too sensual and quick to divorce, while the Druidic sages were excessively cerebral.[16]

In the course of history, however, antidotes had been provided. Christianity had taught the Gauls love and the Romans had given them ideals of discipline, loyalty, and lawfulness. When these additions had been made to the Druidic foundation, the French genius was able to bring into the world the finest ideals of any society, those of chivalry. Martin thus agreed with the earlier admirers of chivalry that it marked a large step forward in the progress of European morals; but unlike them, he did his best to give the credit to his Celtic forefathers. Even before the preaching of Christianity, he contended, the status of Gallic woman was rising, and the Gauls had always been wise enough to revere the natural woman rather than the ascetic virgin. The chivalric respect for woman was a result of both Christian teaching and the Gallic tradition. It arose not in French territory, where the Gauls had mixed with other "races," but in the Gallic areas of Britain, where the Gauls had remained apart. There they combined the Druidic respect for natural woman as a free and equal person with the Christian ideal of love.[17] "It was in the legends of the Kymro-Bretons, that is, of the people remaining purely Gallic, that the romancers, those bards of chivalry, sought the poetic types of love. . . ."[18] What then was the role of the Provençal poets? Martin acknowledged that they had refined and enhanced the poetic types, but even this work he claimed for the Gallic spirit. For "Provence was the Gallic region [that was] the most foreign to Germanic influences. . . ."[19] Searching through classical authors and Gallic traditions, Martin also found evidence that the Gauls had developed the principle of equality—among knights—and the ideals of military honor and devotion of squire to knight long before the appearance of medieval knighthood. The symbol of this equality and fraternity was, of course, the legendary (Celtic) Round Table.[20] Skipping lightly around a dense thicket of

historical materials and problems through which medieval-
ists are still groping, Martin thus captured fraternity and
equality for the Gallic camp.

But to him the most important of all ideals was liberty,
and it too he attributed to the Gauls, locating it in their
oldest beliefs, in the Druidic doctrine of the immortal soul.
No other people, he asserted, had so clearly and fully developed this idea. He made a special point of contrasting Druidism with the eastern religions then enjoying so many admirers. To the pantheist and fatalist beliefs of the Orient, he
opposed the Druidic belief in the human soul which never
lost its individuality and always actively engaged in a struggle against fatality, elevating itself by knowledge and force
through a series of existences, endlessly perfecting itself. For
the Druids this belief was the source of their famous bravery
in battle. For later Frenchmen it was the beginning of their
idea of liberty, a liberty enjoyed by both the divine and the
human personality, both of whom willed and acted not by
necessity, but by choice.[21]

To find his liberalism so firmly rooted in the national
genius and primitive traditions no doubt reassured Martin,
and in turn he proclaimed the discovery to reassure his
readers, to persuade them that liberal ideas were the oldest,
hence the most genuinely French, hence the correct ones for
nineteenth-century France. Martin needed reassurance. Under the July Monarchy he soon felt that the hopes of 1830
had been betrayed, and he joined the opposition, adding his
pen and voice to those calling for an enlarged franchise and
a better balance of the executive and legislative powers. The
Revolution of 1848 brought him new hope, but soon the
victory of Napoleon at the polls and later the coup d'état of
1851 dashed that hope. Tocqueville, equally disturbed by the
failure of French liberalism, turned to historical analysis of
the problem and arrived at a sobering conclusion: the
French were unable to achieve a lasting democracy because
of defects in the French character and society which
stemmed from the fiscal and centralizing policies of the old-

regime monarchy. Martin, in contrast, immersed himself more than ever in his Celtic researches, working to improve —above all—his volume on the Celtic origins of France, writing articles on Celtic folklore and monuments, and traveling to Celtic areas of Western Europe to gather more information.[22] Through such research he sought to demonstrate that liberty was not a fleeting ideal or a recent conception of the philosophes or revolutionaries, and certainly not a contribution of Germanic or other conquerors, but an idea native to the Gallic mind from its inception. His historical conclusions were certainly less penetrating than Tocqueville's, but more encouraging: the most important French idea, liberty, he found anchored securely in the deepest strata of the French past.

As he studied the popular traditions and monuments of Brittany, Wales, Ireland, and Scotland, Martin always looked first for the pure Druidic heritage that had been overlaid with Christianity and popular legend. A complete believer in the theory of survivals, he studied current traditions with a historical purpose—to glimpse in them the old Celtic character and beliefs. His folklorist research in the 1860s included listening to the bards' songs at the Celtic convention in Aberdare, Wales; examining Gallic manuscripts—triads, chronicles, and songs—in the Bodleian library and in Welsh castles; talking with local authorities like Goulven Denis, whom he considered a "living tradition"; and searching out Celtic dolmens, tombs, and altars in the forests and fields of Western Europe. In the same years he encouraged the Celtic peoples to treasure their legacy and defended their folklore and his theories from the assaults of skeptics. He entered the lists of controversy to refute, for example, contentions that the megaliths were not Celtic; that the bardic triads were not ancient oral traditions but rather the recent writings of an individual; that the mythical figures could best be understood by the euhemerist theory rather than by religious and metaphysical interpretations. He also sounded the alarm against the arrogance of positiv-

ism and the cult of the written document. He urged folklorists to study living oral traditions and to respect the populations still preserving those traditions:

> Historical and archaeological criticism has made immense progress;
> as far as technique and what one can call the material of science are
> concerned, today it has methods of a sureness and a soundness that
> our predecessors did not even dream of; it is sovereign with regard
> to facts and with regard to the external characteristics of texts; but
> it is desirable that it not forget that under things there is the spirit
> of things; that such and such a traditional imaginary fact may serve
> as covering for an ideal truth, and that beside written and fixed texts
> there is an animated text which thinks and which speaks, which is
> man.
>
> The man of the old races and of primitive languages as he holds out
> in some back country of the West, remains a living commentary on
> disputed books; it is there that one must have eyes to see and ears to
> hear, and a sympathetic intelligence to understand. If with negative
> criticism and modern *positivism*, you approach these populations
> which have kept the turn of mind, of imagination and of sentiment
> of the ancients, all is closed [to you]; you see nothing, and you deny
> all.[23]

In the last two decades before his death in 1883, Martin
served as mayor of Passy, deputy from the Aisne, and finally
senator in the young Third Republic. Meanwhile he continued to revise his history of France in small ways, and he
wrote an even more popular version. His biographer, Hanotaux, has given an extraordinarily high estimate of Martin's
influence as a historian:

> There is not an educated man who has not gathered in the work of
> Henri Martin the greatest part of his ideas and of his appreciations
> on our history. . . .
>
> His book is now the true foundation of the teaching of the history
> of France. Most of the authors of manuals have drawn from it.[24]

With regard to Martin's Celtic theories, however, Hanotaux was apologetic. Yet if anything distinguished his history from others, it was those very theories. Tendentious,
overstated, and sometimes ridiculous though they were,
they undoubtedly helped to awaken Frenchmen to the im-

portance of Celtic folklore in their past. Martin played a part in the Celtic renaissance comparable to Fauriel's part in the Provençal renaissance.

Martin also reinforced the conclusions of his contemporaries that popular traditions were not the bizarre, fantastic, crude offspring of an infantile mentality, nor a dead hand on the present whose crushing pressure hampered efforts to change. On the contrary, Martin found in ancient Celtic traditions the idea of progress, a sanction for individuality, and the seed of French liberty.

4

Responses of Reason and Faith

1. Quinet: Merlin and his Disenchantment

In the late 1850s and the 1860s, while Michelet and Martin occupied themselves with folklore, Edgar Quinet broke with legend and myth and embraced "science." He broke, in particular, with the Napoleonic legend and Michelet's kind of historical writing. In contrast to Michelet's story of the "heroic days of Liberty" based partly on oral tradition, Quinet presented his own account of the Revolution as a "critical history," beginning with an introductory "critique of the Revolution" and written throughout in "the scientific spirit."[1] His intention was to demythologize, to smash the idols that myth makers like Michelet had set up:

> We remake of our history a goddess Roma, a Minerva-Athena, infallible yet human. These idolatries have fallen, and like the others, they will not rise again. Behold, we are freed from our paganism.[2]

Quinet was turning his back not only on idolatry and Michelet, but also on much of his own work. As a young man in the 1820s and 1830s he had devoted himself not to so-called science and criticism, but to primitive literature and religion. Young Quinet had argued that the old "national" epics such as Homer's were truer than history, and like Ballanche, he had aspired to write epic poetry. One of the epics that he did write, *Napoléon*, he considered a synthesis of popular traditions, the work of a modern Homer.[3] He himself thus contributed to the Napoleonic legend, a growing oral and written tradition idealizing the man as, among other things, a champion of democracy and a martyred French hero. In those years Quinet's enthusiasm for folklore was as great as Michelet's.

And like Michelet, he was led to the study of folklore by an interest in the history of mankind. After enthusiastically reading and rereading Bossuet in the early 1820s, he turned to a more recent theorist of universal history, one who offered an even more comprehensive view of the subject as well as a philosophic understanding of folklore: Johann Gottfried von Herder.

Quinet became acquainted with Herder's writings in 1823, when one of his mother's relatives advised him to read Herder's *Ideen zur Philosophie der Geschichte der Menschheit* in the English translation by Churchill. Late in 1824, the young Quinet began translating the work into French,[4] almost at the same time that Michelet began translating Vico. As Henri Tronchon's *La fortune intellectualle de Herder en France* makes clear, news of Herder's work had been drifting into France for decades before the turn of the century, and under the Empire and during the Restoration his fame was diffused more generally as a result of the writings and conversation of returned émigrés. But Quinet's effort far surpassed theirs, for his was the first French translation of any complete work by Herder. Though the *Ideen* was not one of Herder's studies of folklore, it did contain his views on the primitive mind and literature, and Quinet's important introduction and essay on Herder's other writings (1827) discussed the whole range of Herder's work, from theology to folklore.[5] At the outset of his career Quinet was therefore a mediator between German folklorists and the French. His ambition was to introduce further German thinkers to France,[6] but—for reasons discussed below—his first effort remained his last.

Early in 1825, he met Victor Cousin and Michelet. With Michelet and Jules Simon, Quinet met regularly for philosophical discussions under Cousin's guidance. Cousin encouraged him in his work of translation and introduced him to the writings of other German philosophers—notably Kant, Hegel, and Schelling, together with the philologist Friedrich Creuzer and the Scottish philosophers Reid and Stewart. Michelet, who was then translating Vico, shared Quinet's interests completely, and for the next several decades the two men lived with "the same heart," as Michelet remarked in his dedication of *Le peuple* to Quinet in 1846.[7] Quinet soon found other new friends in Paris—Jean-Jacques Ampère, Ballanche, Fauriel, and Thierry—men who were studying the history and literature of the less cultivated ages, as he was, and who had come to Paris from the provinces, as he had, making it a center of folklore scholarship.[8]

In Germany Heidelberg was the center of such scholarship. There Arnim and Brentano had edited *Des Knaben Wunderhorn*, there Görres had edited and published *Die teutschen Volksbücher*, there Georg Friedrich Creuzer taught, and from there had emanated the *Zeitung für Einsiedler*, in which the Grimms had published their first translations and essays. In 1826 Quinet left Paris for Heidelberg where he stayed for most of the next two years, studying, finishing his translation of Herder, and meeting German scholars. Among them were Creuzer, August Wilhelm Schlegel, and Niebuhr. A few months after meeting the latter, Quinet wrote to his mother that in reading Niebuhr's Roman history he was most struck by the new view of the history of kings as "only a variegated epic born of songs and national traditions"; it was characteristic of Quinet at the time that he did not express any critical judgment but merely commented on the "strange destiny of man"—that a science had to be created to distinguish between the lived and the imagined past.[9]

His remarks about the symbolist mythographer Creuzer,

however, had no such detachment. Creuzer, Quinet wrote to his mother, was the true successor to Herder and the best living representative of the German genius, which was a "mélange of a prodigious knowledge with the imagination and the poetry of Schiller."[10] One bond between Quinet and Creuzer was their common admiration for Herder. In Creuzer's room Quinet noted, there was only one picture, a portrait of Herder. And toward the end of Quinet's stay in Germany, the professor sent his younger friend a similar portrait of their common master. Drawn together by common interests and mutual affection, the two men talked together almost daily; Quinet shared his letters with his friend, translated into French the latter's memoir to the Institut, and sang the praises of the German in letters to France.[11]

In this period of apprenticeship under the Germans, Quinet wrote three brief essays: an introduction to Herder's philosophy of history, a survey of Herder's works, and an essay on the psychological and historical beginnings of religions in primitive man. From his "Introduction à la philosophie de l'histoire de l'humanité" it is clear that Quinet was suffering from the common spiritual malaise of the Restoration and was attracted to the philosophy of history for the consolation it provided. Feeling himself alone and uncertain, lacking the firm supports of an unquestioning belief in God and the rightness of his society, Quinet turned to humanity as a kind of god. Feeling insignificant and insufficient, he wanted to reach out to join hands with his predecessors of every century and society and to assimilate their wisdom. To learn his own identity, he sought to know them, for their thoughts and the consequences of their acts had become a part of him and his world. In himself all the past was summed up. Therefore he could come to know the past and himself through introspection, drawing on the "common sense" described by the Scottish philosophers, as well as on the written records of the past.[12] Quinet's philosophical studies had taught him the identity and unity of the individual, society, and mankind; his all-inclusive sympathy enabled him to feel that identity and unity.

He felt a special attachment to the earliest, most uncivilized man. Later, when he was less sympathetic to the primitive, he wrote apologetically that his education had made a barbarian of him. But he also later recalled that he had had a mind "opened to all that was proud, bold, whole, and—I might say—primitive in the thought of others. Thus I was swept along by an irresistible force toward the great unrefined poets. What was most uncultivated about them was what attracted me the most."[13] Quinet wanted to be a poet himself, and he made the usual association of poetry with youth: "While I have blood in my veins," he wrote to his mother, "I am sticking to poetry." "Later, I will pass to the novel, and with the approach of old age, to history, to philosophy, to prose."[14] Young Quinet, then, felt a kinship with the times that he regarded as the youthful age of humanity, an age of poetry and spontaneity. The study of this age seemingly promised to yield a key to history, which was what Quinet sought above all. Herder's speculations on man's first psychological perceptions especially fascinated him.[15] From Herder he learned that earliest man had had a comprehensive world view, a primitive synthesis, which had been the germ of all subsequent religion and civil history. He learned too that the most deep-rooted, lasting ideals of a race or nation were conceived at the very outset of the nation's life. Quinet took up both these ideas, but it was chiefly the question of national ideals that occupied him through the rest of his career.

Quinet's *Origine des dieux*, one of the essays written in Heidelberg, was a history of those ideals or religions as they emerged in the early ages of mankind. Ten years later, when he was a professor of foreign literature at Lyons, Quinet returned to the subject and developed it further in a book called *Le génie des religions*. In both works he took a broad evolutionary view of religious traditions, including in his discussion dogma, legend, and epic poetry. In both he followed the religious traditions through time in such a way that they appeared in a unilinear order, proceeding from the Orient to the Occident. Quinet respected the individuality and incommensurability of religions, but he also wanted to view humanity's history as the life of a man and as progress.

He held to this idea of organic development unreservedly when he wrote the *De l'origine des dieux* in 1828, showing the religious traditions of man progressing—or better, growing —like an organism from epoch to epoch. They had a life of their own, as he presented them, a long-lasting orderly life without the bizarre, aberrant lapses and erratic departures, the chaos that a philosophe might have expected from the popular imagination. As Quinet remarked, "Isn't it strange that the reign of the impossible, of the marvelous, of the ideal, is incomparably less varied among peoples than that of reflection and of the real, and that the gods live longer than empires?"[16] In no other work did he stress so much the continuity and endurance of traditions, and—not by coincidence—in no other work was he so dependent on German philosophy.

Thoroughly steeped in the language and thought of Herder, Görres, Hegel, and Schelling, this early sketch retraced the course of the "cosmogonic idea" or creation coming to know itself, rising to full consciousness in the historical thought of reflective humanity after long ages of less conscious activity in the inorganic world and the lower orders of the organic world. In the process mankind passed through three psychological stages: first, man was enveloped in nature, his mental activity was limited to sensation, and his religion was pantheism. Then he began to copy nature spontaneously in his thought, creating myth composed of symbols of the physical world outside man. The Indians kept their mythology in that stage, but to the West the Greeks began to project themselves into traditions. As they became more conscious of themselves and desirous of attaining immortality by rising above nature, they personified themselves in gods. To these gods the people increasingly attributed their own historical experiences and eventually mythology grew into epic poetry. Then when the people passed into a reflective stage, epic poetry gave way to history. The myths, then, were symbolic, but there was no one universal principle for interpreting them: in some ages the symbols represented nature, in others history, and sometimes mixtures of the two. Thus in the life of traditions there were major stages, qualitatively different, that succeeded one another over time as human consciousness changed.

On the much debated question of the origin of traditions, Quinet in 1828 echoed Herder: the epic poems, like the original religious ideal, spontaneously emanated from the "soul of a people."[17] The creation of such poetry was the continuing act of a whole people. "Instead of being chained to stone or bronze" in written or pictorial form, the national poem soared in song from forest to forest, across mountains, from island to island. It was put into writing only when the collective breath of inspiration began to fail. Comparing the "impersonal" collective art of creating an epic poem to cathedral building in the Middle Ages, Quinet insisted that the tradition was formed by the genius of all. Orpheus was a personification of generations.

Into both myth and epic, then, were projected the character and experiences of an entire people. A people personified itself and then adored itself in its mythical and legendary form. "It bows down before its own past, it reconstructs it avidly; it makes of itself an idol that it enriches with each conquest of the present";[18] in this way, for example, the migrations, conquests, and labors of the Greek people became part of the story of Hercules. Quinet here conformed to the consensus of his time in finding collective actions and personality rather than individuals in popular traditions. With serene detachment—or fascination—he described the ancient process of collective mythmaking which he was to assail in the 1860s.

As much as any thoroughgoing rationalist, Quinet

wanted to find a historical law, a formula summarizing the total mass of detailed history, but instead of seeking the formula through analysis or abstraction from amassed details, he looked for it, characteristically, in popular poetry, in the tradition created by the popular imagination. Hence for him the epics which in one light were crude historical records were at the same time the eternal ideals of a society. Given the form of art in a people's childhood, they dominated the imagination of the people for the rest of its history. As the stars in their physical movement only approximated the immutable eternally true formulæ of a Galileo or a Kepler, so a nation in its history followed the "living idea" first expressed in the national epic. At times Quinet used figures borrowed from the vocabulary of the arts: for example, he spoke of the Greeks' history as an effort to reproduce in actuality the archetype of the *Iliad.* But more often he spoke in rationalist fashion: there was a logic in the universe, and each people represented an idea in the cosmic syllogism. Whether as a formula or as an ideal, the epic remained truer, purer than history. It was "the substance of the race." In the real world obstacles prevented the realization of the ideal, but the ideal remained the goal toward which history tended or the course which history approximated.[19]

The *Origine des dieux* ended with a call for a new Homer to create a universal epic combining the traditions of all mankind but omitting the supernatural and mysterious. Quinet himself wrote such epics of humanity: his *Ahasvérus*, a radical recasting of his earlier satirical *Tablettes du Juif Errant* (1823), appeared in 1833; and his *Prométhée* in 1838.[20] And he wrote new national epics as well, celebrating a modern hero of democracy in his *Napoléon* (1835) and attempting to weave together the best of all French traditions in his *Merlin l'enchanteur,* his last literary effort. Quinet also took part in the search for old national epics. After returning to Paris from Heidelberg, he began to look for medieval French epics and was overjoyed to discover some apparently neglected ones in the Bibliothèque Royale.[21] Thus he was at once cosmopolitan and nationalist, both a student and an author of epic.

In 1836–37 he turned from the composition of epics to writing a historical study of them, a study which appeared as articles in the *Revue des Deux Mondes* and then as a book, *De l'histoire de la poésie.* In contrast to the earlier sketch, it was a detailed history ranging from Homer, Ariosto, the French medieval epics, the Eddas, and the *Nibelungenlied,* to epic traditions of the Slavs and popular heroic songs of the Bohemians. And it was a critical history. Quinet was no longer enthralled by folklore, nor was he completely affirmative and dependent upon German thought.

Perhaps the first signs of Quinet's rebellion against his German masters appeared in 1828, while he was still in Heidelberg. In a letter to his mother, dated January 5, 1828, he expressed amazement at the "unanimous servility with which one bows without discussion, without preliminary examination, before the German doctrines, to the point of denaturing them by a complete exaggeration."[22] In 1832 he publicly voiced his growing distrust and dislike of the Germans in a pamphlet—and an article in the *Revue des Deux Mondes*—entitled "Germany and the Revolution"; in it he complained of German skepticism and anti-French feelings, and warned of Prussian despotism and militarism. Though he married a German woman in 1834 and made many trips to Germany in the 1830s and 1840s, he was never again an adulatory admirer of things German. Egoistic and always sparing in his acknowledgment of intellectual debts, Quinet became rather spiteful in opposing those whom he had once practically worshipped—notably the Germans and Cousin. Thus in Quinet's arguments against German historical and folklorist theories lurked a personal and emotional antagonism that should be kept in mind as we examine his phase of "refutation."

Quinet's history of epic poetry began with a refutation of Vico's and Wolf's theories on the Homeric epics. To consider Homer a symbol of ancient Greece, he contended, was to substitute an abstraction for a man, a concrete reality. For Quinet symbol was no longer a concrete expression of an idea or emotion, but an abstraction, which for any Romantic was far from the truth. In disputing the views of Vico and Wolf, he was countering the effort to put "abstract forces in the place of man, abolishing life everywhere in history and art."[23] Gravely he warned that Wolf's theory could be extended to all epics and could be used to efface the memory of every epic poet. In the discussion that followed, however, he took a moderate position and accepted much of the Wolfian revision. He admitted that the people had played a large part in the creation of epic—by memorizing the poetry and then by subtly guiding the rhapsodes, encouraging them to elaborate, to alter, or to add to their recitations. And he held that the poems were popular, familiar to Greeks of every city, class, and group. From this idea, however, he argued not the thesis of popular creation, but the thesis of the unity of the full-length epics: scattered local songs, he contended, could never have become the national unifying bond that the Homeric epics were. On the question of the historical Homer, Quinet was adamant: he insisted that a man, an individual genius named Homer, had given the final form to the poems. Using arguments already voiced in France by Fauriel, he contended that the poems had a unity and a brilliance not found in those arising directly from the uncultivated people. He also maintained that the epic in the long form that Homer had given it was preserved for centuries in the memory of the people and rhapsodes even without writing; the absence of writing did not necessitate short, detached songs. Quinet thus reaffirmed the ancient belief in Homer's existence. To forestall a modern effort to transform Homer into a popular tradition, Quinet defended an ancient popular tradition.

If Quinet was unwilling to add to the world's treasure of folk poetry by effacing the memory of an individual poet, he was equally unwilling to add to the stock of popular traditions at the expense of three or four centuries of early history. Hence he rejected Niebuhr's theory that Livy had transcribed into prose a primitive Roman epic composed of once separate popular songs, the songs of Romulus, Tarpeia, Numa, Ancus, Servius, Tarquinius Priscus, and so on. In this case, Quinet held, a German professor was snatching a crown from Virgil to give it to "the phantom" of a Latin Homer, and in the process the ancient knowledge of several centuries of early history was relegated to the domain of folklore. Following arguments already outlined in Michelet's Roman history, Quinet contended that the Romans lacked the conditions necessary for the creation of a popular epic. Rome was "predestined to prose," to writing, to legal and political preoccupations. The Romans did not sing; they wrote and they legislated. Moreover, the people—the Roman plebs—were not free and independent; hence, unlike the Greeks, they did not spontaneously break forth in song or proudly recount the heroic deeds of their betters.[24]

When Quinet reviewed theologian David Friedrich Strauss's *Leben Jesu* in 1838, he chose to regard it as still another German effort to transform an individual into folklore. In fact, Strauss did not deny the historical existence of a man named Jesus; rather he argued that the Biblical stories about the man had been created by the popular imagination of the Jewish people working on a stock of religious traditions which included above all the messianic idea. Though in his attack on German symbolism and skepticism Quinet lost sight of this fact, at least he clearly saw the difference between the new threat to Christianity and that of the philosophes. Strauss, he explained, was not simply denying the supernatural by arguing that it was contrary to *bon sens* and that the believers were deceived or benighted. Rather Strauss saw the familiar biography of Jesus as a tradition formed by an entire people who had accepted it for reality —without conscious deception, fabrication, or imposture. It was folklore, a concept which the philosophes had not understood.

What Quinet disliked about Strauss's work was its tendency to strip a tradition down to only the most ordinary events and to treat concrete details about a hero as symbols in a myth, symbols representing abstract ideas. As in his defense of Homer, Quinet argued that there *had* been extraordinary men capable of extraordinary achievements, and that the traditional account of Jesus' life was fundamentally historical. Jesus' first call to the disciples by the Sea of Galilee and their immediate acceptance, for example, did not need to be regarded as mythical if one imagined the personal magnetism of such a man. Similarly, the story of the temptation in the wilderness did not need to be accepted as a supernatural event or dismissed as fantasy, but might be considered a reality within Jesus' mind. To reduce such events to an idea was to impoverish history and to lend to Christianity a double truth, one for the masses, another for the priests or intellectuals—a move which the democrat Quinet could not abide.[25]

Quinet's reply to Strauss, the first by any Frenchman, was clearly not the protest of a threatened fundamentalist; Quinet was defending not belief in the supernatural but rather his idea of the individual's importance in history and was protesting against efforts to strip history of the extraordinary. Quinet was objecting, as Thierry and Barante had done before him, to historical determinism and to preoccupation with society's part in the movement of history and the creation of art—all of which seemed to obscure the idea that the individual decided and acted for himself (a familiar French philosophy of our own century). God, humanity, impersonal historical forces—Quinet would allow none of them to overshadow the individual's action and free will. On this matter, he never wavered. In 1828 his most important point of disagreement with Herder was that divine intervention was not necessary to set human history into motion and to set it apart from the rest of creation;[26] he held that all through history there had been a continuous assertion of human will against nature—indeed the individual will and act had been the distinctive facts of human history.

About the time that Quinet emerged from his apprenticeship and took a sharply critical view of the Germans, he also became openly critical of the French government and of the Church. His disillusionment with the July Monarchy set in quickly, although he somewhat restrained his criticism in the 1830s perhaps in the hope of getting a teaching appointment in the University. In his attitude toward the Church, he had probably never been wholly orthodox and certainly never devout, but it was only in 1831 that he began to state unequivocally—notably in an article "L'avenir de la religion" in the *Revue des Deux Mondes*—that Catholicism would perish and that a new religion would emerge from the New World.[27] Finally, he also became increasingly discriminating in his attitude toward history. Though he still maintained in 1838 that as a human being nothing was alien to him, he now tended to judge the past as the philosophes had, by what was still acceptable and what was not.

In Quinet's *Histoire de la poésie* is found the rationale for his new critical attitude: by 1836 he had arrived at a new understanding of the individual's relationship to tradition. And with this understanding he clearly valued folklore less and independent individual thought more than he had in the late 1820s. He no longer stood in awe of tradition and its organic continuity, its enduring life over the centuries. Rather he now admired the individual who transformed tradition. The great artist, he held, created a masterpiece by expressing that tradition in a new form, thereby altering the tradition and breaking away from the old orthodoxy. The artist, then, was always tending toward heresy, and the brilliant periods of artistic flowering—contrary to the belief of his contemporaries—were not the religious periods, but times of growing doubt and dissatisfaction with the old tradition. Art must break away from cult and liturgy to be great in its own right. "The priest creates symbols, the artist destroys them."[28] Quinet now expounded the view of the artist as a revolutionary.

Quinet identified the French genius with this kind of revolutionary. Hence the French genius did not emerge back in the Druidic forests; in fact, he maintained, the Celts had surrendered their particular identity when they accepted the gods of Rome. Quinet found the roots of modern France in the seventeenth century, which he considered a preparation for the Revolution. For it was in the century of Louis XIV that Frenchmen turned their backs on the feudal past. Rejuvenated and liberated by the break with tradition, they created a French literature that was "an act of choice and free will, not of necessity and tradition."[29] They chose the ancestors they wanted from all the past—Oriental, Greek, Roman, and feudal. Yet even in the Middle Ages, he contended, the French genius was already apparent. Even then the Frenchman was more inclined to action than the German. To illustrate, Quinet pointed to French and German versions of the same medieval tradition: the German Tristan and Iseult drank an enchanted brew and went deep into the woods carrying a harp and occupying themselves with love and reverie, while the French Tristan quickly tired of solitude and meditation, took his bow and hunted industriously, and eagerly sought to return to the tournaments of his paladin companions.[30] The French genius, Quinet asserted, was the first to enter the real, the modern world, to leave behind the dream world of the Middle Ages, to substitute the fabliau for legend, and woman for the Church. France had left behind the enchanted forest of the Middle Ages, he reminded his readers, and there could be no turning back.

If, in truth, the Middle Ages were the cradle of popular beliefs and of instinctive poetry, the century of Louis XIV is what separates us from them irrevocably. About that time France tasted the fruit of the tree of knowledge of good and of evil. It cannot return to its age of innocence. Austere, inexorable, the epoch of Louis XIV is like the angel with the flaming sword, which closes on us the doors of this mystical Eden. Every time the people begin to falter, and turn their heads regretfully toward this lost paradise, the great century rises up

of itself and makes the return impossible. None of us will re-enter the
Eden of poetry and of faith of our ancestors.

Epic of past days, trouvères, chivalry, enchanted loves, legends,
spells begun, phantoms, sketched images, poetry which could have
been, which has only half been, drift, wander in the limbo of empty
memories. In vain you ask to be born; it is too late; a world separates
us from you.[31]

Quinet now repudiated both the Middle Ages and its Romantic admirers.

In the *Génie des religions* (1842), he singled out for criticism
two other groups of men equally misunderstanding history.
One of them was composed of the Catholic philosophers
who reduced all pagan beliefs to a single set of dogmas and
failed to see the development and progress of pagan religions
that anticipated and prepared the way for Christianity.
Quinet mentioned Schelling and Görres by name, but may
well have intended his strictures for Ballanche as well. The
second group was composed of rationalist and eighteenth-
century writers whose idea of primitive times sharply differed from Quinet's. One of them was Voltaire, whom
Quinet incorrectly saw as purely a scorner of paganism, a
man who attacked Christianity by showing its similarities
with pagan religions and then by ridiculing the latter, meanwhile failing to see the more constructive and progressive
side of paganism. But to Quinet an even more pervasive fault
of the rationalists—and here he singled out Rousseau—was
their habit of ignoring traditions and thinking of primitive
man abstractly as a figure who reasoned and in a calculating,
mechanical way formed society, institutions, his dwellings,
and his art from simple, crude beginnings.

Quinet argued that the reflective, critical mentality, the
genius that decomposed could not have been responsible for
the great creative work of forming society, institutions, and
art. Inspiration, instinct, the sentiments were the creative
faculties. By a "divine instinct" man tended toward society,
humanity, and God. The early period of mankind, in sum,
was dominated by imagination, poetry, and religion. To sup-

port his argument, Quinet—characteristically—cited the traditions which preserved the memory of "chosen men, poets, prophets, seers, priests," as the inspired teachers, judges, and artists of antiquity.[32] Orpheus, Hermes, Manu, Zoroaster—not the rationalist, isolated individual entering into a social contract—had led mankind forward toward civilization from primitive conditions. Indeed mankind in its infancy was so rich in this kind of inspiration and creativity that it was capable of great works. It did not content itself with crude huts and infantile literature:

> The pyramids of Egypt, the temples of Thebes, those of Persepolis, the monuments of Mycenæ—there are the first huts of mankind; and, in another order of things, the books of Moses, the poems of Homer, there are the books with which the child learns to read.[33]

Later in his life, Quinet had doubts about the greatness of the infant man's works, but he never doubted the importance of the ideal, of religious sentiment and dogma, in the history of man. He never repudiated the thesis of his most complete study of religion, the *Génie des religions*, the thesis of the all-importance of religion as a social determinant throughout history: from religion came, "like so many necessary consequences, political institutions, arts, poetry, philosophy, and even, to a certain extent, the succession of events."[34] Quinet was not entirely consistent, sometimes suggesting that the geographical configuration of a country determined the kind of society that developed there. But certainly the thrust of his work was that the religious belief, or ideal, of a people was the key to a nation's gods.

Such an ideal was always necessary for the life of a people, Quinet was convinced. "Idols" like the Saint-Simonian material progress and the *ersatz* god, humanity, could not satisfy him—nor, he believed, a nation—for very long. Genuine religious ideals were a partial revelation of the infinite; they were sublime moral ideas, goals to which man aspired but could never fully attain. Quinet further believed

that the nation's ideal should always be evolving toward a
higher ideal, a more inclusive one, or else moral progress
ceased and religion became what he called "Jesuitism," adherence to the letter rather than the spirit, satisfaction with
a narrow orthodoxy, and the cult of a sect rather than an
ever more universal and ever higher ideal. Thus he preferred
Vico to Bossuet and Loyola, for the former had urged the
Church to enlarge its purview, to recognize the divine wisdom in pagan beliefs and legends.[35]

Quinet wanted the new religious ideals to emerge spontaneously, as the religions and literature of primitive times
had emerged according to the common Romantic view. In
that way, he held, the modern ideals or dogmas of liberty,
democracy, and the unity of modern civilization had already
established themselves. The new religion that expressed
them best was flowering in the New World, and appropriately it was a blossom on the traditions of both the Occident
and the Orient: the truly modern religion for Quinet was the
transcendental Unitarianism of New England. In France,
meanwhile, the urgent task was to shake off the grip of a
superannuated and ossified religion, Roman Catholicism.
Quinet did his part by joining Michelet in denouncing "Jesuitism" from his professorial pulpit in the Collège de France
in 1843–45[36] and by zealously working for a complete separation of Church and State in government and education.

So from 1828 to 1848 Quinet moved step by step from an
all-embracing sympathetic attitude to a critical and exclusive one. He broke his ties with his masters, the Germans
and Cousin, and he also moved into opposition to the
Church and the July Monarchy. Like the protagonist of his
semi-autobiographical prose epic, *Merlin l'enchanteur* (1820),
he became disenchanted—not that he lost his magical powers, but he progressively shed what he came to regard as
illusions. Little by little Edgar Quinet freed himself from
the spell under which he had so happily taken his early
lessons in history, philosophy, and folklore.

Louis Napoleon's victory at the polls in December 1848,

brought further disenchantment. Quinet could no longer accept the Napoleonic legend which he once had helped to propagate. With remarkable swiftness, he observed in 1849, the flesh-and-blood Napoleon in power had dissipated the legend, indeed the "superstition":

> The legend of Caesar governed for 600 years; that of Charlemagne dominated, in reality, all the Middle Ages; the superstition of the Napoleonic legend has vanished before reality in a few months.[37]

After the coup d'état in 1851, Quinet went into exile and remained outside France until the fall of the Second Empire in 1870. When he prepared an edition of his collected works in 1857, he considered suppressing his poem *Napoléon* but decided not to, confident that the "modern spirit" together with the reality of a new Napoleon in history had effectively nullified the legend:

> The naïve imagination of the people will not draw from it new epic cycles, as one believed for a moment.
>   The interest that one can find in this poem lies, in part, it seems to me, in the ingenious attempt that the author made to fix a legend that the modern spirit, with its rigorous exactitude and its sure means of criticism, prevented from being established.[38]

Two years earlier, in this same critical mood heightened by disillusionment, anger, and sadness, the exiled Quinet had written his most thoroughgoing work of historical criticism, his brief "Philosophie de l'histoire de France."[39] In it he lashed out against the historians of the first half of the century for their fatalistic and providential views of history, their practice of blithely finding the germ of liberty in the French past, whether in the time of the Druids or of Saint Louis, and then suggesting that even centuries of absolute rule had in some way led to liberty in the Revolution. What Quinet opposed was the idea that whatever had happened was right and that every institution and event had a necessary place in the course of history. In these schemes the failures of the States-General were excused as premature, the French rejection of Protestantism was interpreted as evidence that Protestantism was wrong, and the dictator Napoleon was deemed necessary to save liberty. Marshalling the language and critical spirit of the Enlightenment, Quinet denounced such "superstitions" and "idols."

In the same spirit in 1865 he again attacked the idol makers among historians, as we saw at the beginning of this chapter. His history of the Revolution, in which that attack was launched, was thus the fruit of a long-growing conviction that he must judge history critically and range himself against modern legend and against modern efforts to reinterpret old literature and history as folklore. In his last study of ancient folklore, Quinet moved even further from his early position. But that work, his *Esprit nouveau*, belongs to the period of the late 1860s and 1870s. Before turning to it, we should first consider a forceful Roman Catholic reply to Quinet and to other historians of the first half of the century.

2. Ozanam: Christianity and Folklore

In the first half of the nineteenth century, the Church in France had a particularly valuable advocate in Frédéric Ozanam. He was both a liberal and a fervent Roman Catholic, an uncommon combination in the half century after the Revolution. He was a professor in the secular University and an able scholar of history, literature, and religions. Ozanam, in short, was a Roman Catholic who could answer the Martins, Michelets, and Quinets of the day on their own ground. Born in 1813, he had none of the antirevolutionary passions of a Bonald or a Maistre, and when he began to write in the late Restoration, he did not join in his elders' debate on the French Revolution. Though in his youth he associated himself with the older generation—Ballanche and Eckstein, Görres and Friedrich Schlegel—in the search for a primitive religion, he did not linger long in the twilight of prehistory and ancient history. Ozanam became most con-

cerned with the traditions of the European Middle Ages—
the barbarian and Christian legends, epics, and religions of
the first fourteen centuries of our era. He chose to defend the
Church's historical role in the very period in which anti-
clericals from Voltaire to Quinet had condemned it most
vehemently.

In Ozanam's youth a love of the Church had been instilled in him by his devout middle-class parents and his
clerical teachers in the Collège de Lyon. When he began to
examine his beliefs for himself in his fifteenth year, his un-
tested faith disintegrated. Plunged into an abyss of doubt, he
desperately sought the way to a new spiritual certainty acceptable to his reason. With the guidance of a gifted teacher
of philosophy, Abbé Noirot, he succeeded in finding his way
back to the Church and thereafter clung to its teaching with
an intense loyalty, knowing that it alone stood between him
and the torment of an uncertainty he could not bear. Emerging from his crisis in 1829, he began writing a "Démonstra-
tion de la vérité de la religion catholique par l'antiquité des
croyances historiques, religieuses et morales."[1] This particular work remained in partially completed manuscript form,
but the defense of his faith in a similar vein continued to
occupy him for the rest of his life.

Ballanche had provided Ozanam with an example to follow. It is clear that Ozanam knew of this example. In 1831
he wrote to a friend about his belief in a current "palingenesis," a new society emerging from the old; during such times
one should search through all the ruins of the past for truths
that might aid in the reconstruction of society. By ruins he
meant above all the religions of the past, and by truths he
meant primitive revelation. "I am therefore going through
the regions and centuries," he continued, "stirring up the
dust of all tombs, digging in the debris of all temples, exhum-
ing all myths, from the savages of Cook to the Egypt of
Sesostris, from the Indians of Vishnu to the Scandinavians
of Odin."[2]

But his father wanted him to study law rather than religious traditions. Yielding, Ozanam studied two years in Lyons under an *avoué* and in 1831 went to Paris to prepare for a doctorate in law. Yet in the same years he continued to study literature and religions. Translating Lapland mythology, writing on the doctrines of Lao-Tzu and Confucius, Buddhism, and the mythology of India, he sought corroboration of his Catholic faith, as he had planned, in all centuries and localities.[3] At first Paris seemed to him cold, corrupt, and hostile to his religious spirit, but soon he made notable friends of his own persuasion—Ballanche, Chateaubriand, Montalembert, and André-Marie Ampère. A former Lyonnais and an ardent Catholic, the scientist Ampère invited young Ozanam to live in the room of his son, Jean-Jacques Ampère, who was then across the Rhine studying German literature.[4] Ozanam lived there two years and made good use of the younger Ampère's excellent library, which was rich in books on Scandinavian and German mythology and epic literature.

Several months before the young provincial moved to Paris, he published his first defense of the Church. It was an answer to the Saint-Simonians, whose idea of progress, if realized, seemed to Ozanam to threaten property, the family, and of course traditional Christianity. In his "Réflexions sur la doctrine de Saint-Simon"[5] (1831), he signaled these threats and pleaded for a less materialistic, more moralist and spiritual kind of progress, to be achieved through the Church. Ozanam certainly did not find fault with the Saint-Simonian concern for "the poorest and most numerous classes"; he himself was distinguished by the same concern and is remembered especially for his part in founding the Society of Saint-Vincent de Paul. But Ozanam's remedy was more voluntary charity and aid from the Church. His response to the Saint-Simonians can be summed up in the phrase "Progress through Christianity," which was both the title of an essay he wrote a few years later (1835)[6] and the major theme of his historical writing over the next two decades.

Another challenge to Christianity came from literary, historical, and folklorist scholars who—as we have seen—identified Christianity with mythology and minimized or denied the Church's historical contribution to French civilization. Ozanam answered them in his capacity as a professor of literature at the Sorbonne from the early 1840s until his death in 1853. His career in law had been brief: in 1836 he received his doctorate in law, practiced for three years in Lyons, and in 1839–40 taught commercial law there. Somehow in these same years he prepared his two theses for a doctorate of letters and received the degree in 1839. Literature was always his preferred subject, and law had been more his parents' choice than his own. When an opportunity arose for him to devote himself fully to letters, he grasped it. His parents having died in the late 1830s, and his mind at last certain as to his vocation, Ozanam was free to compete for the post of *suppléant* to the ailing Fauriel, professor of foreign literature at the University of Paris. Ozanam won the appointment and in the year 1841–42 lectured on medieval German literature.

Two of the most important parts of the course appeared as articles between 1841 and 1843: an introductory survey of German literature and a study of the *Nibelungenlied* and the origins of epic poetry.[7] In both Ozanam responded directly to the German theorists. Without Quinet's personal animosity toward the Germans, he was as disturbed by their wide-ranging skepticism, their philological criticism that first put a collective anonymous author in the place of Homer and thereafter apparently knew no bounds. In the chairs of Göttingen and Leipzig, Ozanam observed with alarm, "half of the writings of Aristotle have been contested; twenty-five dialogues of Plato have been denied, for the sole reason of the diversity of opinions and of the inferiority of style. At this rate, what will become for posterity of the theater of Corneille between *Le Cid* and *Pertharite*, or the writings of Montesquieu between *Le Temple de Gnide* and the *Esprit des Lois?*"[8] Deploring this "sad game" of demolishing "old glories," Ozanam likened the skeptics to the young vandals who threw stones at the statues of kings and popes in cathedrals, and he echoed Fauriel's and Quinet's protest that the German theorists were losing sight of an individual genius in their new consciousness of the artist's dependence on tradition.

A work of art, Ozanam argued, did not spontaneously emerge from a long tradition; it was not a necessary result of national character embellishing a long-transmitted memory of historical events and dreams, reflecting in some way a geographical setting; it was rather the creation of an individual who had worked to give an artistic form to a tradition, who had been set free to select, reject, and modify. Ozanam recognized that the Middle Ages were not dominated by a small number of eminent men as were the classical ages of Pericles, Augustus, Leo X, and Louis XIV. Medieval legends and epics were indeed "collective" works in the sense that they were composed of ideas taken from a common stock of beliefs shared by a whole society. But a work of art in its best form was not simply the product of a tradition. Lachmann to the contrary (or better, the Grimms, whom Ozanam did not mention), the *Nibelungenlied* was the creation of a free, distinct personality, as was Dante's *Divine Comedy*. Like Quinet, Ozanam feared that the idea of the collective creation of epic would weaken belief in individual freedom of action: if one became convinced that individuals were mere agents of impersonal historical or literary forces in past societies, one might be inclined to accept servitude in the present. Furthermore, and here he went beyond Quinet, he feared that the denial of human personality in art would lead to the denial of the divine personality in the universe—to pantheism.[9]

Though Ozanam passed quickly over the religious grounds for his objections to the German theories, his concern for the faith was probably strongly felt here as elsewhere. Unlike Quinet, he accepted the Biblical accounts of Jesus' life as literal historical records: he did not balk at belief in miracles nor did he treat them as merely psychological realities. He agreed with Quinet, however, on the origins of the new skepticism: he too believed that the literary criticism regarding Homer had prepared the way for skepticism about historical events, first about the events narrated in the early Roman annals and then, still worse, about the events relating to the towering historical figure of Jesus. Unwilling to have the historical origins of his religion put in doubt, Ozanam was immediately antipathetic to the new criticism. Shocked by the "scandal of Strauss," he opposed any attempt to make long-accepted history fade away in "the nebulous light of myth and symbol."[10] His religion was at stake, as Quinet's was not.

Ozanam was also disturbed by the nationalism of the German scholars who vaunted the barbarians' liberty; gloried in their pre-Christian beliefs in divinity and immortality; and extolled the *Nibelungenlied* as the incomparable masterpiece of the Middle Ages. Ozanam could have named French counterparts for each of their boasts but he did not, perhaps from a desire to avoid controversy with his own associates, perhaps simply because the nationalism of foreigners—Germans, and Protestants at that—was more grating to him than that of Frenchmen. But by implication Ozanam objected to nationalist claims *tout court*. The Franks were German, he reminded his reader, but they had assimilated with Gallo-Romans to form the French people; hence the epic of the Nibelungs belonged to both France and Germany. Similarly, the French chivalric epics belonged to no one people, but immediately became the property of "the European family." Always stressing the common "infancy" of European peoples in the Middle Ages and their common education under the tutelage of the Church, Ozanam maintained that the Germanic fables, the Carolingian cycle, the Breton cycle, the Spanish *Romancero* and Camoëns' *Lusiades* all formed one great epic. He further maintained that in this epic and indeed in medieval history as a whole there was one dominant theme: the conflict between barbarism and Christianity, the latter being synonymous with civilization.[11] That was also the theme of his courses given at the Sorbonne in the late 1840s and published in four volumes: *Les Germains avant le christianisme* (1847), *Civilisation chrétienne chez les Francs* (1849), and two posthumous volumes entitled *La civilisation au cinquième siècle* (1855).

To demonstrate the fraternity of all European peoples, Ozanam called attention to similarities in their myths and religious doctrines as well as in their languages and institutions. His comparative mythology provided thus no small part of the supporting evidence, since he had long taken special interest in the subject. To argue the unity of the German and Scandinavian peoples, for example, he pointed to their common tradition of the hero called Sigurd in the Scandinavian Eddas and Siegfried in the epic of the Nibelungs. Discounting the possibility of diffusion of the tradition from people to people, he maintained that the myth was most likely a precious inheritance from common ancestors, since it was found throughout the North of Europe, since it had endured from the most remote antiquity to the present, and since it had withstood changes of religion, dialects, and manners through the centuries. A variant of the tradition, indicating the Germans' kinship to the Slavs, was the Polish tale of King Crocus, who killed a deadly serpent and then was himself murdered by his brothers' emissaries. Comparing Celtic gods and doctrines to those of the Germans, Ozanam further argued that the Celts were part of the same family.[12]

But the northern peoples were only a part of a still greater fraternity, that of all Indo-Europeans, who had originated in a common central-Asiatic cradle. "All the historical researches of the nineteenth century tend to demonstrate the dogma of fraternity, of universal solidarity," Ozanam declared amid the unprecedented clamor of nationalist historians.[13] One branch of those historical researches was of course the search for analogies in traditions—for Ozanam analogies above all between religious traditions. The differences in beliefs he attributed to particular national characters and histories; the similarities to a common origin and common religious instruction through a primordial revelation. The doctrines that Ballanche had sought in the most ancient myths Ozanam now found lingering on in popular traditions even of medieval times and later. In the folklore of European peoples, that is, he discerned the primitive doctrines of a supreme god, a trinity, a golden age in the past that was ended by the crime of a woman; the death and return of a god-victim who thus overcame the power of death; and the judgment of souls in another world. The symbolic expression of such beliefs, he found, took many forms. The idea of a war between good and evil, for example, was variously represented as a conflict between Volsungs and Niflungs, Ormuzd and Ahriman, black elves and white elves, or as the combat of a serpent or dragon against Hercules, Cadmus, Bellerophon, Beowulf, the Danish kings Frothe and Fridleef, the Lombard king Otnit, and other popular heroes. Apollo, the Celtic Saint Samson, Jason, Achilles, Perseus, and Siegfried all had similar destinies, Ozanam noted, despite their obvious differences. Gods or offspring of the gods, these heroes (except Achilles) fought serpents or dragons and in most cases also encountered a *femme fatale*. The heroes died, most of them after a betrayal; they then descended to hell, but soon—according to popular belief—returned to life or to immortality.[14] In the Indo-European family, Ozanam concluded, the eternal subject of epic songs was "always the struggle of good and evil, of light and darkness, of life and death: on the one side, the power of evil introduced under the figure of the serpent, with the aid of woman; on the other side the hero, the incarnation of divine nature, undergoing death in order to conquer it, and to expiate an ancient curse."[15] A universal religion, then, and not a nationalist "ideal" was "at the bottom of all epics." The divine epic of the struggle, fall, and redemption had captured the popular imagination everywhere.

But unfortunately through the centuries the dogmas had

become overlaid with superstitions and the fantasies of un-
disciplined minds, particularly in unstable societies where
no authority had kept check on the popular imagination and
in societies whose priestly caste had been destroyed or seriously weakened, as with the Franks, Alemanni, and Bavari-
ans. The Scandinavian god Odin, for example, was originally the just and good supreme God revealed to man in the
beginning, but in the minds of the violent people of the
North he himself became violent and the dispenser of misfortune or sickness, and death as well as good. Ozanam
thought of the barbarians as children who lived according to
sense impressions rather than ideas. Unable to appreciate
the austere dogma of one transcendent God, such men
deified what struck their senses—natural phenomena like
thunder, lightning, fire, earth, and sea—and they attributed
to such phenomena both the characteristics of God and the
physiognomy and weaknesses of man. After the gods had
become as evil and capricious as man himself, the primitive
feared them and tried to appease them with human sac-
rifices, to learn their will through augurs, and to command
them through magic formulae and potions. In adoring nature, man worshipped life itself, and in the process he gave
vent to his sensual desires, reenacting the mythical loves of
the gods in religious prostitution, making a cult of the phal-
lus, and seeking love potions from sorceresses. In general,
primitive man, or a degenerate pagan like a Roman of the
late Empire, did not bridle his imagination or his natural
passions but gave them free rein. He did not try to conquer
nature by laborious observation and experiment, by prayer
or virtue, but by quick and easy magic. To Ozanam non-
Christian folklore, in short, was the creation of fallen man
who lacked the self-discipline of the civilized, who did not
check his appetite for gold, blood, and flesh, and who consequently lived in a disorderly society.[16]

Ozanam did not ignore the beauty of some Greek and
Germanic deities and the art inspired by them, nor the lofty
sentiments expressed in traditions like the Eddas, the vir-

ginal modesty that prompted Brünhilde to place a golden
sword between her beloved and herself, the tenderness of
the love that moved her to throw herself on Sigurd's funeral
pyre, the filial devotion of Sigurd that roused him to seek
vengeance for his murdered father. Ozanam also recognized
that traditions like the Slavic epic songs formed a strong
bond, indeed in their case the strongest bond, unifying a
barbarian people in one society.[17] Nonetheless, he could not
pass lightly over the grave shortcomings of such traditions.
Folklore, he insisted, was not so effective a civilizing and
unifying power as some had maintained, for it was inextrica-
bly bound to the existing order with all its defects. Popular
poetry and beliefs merely reflected the untrammeled passions and disorder of paganism.[18] Being a popular creation,
folklore celebrated the heroes consecrated by tradition and
it depicted the folkways already well rooted in the society.
How could it elevate a people's morals? How could it civilize? Underlying this criticism of folklore were assumptions
about God and history which differed from those of other
scholars already encountered in this study. Ozanam accepted neither Ballanche's view of pagan poet-prophets
civilizing a people with poetry and revealed dogma nor Michelet's and Quinet's identification of God with ideals that
unfolded in human history and manifested themselves in
folklore. For Ozanam, a personal God in the beginning had
intervened from outside history to reveal truths to his creature; the best man could do was to preserve the revealed
dogmas as pure ideas, free from anthropomorphic fables—
that is, to discipline his imagination or at least to discipline
his appetites so that the fictions springing from his imagination might be morally uplifting. In sum, man should become
civilized.

Unlike most of the other students of folklore figuring in
this study, Ozanam sided completely with civilization. In
varying degrees Ballanche, Barante, Fauriel, Michelet, and
Quinet regretted that in the process of becoming civilized
man had lost spontaneity, vigor of imagination, and poetic

fecundity. Recognizing within themselves the *homo duplex* that Michelet best described, they yearned for an inner harmony and a directness in the expression of emotion and imagination. Though they did not admire a mythical savage who was virtuous or blissful, they did look fondly on a perhaps equally mythical primitive who was unpretentious, at peace with himself, honest and open in his response to the world–that is, "naïve" and "natural," as they said, rather than artificial and calculating. And though none of them was willing to undo the progress achieved in the West during the last several thousand years, they did view it with mixed feelings. Ozanam, in contrast, neither admired nor disdained the barbarians, but had only concern for civilizing them. More specifically, he did not admire their spontaneity; he regarded it as a lack of discipline, indeed, the hallmark of barbarism. No philosophe believed in progress more fervently than the loyal Churchman Ozanam, but for him progress was the arduous course prescribed by the Church: the goal was the victory of the spirit over the flesh and man's submission to dogma and law. For him progress was the fruit of faith, self-discipline, hard work—the price of fallen man's regeneration—and adherence to law and religious precept.[19]

A teacher of German medieval literature, Ozanam admired the barbarians' fables for their aesthetic merits, yet he would not allow himself to value them more than the literature fashioned by an individual who laboriously strove to perfect a tradition, to write his thoughts in an orderly, disciplined form. Like the philosophes, Ozanam wanted to restrain the human imagination, not, however, because it confounded reason, but rather because, unless checked, it beclouded dogma and became an instrument of immorality. To be sure, Ozanam was careful to point out that the advance of civilization and Christianity did not mean the death of the imagination: when the Church performed its great mission of civilizing Europe in the Middle Ages, it did not set out to destroy classical pagan traditions; it made their immorality and error clear and "purified" them. Yet that purification did entail the repression of natural appetites. Ozanam approved. Civilization as well as Christianity required sacrifice, and part of the sacrifice was spontaneity.

Ozanam considered the struggle against barbarism an eternal one. In the role of historian, he wrote the history of one momentous campaign in the struggle, the medieval campaign in Western Europe. In his own life, he engaged in the struggle personally by working to civilize the barbarian in himself, checking himself with the severity and moral rigor of a Puritan, forcing himself to work relentlessly, chastising himself for his idleness and weakness *(mollesse)*—such as staying in bed too late and spending time in conversation with friends.[20] In his society, too, he sought to civilize the barbarians—that is, the common people. Ozanam believed that the Church should break its ties with the kings and conservative governments of Europe and "pass over to the side of the barbarians," as he wrote in early February 1848,[21] in order to minister to them, educate them, support their claim to a larger role in public affairs, ensure them against poverty, assure them of work, and win them from the paganism of the time. To him the modern paganism was not so much a matter of popular superstitions as it was the doctrines of the educated pagans—the Saint-Simonians and their "rehabilitation of the flesh," the German philosophers and their new pantheism, the socialists and their apotheosis of the state,[22] but it was nonetheless as alien to Christianity as ancient paganism.

Even though in the nineteenth century pagan folklore was not the great threat to Christianity, one of the prominent modern pagans (Strauss) had identified the early history of Christianity with mythology and so Ozanam took pains to contrast the two. In his *Civilisation au cinquième siècle*, in particular, he pointedly described early Christianity as austere dogma and historical "fact." For three centuries, he contended, the historical account of the canonical Gospels was so overpowering that Christians could not bring themselves to create poetry or fictions. Whereas the pagan gave free rein to their imaginations and desires and created charming fictions in poetry, the Christians appealed to reason, called for mortification of the flesh, and limited themselves to prose in which they related a stark *history* lacking sensual interest.[23] When one considers the unwillingness of the liberal and learned Ozanam to admit the presence of legend in the Gospels, one can perhaps understand better why Renan's *Vie de Jésus* produced such a shock to Frenchmen a decade after Ozanam's death.

Ozanam did acknowledge, however, that after the first several centuries Christians had created a folklore, a popular poetry that was written on the walls of catacombs and later on the walls of churches. He was fond of this Christian literature, so infused with an absolute and indomitable faith. Through an application of the *cantilène* theory, he even raised the scattered legends and poems of the Christians to the status of an epic cycle, to be ranked alongside those of the Carolingian and classical heroes.[24] All through his brief career Ozanam studied this devout literature intently. For his Latin thesis, revised and published in 1845 as "Les sources poétiques de la *Divine Comédie*" in *Dante et la philosophie catholique au treizième siècle,* he surveyed a wide range of medieval literature—popular mystery plays and legends of the saints, as well as Eddas and poems of the trouvères—to trace the theme of heroes' descents into hell. When he went to Italy in late 1846, supposedly to rest for his health's sake, he collected legends and popular poems about Saint Francis which he found inscribed on the walls of catacombs and basilicas and written in books in the libraries, and he returned to France to write his *Poètes franciscains en Italie au treizième siècle,* published in 1847.[25] In his *Civilisation au cinquième siècle,* he closely examined Christian poetry and legend from the time of the persecutions through the fifth century. And in 1852, the year before his death, as he traveled through northern Spain, he inquired into the legends of the places he visited, and later in his "Pèlerinage au pays du

Cid" (1853) laced his travel notes on Castille with references to the story of the Cid and other legends, combining his remarks on the Hospital de Rey, for example, with the legend of Saint Amaro washing the feet of pilgrims there, and his observations on Spanish mountains and swift streams with the legend of Saint Bona of Pisa, whose passage across one dangerously weakened bridge had been safeguarded by the miraculous appearance of Christ and the saints.[26]

Ozanam had no objection to such Christian folklore: he accepted it; indeed he loved it. It was morally pure: the people projected neither malevolence nor sensual desires into these traditions. The tellers of the legends were not deliberately deceitful, but "naïve," disinterested, innocent. Hence there was no reason for them to restrain their imagination. They were answering a natural human need for moral beliefs. They were creating the imaginative past necessary for such glorious institutions as the Church and chivalry. Medieval tales of miracles simply did not astonish or disturb Ozanam. He treated them as a commentary on the faith of the believers and the greatness of the individuals inspiring them. For example, when reviewing the familiar stories of beasts pacified by the saints—Saint Gall appeasing the bears in the Alps, Saint Columoan drawing wild animals around him in the Vosges forests, Saint Francis leading the lambs and swallows across the plains of Umbria—his comment was that the real miracle of the Middle Ages was the missionaries' ability to pacify and civilize barbarians who were wilder than any beast.[27] In the presence of men of such faith, Ozanam, a man of faith himself, reverently withheld critical judgment.

Even dearer to him than the popular traditions were the finished works of Christian art, the definitive forms given to traditions by men of genius. One such work was the *Fioretti de San Francesco*, which Ozanam hailed as a "little epic" of Christian poverty, the finest fruit of the numerous legends and poems about Saint Francis;[28] Ozanam translated a part of the poem and published it in his *Poètes franciscains*. Another work of this kind, and the most important one to Ozanam, was the *Divine Comedy*. Ozanam's study of it extended over his whole career. After writing a thesis on Dante and his great poem, he lectured on the subject in 1844–45, continued to do research in the poetic sources of the work, and spent seven years translating and commenting on the "Purgatory." In Ozanam's defense of Christianity against students of popular literature, the *Divine Comedy* was a prime exhibit. It was a brilliant imaginative epic of *Christian* literature that he proudly ranked above Provençal poetry and the *Nibelungenlied*. Examining Dante's philosophy, Ozanam found it orthodox, not heretical as Quinet's theory of the artist would have it. In politics, similarly, Dante was not revolutionary, contended Ozanam; rather he was politically independent, siding with the Guelphs in his respect for the Church and in his attack on feudalism, but siding with the Ghibellines in his monarchist loyalties and dislike of France. Furthermore, though a man of genius, Dante wrote in the popular language and drew on a long tradition of popular literature. He did not depart from popular traditions; he completed them.[29]

Since Ozanam believed barbarism and paganism to be eternal problems, eternal challenges to civilization, the Revolution and June Days of 1848 were readily understandable to him within his old world view. If anything, those events strengthened his belief that the Church must "pass over to the barbarians," in order to educate and to civilize them. From the early 1830s on, he had always tried to reach the common people both in his charitable work and in his teaching. After 1848, he was perhaps more aware of the difficulty of the task and less optimistic about rapid or steady success, but he was more than ever convinced that the Church must throw in its lot with the people, as it had done with Clovis and the barbarian Franks in the fifth century.

Ozanam died at the young age of forty with his hopes unfulfilled. The Church did not go over to the "barbarians." On the contrary, it was more than ever alienated from them as a result of the events of 1848. Pope Pius IX cast off his liberal policies, and in France the men of Louis Veuillot's animus gained in strength. The Church did continue to educate, of course, but it suffered severe setbacks in the next sixty years, especially under the Third Republic. In France, it turned out, the "barbarians" were educated not so much in the Christianity loved by Ozanam as in the secular and nationalist kind of history and folklore taught by Martin, Michelet, and Quinet.

5

L'esprit nouveau

French historical writing of the first two-thirds of the last century has been judged to be notoriously uncritical, and rightly so by later standards. Yet even in that Romantic age there was no complete surrender of reason to fancy, rigor to vagueness, and criticism to mythmaking. The men who were so fond of the imagination and poetry commonly believed them to be in their death throes. Few doubted that science was destined to dominate the intellectual life of the future, and fewer still dared to defy that prospect. Fauriel, for one, did not indulge in regret that his was an age of science—meaning both natural science and philology—an age in which critical judgment and prose were replacing imagination and poetry. Even a man so steeped in myth as Ballanche looked eagerly to science to confirm and add to his divinations, and even he urged that henceforth the investigation of antiquity be carried on with all the combined resources of paleontology, philology, and historical scholarship. In the latter part of his career, Thierry also paid homage to science, and he turned from imaginative narrative to historical work more befitting the scientific age—collecting and editing documents and writing critical essays on them. Martin, too, turned from his early romantic writing to work of a more "scientific" nature; from the 1860s to the end of his life in 1885 he followed with close interest the archaeological and anthropological research of the times, took part in it himself, and in 1878 became president of the French Society of Anthropology. During the years of the Second Empire, Michelet, for his part, took time from his historical studies to write popular books on nature and the natural sciences: *L'oiseau* (1856), *L'insecte* (1857), *La mer* (1861), *La montagne* (1868). In addition, he wrote *La sorcière* (1862) in order that the victorious "new spirit" of science might not forget its medieval advocate, the sorceress, and that it might never mistake its irreconcilable foe, the Church.

Several major events in French national life furthered the development of a more sober and critical "scientific" attitude. Many Romantic hopes and dreams were shattered in 1848 when a revolution once more failed to bring France a stable liberal government and a fraternal, egalitarian society. For many Frenchmen disillusionment with revolution was followed at some point during the next twenty-two years by disillusionment with Louis Napoleon, who as President and then Emperor failed to live up to the Bonapartist legend that promised order and liberty, glory and victory. Not only did a Napoleon meet humiliating defeat on the battlefield in 1870, but the democratic leader Gambetta also failed to repulse the enemy in the heroic manner of the revolutionaries of 1792. Then the next spring the revolutionaries of the Paris Commune failed to realize their dreams of a democratic or socialistic decentralized France. Writing in the wake of France's defeat in the Franco-Prussian War, the politically conservative historian Ernest Renan concluded that these events had "fatally wounded" legend in modern France. The legend

of the Empire has been destroyed by Napoleon III; that of 1792 has received the *coup de grâce* from M. Gambetta; that of the Terror (for even the Terror had its legend) has had its hideous parody in the Commune; that of Louis XIV will no longer be what it was since the

day that the descendant of the Elector of Brandenburg set up again
the empire of Charlemagne in the hall of mirrors at Versailles.[1]

1. Renan and Biblical Legend

During the previous decade, in his historical writing of
the 1860s, Ernest Renan had clearly revealed that he was
captivated by the new spirit. His admiration for the natural
sciences was indeed so great that he felt uneasy about the
value of his own pursuits—history, literature, and philosophy; his own work seemed to pale in comparison. His un-
easiness was expressed explicitly in a letter that Renan
wrote from his native Brittany to his closest friend, the
scientist Marcellin Berthelot, in August of 1863.

> Here beside the sea, recalling my oldest ideas, I am filled with regret
> for having preferred the historical sciences to those of nature, espe-
> cially to comparative physiology. Formerly, in the seminary of Issy,
> these studies excited me to the highest degree; at Saint-Sulpice, I was
> diverted from them by philology and history; but each time that I talk
> with you, with Claude Bernard, I regret that I have only one life, and
> I wonder if, by devoting myself to the historical science of humanity,
> I have taken the better part.[2]

Renan went on in this letter to justify research in history
and mythology by arguing that all the sciences together
were needed to enable man to understand the totality of the
developing universe; his chosen subjects after all occupied a
place in a hierarchical scheme of sciences reminiscent of
Comte's.

As the letter indicated, Renan's admiration for science
dated from the early 1840s, when he was a seminary student
at Issy. It had reached a peak perhaps in 1848, when he wrote
his *Avenir de la science*. Although his interest was thus not
new, there was a special reason why in that summer of 1863
he was looking so enviously on the impartiality and dignified
serenity of scientific work and was justifying his own pursuits. In June his *Vie de Jésus* had appeared, touching off a

fierce storm of controversy which Renan attempted to escape by leaving Paris for Brittany.

In that controversial biography of Jesus, Renan had reexamined the gospels with a critical spirit backed by knowledge of recent German Biblical exegesis and recent folklore theories. His book both pleased and unsettled its readers as few other books of the century did. A graceful literary masterpiece suited to the tastes of the time, it became an immediate best seller[3]: ten editions, or 50,000 copies, were sold the first year. It also became one of the most hotly disputed books of the century.

What was most disturbing was, of course, Renan's conclusion that the supernatural and miraculous incidents in Jesus' life were not history but legend. Renan was not scornful of legend—far from it. As a student, both before and after his decision to leave the seminary in 1845, he had had a special fondness for myths, legends, and primitive epic poetry, particularly for the folklore of his Breton forefathers. When he wrote in his notebook in 1845 "Oh how I love this first literature, naïve expression of man," he was not voicing an ephemeral, capricious love.[4] He followed it up with serious study, as his notebooks demonstrate with their comments on the principal accepted ideas on primitive literature—its spontaneous and collective nature, the *cantilène* theory of epic, and the idea of epic as a people's ideal. He had gathered such ideas from his reading, notably in Herder, and from the lectures of his Sorbonne professors—Géruzez, Egger, and (probably his favorite) Ozanam.

Though he thus loved legend and epic for their beauty and sentiments, Renan did not want to write legend. He wanted to write history—a history of Jesus' life, and, quite distinct from this, an account of the "formation of the legendary cycle of the resurrection," all to be a part of a multivolume history of the origins of Christianity. Much of the legend was immediately distinguishable to Renan: the miracles and the supernatural were *ipso facto* legendary. No miracles had ever taken place before a scientific assembly under controlled conditions, he argued, and most often it was the people, having an insatiable need to see something divine in great men and events, who created the legends after the event.

> Until the world becomes radically different, we shall maintain there-
> fore this principle of historical criticism, that a supernatural narra-
> tive cannot be admitted as such, that it always implies credulity or
> imposture, that the duty of the historian is to interpret it and to find
> out which part of the truth, which part of error it may harbor.[5]

Beyond this initial exclusion of the miraculous, it was necessary to examine the texts and to try to learn how they came to be written, by whom, and when. Renan did so and concluded that the Gospels contained—to varying degrees— popular traditions which had circulated orally for decades after the crucifixion. He further concluded that both oral and written versions were collective works, and that the oral traditions were long considered more important than the written ones:

> Since people still believed the end of the world imminent, they cared
> little for composing books for the future; it was a matter only of
> keeping in their hearts the lively image of the person whom they
> hoped to see again soon in heaven. Hence the little authority which
> the evangelic texts enjoyed for a hundred and fifty years. People had
> no scruples about inserting additions into them, combining them
> diversely, completing one of them by the others. The poor man who
> has only one book wants it to contain all that touches the heart.
> People lent these little booklets; each transcribed in his copy the
> words, the parables which he found elsewhere and which touched
> him. The most beautiful thing in the world thus emerged from an
> obscure and completely popular elaboration.[6]

The result was legendary biography, like the medieval lives of the saints. The popular imagination took an exemplary figure and improved upon it, making it a perfect model of saintliness. In this way within twenty years or so after the crucifixion, Jesus had become a legend; again and again his biography had been embellished with anecdotes that

brought out a character trait or showed him to be the fulfillment of ancient prophecies.

Renan cautioned students of legend against adopting any
one simple explanation for all legendary elements: the motives behind the creation of fictional anecdotes were numerous. As a biographer, however, Renan was not so much
interested in the motives of the legend makers as in the
information conveyed about the protagonist of the legend.
That information, he knew well, was certainly neither precise nor detailed. The popular memory was notoriously
inexact regarding minutiae: it confused places, changed
around the chronology of events, and altered the speeches
purportedly quoted. But Renan was not particularly interested in this kind of information. Rather he was looking for
the same kind of historical truth that Thierry and Barante
had sought decades before: the truth of "color," of emotions,
in this case the impressions felt by Jesus' companions. What
Renan hoped to capture and convey was not an annalistic or
accounting-book precision, but rather "a superior truth": a
living image of a man, "truth rendered expressive and speaking, elevated to the height of an idea."[7] That was exactly the
truth found in legend. Renan assumed that a man's character
was a harmonious whole, pervaded by a readily recognizable
spirit, and that the historian who conveyed that spirit was
conveying the essential truth. Even though the details by
themselves might be fictions created by the popular imagination, such fictions were true if they served to bring out the
character or the spirit of the legendary figure.

With this idea of truth in fiction, Barante had justified his
dependence upon tradition for conveying the spirit of an
age, and Thierry had justified the use of folklore for conveying the national spirit or character. Thus Renan, despite his
ostensible scientific rigor and critical attitude toward legend, retained the subjective, romantic, intuitive method of
arriving at the truth about a man's character through the
reading of folkloric sources.

Though he would judge the marvelous by present standards, he made a point of *not* judging human character by present standards. Under the Second Empire Renan developed a strong elitist disdain for the mediocrity of his times and found in Jesus a truly great man of whom there was and could be no modern counterpart. In Jesus' time, Renan held, the potentially great man was not levelled to a commonplace stature by a uniform education, nor was he hampered by an overbearing society trying to impose equality on the naturally unequal; in Jesus' time the great man was free to rise to the heights of grandeur. Modern men should therefore not allow their distrust of legend to blind them to human greatness in the past. "Our civilizations, ruled by a sweeping regulative administration, could not give us any idea of what man was in epochs in which the originality of each had a freer field to develop."[8] Here Renan was protesting not only against the social and political climate of his times, but also against the tendency of men like Michelet and Strauss to regard great deeds and great men as symbols of their times or the people, and thus to shift the emphasis from the hero to the sentiments and ideas of the masses. Renan was willing to humanize a legendary hero, a son of God, but not to admit that individual greatness was due to the people or to the popular imagination.

Some thirty years before, Michelet in summarizing the message of the *New Science* had written that "humanity is divine, but there are no divine men at all."[9] Strauss's book on Jesus had been translated into French in 1839–40 by Littré. Nonetheless, it was Renan's book that brought on the storm. No book on history and folklore in the nineteenth century reached such a large public as his. None did more to popularize the new Biblical exegesis and to acquaint the public with questions of historicity and the popular imagination. And none made the public so aware of the readiness of recent scholars to regard the popular imagination as the author of ancient texts. Of course, Renan's book dealt with the most widely and fervently revered figure known to its readers, and it set forth with a new confidence the refusal of philosophes and positivists to admit the supernatural into historical writing. Thierry and Michelet had also left out the supernatural and had limited their comments on legends of miracles to observations on the faith and emotions that were the conditions for such beliefs. But Renan went beyond them into a discussion of mental conditions that bristled with references to recent pyschological studies of sectarian religious behavior and "madness." Much more self-consciously, much more conspicuously than the historians writing during the Restoration and the 1830s, Renan was a devotee of the new spirit.

2. *Quinet's New Spirit*

None of the historians, however, gave himself over to the "new spirit" so completely as Edgar Quinet. We have already noted his disenchantment with legend and with popular traditions generally, his ever more critical attitude, and his preference for art wrought by an individual. In the last decade of his life, when he became a devotee of science, he moved still further from his early beliefs about folklore. Quinet's final thoughts on myth, legend, and epic may be found in two of his last books, *La création* (1870) and *L'esprit nouveau* (1874), the latter published one year before his death. In both Quinet revised his thought in the light of recent discoveries in the natural sciences. *L'esprit nouveau* in part restated the thought of *La création* and in part carried the reexamination of history forward in time, spelling out the implications of the natural sciences for the literary, philosophical, historical, and political thought of Quinet's own time. Both books had an obvious ancestor in Herder's *Ideen*, but in Quinet's desire to make clear the newness of the *esprit nouveau*, he failed to acknowledge his intellectual debts. In any case, the science he was now popularizing was certainly post-Herderian: cited, among others, were Alfred Russel Wallace, T. H. Huxley, Claude Bernard, Charles Lyell,

Geoffroy Saint-Hilaire, Sir Francis Galton, Louis Agassiz, and Charles Darwin.

In these two books, then, Quinet revised many of his earlier ideas about myth and primitive man in order to be in step with the findings of natural science. He still had sufficient independence of mind to reject the conclusions of science when the impression given by early myth seemed to him more correct: for example, he refused to believe that man had first appeared in the cold, silent glacial epoch from which the earliest human skeletons known at that time apparently dated, preferring instead the evidence of the myths that man's first environment had been a warm, smiling nature of birds and flowers.[10] However, on the nature of primitive man Quinet had new views that were based on science, not myth. He now considered the ideas current in his youth to be erroneous, and he spoke of Schelling, Creuzer, and Ballanche as mistaken men, without noting that he himself had held the same ideas:

> In my youth, most scholars lived still on this foundation of illusions: the wisdom of a primitive people. Their thought was plunged into darkness by it. I have seen these fantasies dissipated in the light of the new spirit.[11]

An illusion of the same order, he believed, was the eighteenth-century idea of a good, wise, and innocent savage. Quinet now believed—mistakenly, according to our present understanding—that the contemporary "savage" and the ancient primitive were naked, scarcely admirable creatures, without family or love, certainly with no "almost divine language," and without any profound religion.

On the contrary, their religion was infantile: it included the worship of evil spirits and fierce animals.[12] The ancient nature gods were neither symbols, as the philosophers of Quinet's youth had held, nor "metaphors," confusions in language, as Max Müller was then arguing. "Tertiary or quaternary man"—Quinet now unfailingly placed his primitive in a geological period—really believed that a trident-bearing god made the flood-waters rise and that an opposing god pushed them back. The reality here was not a dogma or a sentiment or an ideal, but a geological phenomenon. What the popular imagination pictured as a combat of Poseidon against Pallas-Athena, Helios, or Hera for parts of the Greek peninsula was really a periodic flooding; geological probings, Quinet pointed out, had revealed alternating strata of debris from sea water and fresh water "up to the end of the Pliocene epoch."[13]

Other gods now appeared to have originally been the menacing animals against which early man struggled for existence. Again Quinet denied the presence of symbol or "metaphor." Fearful, helpless primitive man actually worshipped fierce animals, creating for himself "carnivorous gods, with heads of wolves, bears, lions, gorillas, bulls, and crocodiles." By so flattering the beasts, he believed that he was appeasing them: "not daring to attack them, he adored them."[14] Religion, then, was conceived as a means of survival against giant tooth and claw. The same flesh-and-blood animals that inspired early religion were also the real bases of the imaginary monsters that figured in many myths. Quinet even ventured to identify the real animals disfigured by the imagination, discerning in the satyrs, for example, the monkeys of Pentelicus, in the unicorn the plain old rhinoceros, in the goat Amalthea (Zeus' foster mother) an antelope.[15]

Similarly, the imagination of man had metamorphosed gigantic bones uncovered in the earth. Just as the French peasant in the nineteenth century found the spiral shells of ammonite and imagined a mysterious diamond-bedecked serpent, so the Cuviers of ancient Greece imagined animals and men to which the large bones once belonged, thus conceiving legendary giants with serpents' feet, Titans, Minotaurs, Cyclops, and Lestrigons. Such monsters were the ones that the heroes of tradition—Hercules, Theseus, and Perseus—had fought and slain in order to make the environment safe for Homo sapiens in the tertiary or quaternary epoch.[16]

Besides paleontology and geology, archaeology also suggested to Quinet a new insight into the origin of popular beliefs. Homer he now saw as an early Schliemann who had observed ruins and scattered weapons on the site of early Troy, had mentally dug through the strata, and then had restored (in verse) the scenes that must have taken place there. Quinet noted that Homer had gathered legends from other men and taken over the earlier tradition of a war of the gods, but these sources did not seriously interest Quinet at this time. For him now the reality consisted in the ruins, and Homer figured there as a poetic archaeologist.[17]

When Quinet made a last defense of the historical Homer, he again drew his arguments from the natural sciences, guided as he was by the new spirit. In *La création*, he contended that a species did not arise from a collective being or a group, but from an individual, a particular mutant; hence Homer, who was the original specimen, the common ancestor of the "species" Homerides, was an individual.[18] In the *Esprit nouveau*, Quinet saw the question not as one of the origin of species, but of germination and organic growth. If there had been many authors of the Homeric epics, he argued, there would have been no concentration of force, no continuity of life: epic grew in the mind of the poet as the tree grows, adding rings year by year. The epic poet, like the tree, must be an individual.[19]

Just as Quinet's views on myth, legend, and epic poetry were now rooted in the solid ground of the natural sciences, so too were many of his old cherished personal beliefs. Quinet now held that the ideals of justice, love, and beauty were not uniquely human sentiments and definitely not special gifts of the Creator to man, but were common to every living creature, being merely more consciously developed in man than in other forms of life. Quinet's dislike for the Middle Ages also had acquired a foundation in nature and science:

adopting a Lamarckian use and disuse theory of organic development, he argued that "humanity, by forbidding itself to think for a thousand years," had brought on a reduction in the "cerebral mass" of most men in that period, a diminution of the cranial capacity; hence the bad art of the times. His belief in democracy was similarly bolstered by new knowledge that hereditary elites, resisting new ideas, inevitably atrophied intellectually and then degenerated physiologically; the Revolution of 1789 therefore merely established in law what was already the physical constitution of the French nation.[20]

Edgar Quinet, a man of headlong enthusiasms, many times disillusioned, a man remembered for his attacks on the idols of his contemporaries, died an unrepentant idolater of science.

3. Criticism in History and Folklore

"The spirit of our times is essentially a critical spirit," observed G. du Fresne de Beaucourt in 1866, writing in the first volume of the new *Revue des Questions historiques* (p. 6). This new journal, he hoped, would help to satisfy the need for revisions in historical thinking. In the same year the founders of the *Revue critique d'histoire et de littérature* held the same hope for their new journal. Ten years later, the new *Revue historique* gave further expression to the new critical, scientific spirit: "To the development of the positive sciences which is the distinctive characteristic of our century," wrote the editor, Gabriel Monod, "corresponds, in the domain that we call *literary*, the development of history, whose goal is to submit all the manifestations of the human being to a scientific knowledge and even to scientific laws."[21] Together with the creation of the Ecole Pratique des Hautes Etudes (1868) and the newly instituted critical study of French historical sources at the Ecole des Chartes (1882), these journals contributed significantly to what Louis Halphen has called "the reign of criticism" during the last third of the nineteenth century.[22]

Historians of this period—Hippolyte Taine, Albert Sorel, Alphonse Aulard, Gabriel Hanotaux, Ernest Lavisse, Fustel de Coulanges, Gabriel Monod, Léopold Delisle, Paul Fabre, Emile Bourgeois—put no easy trust in popular traditions. Impressed by the Germans' exacting scholarly methods, French historians more than ever before valued heavy, careful documentation, often meaning official or government documents. They profited now from the use of new research tools, such as a catalog of the manuscripts available in French public libraries and up-to-date bibliographical works. They prided themselves on their critical examination of the sources, and they narrowed their research and writing to more and more specialized subjects in order to meet their new standards.[23] None of them wanted to write legend, as Michelet did, or blithely to reproduce "tradition." None wanted to continue the marriage, or the confusion, of history and folklore.

Among folklorists, too, a new critical spirit was in evidence. In the 1860s the French Macphersons of the first half of the century began to be exposed. Garay de Montglave was identified by J. F. Bladé as the recent author of a Basque song purportedly dating from 778. Through unsolicited confessions, the hoaxes of Jules Travers and Mérimée also came to light. But the most shocking revelation was that the leading Breton folklorist, Hersart de La Villemarqué, had taken excessive liberties—in fact had perpetrated a *supercherie*, a fraud—in collecting and editing the popular traditions of Brittany.[24]

One impetus for more carefulness and thoroughness in folklore research had come from the government in the previous decade. On September 13, 1852, the regime of Napoleon III decreed that work should begin on a *Recueil des poésies populaires de la France*.[25] Not since Charlemagne had a French government made an effort of this kind. Primary school inspectors, for example, received the following orders:

> In your rounds question the poorest inhabitants of the villages where you believe that religious or martial songs, festival songs, ballads, historical narratives, legends, stories or satires have been perpetuated by oral tradition. Try to capture them in their primitive form; and when no rule can help you in your transcriptions, do whatever you can to recall faithfully the local pronunciation by the spelling that you adopt; always add a literal translation; finally, do not neglect to remember, as well as you can, the facts to which the collected pieces relate, the authors to which they are attributed, and at least the probable epoch to which they go back.[26]

For the further guidance of the participating researchers, Jean-Jacques Ampère issued official instructions with examples the following year.

During the last third of the century, the folklorists of a new generation—Cosquin, Rolland, Saintyves, Bladé, Luzel, Gaidoz, Sébillot—strove to be conscientious, methodical researchers.[27] They were anxious to preserve from loss as many living traditions as possible, yet they were concerned about the accuracy of the version recorded. Like the historians of the period, the folklorists founded professional journals: *Mélusine* (1878), the *Revue des traditions populaires* (1887), and *La Tradition* (1887), which all urged greater care on collectors of folklore. In the same period new journals in related fields also encouraged the more scholarly study of folklore: among the most important were the *Revue celtique* (1870), the *Revue des langues romanes* (1870), Gaston Paris' *Romania* (1872), and the *Revue de l'histoire des religions* (1879). And a new generation of critical philologists—among them, the partly German-trained Gaston Paris—began to make distinguished contributions to folklore scholarship—Paris' pathbreaking history of the Charlemagne legend (1865), for example.

In an article that appeared first in the *Revue critique* and later in the first issue of *Mélusine*, Paris insisted not on the aesthetic reasons for treasuring popular poetry, but on the "scientific" ones. "There are still people who are astonished to see this heavy word applied to things so frivolous and vulgar in appearance," he recognized, "but it is not less true that popular poetry has a scientific interest of the greatest order, to such an extent that a separate science is being constituted around it."[28] By 1885 the Count Puymaigre could report: "The new science has made . . . great progress." In fact, he even feared that it might advance too quickly, becoming an *affaire de mode* in danger of "amassing more materials than can be classified and assimilated" with care.[29] The folklorists of France, in short, were establishing new standards of scholarship, were increasingly concerned with questions of methodology, and were forming a distinct identity, a discipline of their own. They were no longer to be considered amateur antiquarians or simply historians of "that other history," as Michelet called it, the history preserved by the popular memory and imagination.

In some cases, the folklorists not only distinguished themselves from the historians but did so with a vengeance. Note, for example, the amateur folklorist Antony Dessaix's reaction to the increasingly professionalized, critical history:

> The clients of history could be only decrepit old men; the friends of legend are the child, the woman. Woman and children have an easy smile, and we love to meet pleasant faces.
> Let's then go to legend and leave history with its frowning look, which resembles the misanthrope of Molière, that singular *bonhomme* who was happy to have lost his trial in order to have one more injustice with which to reproach humanity.[30]

For the professional folklorists, perhaps the most decisive declaration of independence from the historians was issued early in this century by Arnold Van Gennep. In defining the scope and methodology of folklore research, he aligned his discipline with anthropology and sociology (even biology) to emphasize that it was the study of living traditions by direct observation in the field. He rejected completely the association of folklore research with historical study, the latter in his view being merely a study of the past preserved in libraries and archives. In his brief introductory work *Le folklore*, Van Gennep rejoiced that folklorists were gradually being cured of "the malady of the nineteenth century which one can call the historical mania."[31] Van Gennep's declaration was the culmination of a separation long developing in France. In the last third of the nineteenth century the relationships between historians and folklorists as well as between their respective disciplines were neither so close nor so cordial as in the preceding two-thirds. The "new spirit" could inspire Quinet to a new synthesis, but it could also inspire a divisive specialization.

Yet in the course of the century much had been gained of lasting value to the study of history and folklore. Even though the historians' interest in folklore was not commonly shared by their immediate successors, they had founded a tradition of historical research, which could be later resumed and better developed. Historians had eloquently stated the importance of understanding popular traditions for understanding history, and they had given numerous examples of the uses that can be made of such traditions. By 1862 a folklorist, Damase Arbaud, could write: "Far from us are the times when history was only a gallery of ingeniously numbered portraits, a theater in which characters in court or battle dress came to display their passions, and too often their vices; new democratic ideas have made us remember that around them, below them if you prefer, there was a nation that had its interests, its manners and morals, its needs, its beliefs. . . ."[32] Jacques Bonhomme and his folklore had at last gained a place in French historical thought.

6
Conclusion

The new idea of historical truth expounded so clearly by Thierry and Michelet had provided new grounds for studying popular life and folklore. "It is incontestable," the folklorist Saintyves has concluded, "that romanticism and its conception of a concrete and picturesque history turned toward the people and their folkways truly prepared minds for the study of folklore. . . ."[1] More directly, the historians encouraged and aided folklorists of the time, and the folklorists often acknowledge the help received. The Breton La Villemarqué, for example, gratefully praised Ozanam's precept and example in treating legend.[2] He paid tribute also to Augustin Thierry, "the historian who has shown so well the use that one can make of popular poetry. . . ."[3] Another early Breton folklorist, Emile Souvestre, owed much to Michelet. Souvestre adopted his friend's ideas of symbolic interpretation and of folklore as a source for the history of the people; fittingly, he dedicated his *Foyer breton, contes et récits populaires* to the historian.[4] Souvestre admired Fauriel, too, and held up the *Chants populaires de la Grèce* as an example of what should be done for the songs of all peoples.[5] Still another of those industrious Breton folklorists, Narcisse Quellien, acknowledged in his *Chansons et danses des Bretons* the encouragement of Henri Martin:

I have undertaken to add to . . . the researches [of Luzel and La Villemarqué] on the counsel of an illustrious and constant friend of the Celts: more than once M. Henri Martin asked me why Brittany remained behind the Irish and Welsh. "These have had their popular and national repertory for a long time," added the lamented *celtisant.* "Meanwhile there are such beautiful melodies among the Bretons!"[6]

At the same time, of course, the historians made a notable contribution to historiography. By their example and programmatic statements, they made it clear that folklore should be taken into account in any attempt to understand the historical life of societies. They did not all have the same kind of historical interests, nor did they seek the same kind of historical truth in folklore. But whatever it was that they wanted to know—popular sentiments, folkways, dogmas, even a narrative of events—they looked for it in popular traditions.

The spirit in which they studied traditions was far from exclusively nationalistic. Having long enjoyed national unity and an almost universal admiration for French culture, Frenchmen in general did not feel a need to treasure and to exalt French folklore in the way that the Grimms and their Finnish, Norwegian, Irish, and Russian counterparts did as students of their respective national traditions. In French historical writing, to be sure, nationalism was evident: Michelet and Martin glorified the legendary and historical heroes of their nation's past with unmistakable fervor. But alongside such nationalism was a strong regionalism, to which almost all French folklorists and, as we have seen, a number of eminent historians contributed. Fauriel, for example, helped to strengthen Provençal consciousness, while Henri Martin, despite his stridently nationalistic assertions, celebrated a Celtic folklore that was identified as much with Brittany and non-French lands across the Channel as with France. At the same time, a cosmopolitan spirit inspired some notable students of history and traditions. Devout Roman Catholics like Ballanche and Ozanam dedicated themselves to the study of "universal" traditions. Fauriel and Thierry gave their sympathy impartially to the traditions of oppressed and struggling nationalities everywhere. And Michelet combined his intense love of the French past with a respectful and scholarly interest in the traditions of all peoples.

Clearly these historians, unlike the philosophes, shared a basic sympathy for folklore. Not only did they value old traditions, but several of them sought to imitate those traditions in their own writing. While Thierry adopted the *cantilène* method of composing epic, Ballanche and Michelet strove to write with a spontaneity and simplicity that they believed characteristic of popular literature. A number of the historians obviously wanted to give France a new folklore, above all new symbols and legends. Thierry's and Barante's legends of Jacques Bonhomme and Michelet's legends of democratic heroes and the revolutionary people were clearly efforts of this sort. Some of the other works of the period can be considered new myths—epic stories and historical images suggesting the origins and the end of their society. Such were Ballanche's theories of social palingenesis and Michelet's epics of liberty. As Cousin presented a new eclectic philosophy and Hugo *La légende des siècles,* historians provided new universal philosophies of history that offered new assurance and orientation to the spiritually anxious, to those yearning for new wisdom drawn from the experience of all the past.[7]

Yet a sympathy for traditions did not mean full opposition to the Enlightenment. Ballanche, Barante, Fauriel, Thierry, Michelet, Quinet, and Ozanam were not Romantic reactionaries. They did not view folklore as a restraining social burden, a heavy collective hand of the past limiting change and preventing individuals from leaving socially and historically sanctioned paths. Rather they were preoccupied with the spontaneity of folklore's origins and its unceasing change in response to a changing popular life and historical events. Unlike the Grimms, they believed in "progress."[8]

The folklore they admired did not seem to them at all incompatible with their ideals of liberalism, self-determination, and a rising level of morality. On the contrary, much of that folklore seemed to have furthered those ideals.

In a sense these men could afford to be sympathetic to folklore because the Enlightenment had done its work. Michelet, for example, could rehabilitate sorcery because there was no longer a danger that sorcery would be widely practiced. The old folklore was dying. Education, improved means of communication, and better transportation—especially the railroad—were fostering a uniformity of culture that saddened and troubled Laisnel de La Salle[9] and countless folklorists after him. Even the "popular images" of Saint Corentin, the legendary wandering Jew, Saint Michael slaying the dragon, and other heroes—which for centuries had been hawked through the countryside—began to disappear rapidly in the second half of the century.[10] The historians were aware of such changes; hence they could study popular beliefs in a way that, say, Bayle could not.

They could not, however, relegate folklore completely to the past. The Napoleonic legend served as a reminder that prominent figures could still become enveloped in fictions, and in the more remote areas of France, the ancient traditions still commanded belief. In Normandy, for example, through most of the nineteenth century mothers still made a pilgrimage to the Dylan stone, placed a branch on the dolmen, and walked around it backwards nine times, in order that their sons might draw a good lot and be able to perform their military service in their home *pays*.[11]

Partly from their awareness of this living folklore, partly from their remarkable historical imagination, partly from their consciousness of their own society's need for common unifying beliefs, the historians had a lively sense of the effects that popular traditions had had on societies throughout history. True, they did somewhat neglect the malign effects, the foolish "chimeras" that had aroused the philosophes' ire and indignation—beliefs in black magic and

witches, fortune tellers and miracle makers. These Romantics also slighted the weird and fantastic, stories of were-
wolves and ogres, the Père Fouettards and the garafatounas,
for example. Often uncritical, they gave to men of the past
the benefit of the doubt, refusing to accept Francis Bacon's
belief that man has "a natural though corrupt love of the lie
itself." All in all their aim was not to repudiate the Enlightenment, but to redress a balance. They were eager to show
the constructive contributions of the popular imagination to
literature, law, historiography, and religion. They went to
lengths to demonstrate that popular traditions had been not
merely a source of stability in past societies, but also a vehi-
cle for change, a means of raising the level of civilization.
They were all convinced, finally, that fictions, weird or
prosaic, had always been a part of man's world and must be
studied seriously, sympathetically by anyone wishing to understand that world.

The French have long distinguished themselves in this
kind of study, as Arnaldo Momigliano has observed in a
recent collection of historiographical essays:

> It is France, from the Abbé Bremond onward, which has produced
> explorations of states of mind, of paradigmatic legends and collective
> religious phenomena for which it is difficult to find parallels else-
> where (for example, A. J. Festugière on the history of Graeco-Roman
> religion, R. Folz on the legend of Charlemagne).[12]

While mentioning Henri Bremond, author of a monumental
Histoire littéraire du sentiment religieux en France (1916–36), he
might well have added Marc Bloch on the belief in the "rois
thaumaturges," and he might have extended his view back
into the nineteenth century to include Gaston Paris' work
on the Charlemagne legend. For historical perspective one
should look still further back to the generations responsible
for the great transition between Voltaire and the Abbé Bremond—the generations of Ballanche, Fauriel, Michelet, and
Ozanam.

Bibliography

I. GENERAL WORKS

A. Secondary

Bertier de Sauvigny, Guillaume de, *La restauration*. Paris, 1955.

Boas, George, *Vox Populi: Essays in the History of an Idea*. Baltimore, 1969.

Cellier, Léon, *L'épopée romantique—Ballanche, Quinet, Soumet, Constant, Hugo*. Paris, 1954.

Charlton, Donald Geoffrey, *Secular Religions in France, 1815–1870*. London, 1963.

Dansette, Adrien, *Histoire religieuse de la France contemporaine*. 2 vols. Paris, 1948.

Cogordan, George, *Joseph de Maistre*. Paris, 1894.

Derré, Jean-René, *Le renouvellement de la pensée religieuse en France de 1824 à 1834*. Paris, 1962.

Fisch, Max Harold, Introduction to *The Autobiography of Giambattista Vico*. Translated and edited by Max Harold Fisch and Thomas Goddard Bergin. Ithaca, New York, 1963.

Gay, Peter, *The Enlightenment, an Interpretation: The Rise of Modern Paganism*. New York, 1966. A major work that deals with the opposition of the Enlightenment to the mythopoeic mind.

Gossman, Lionel, *Medievalism and the Ideologies of the Enlightenment: The World and Work of La Curne de Sainte-Palaye*. Baltimore, 1968.

Greene, Christopher Morrill, "Historical Consciousness and Historical Monuments in France after 1789." Unpublished Ph.D. thesis, Harvard University, 1964.

Guérard, Albert Léon, *Reflections on the Napoleonic Legend*. New York, 1924. A lively, thoughtful discussion of the legend's origins and cultivators. I have profited particularly from Guérard's reflections on legend and historical truth, and the section on Quinet as a "prophet" of legend.

Hunt, Herbert James, *The Epic in Nineteenth-Century France: A Study in Heroic and Humanitarian Poetry from "Les martyrs" to "Les siècles morts."* Oxford, 1941.

Kohn, Hans, "France Between Britain and Germany," *Journal of the History of Ideas*, XVII (June 1956), 283–99. The attitudes of French intellectuals and government officials in the first half of the nineteenth century.

Libby, Margaret Sherwood, *The Attitude of Voltaire to Magic and the Sciences*. New York, 1935.

Lovejoy, Arthur O., *Essays in the History of Ideas* (New York, 1960).

Maigron, Louis, *Le roman historique à l'époque romantique: essai sur l'influence de Walter Scott.* New ed., Paris, 1912.

Manuel, Frank E., *The Eighteenth Century Confronts the Gods.* Cambridge, Mass., 1959. Excellent intellectual history. Particularly relevant to the present work for its presentation of eighteenth-century thought on myth and the primitive mind.

———, *The New World of Henri Saint-Simon.* Cambridge, Mass., 1956.

Pinard de la Boullaye, Henri, *L'étude comparée des religions.* 3rd ed. 2 vols. Paris, 1929.

Reynaud, Louis, *L'influence allemande en France au XVIIIᵉ et au XIXᵉ siècle.* Paris, 1922. A useful survey; sometimes obtrusively anti-German.

Ripert, Emile, *La renaissance provençale, 1800–1860.* Paris, [1917].

Schwab, Raymond, *La renaissance orientale.* Paris, 1950.

Soltau, Roger, *French Political Thought in the Nineteenth Century.* New Haven, 1931.

Swart, Koenraad W., *The Sense of Decadence in Nineteenth-Century France.* The Hague, 1964.

Tonnelat, Ernest, *Les frères Grimm: Leur Oeuvre de jeunesse.* Paris, 1912. A judicious study of the highly productive formative years to 1822.

Tronchon, Henri, *La fortune intellectuelle de Herder en France: La préparation.* Paris, 1920.

———, *Romantisme et préromantisme.* Paris, 1930. A collection of excellent essays.

Van Tieghem, Paul, "La notion de vraie poésie dans le préromantisme européen," *Revue de Littérature comparée,* I (1921), 215–51.

———, *Ossian en France.* 2 vols. Paris, 1917.

———, *Le préromantisme, études d'histoire littéraire européenne.* 2 vols. Paris, 1924–30. An anthology of essays, among which is "La notion de vraie poésie" cited separately above.

Viatte, Auguste, *Les sources occultes du romantisme, 1770–1820.* New ed. 2 vols. Paris, 1965. An important study, especially helpful in illuminating the thought of writers from Lyons, such as Ballanche.

Weil, Georges, *L'éveil des nationalités et le mouvement liberal, 1815–1848.* Paris, 1930.

Wright, Gordon, *France in Modern Times: 1760 to the Present.* Chicago, 1960.

B. Primary

Chateaubriand, François Auguste René, *Etudes historiques.* New ed. Paris, 1872.

"De la propagation des livres irreligieux depuis la Restauration," *Le mémorial catholique,* II (May 1824), 261–99.

Denis, Ferdinand, *Journal, 1829–1848.* Fribourg, 1932. Denis mentions many famous names, but adds only a little to our knowledge of his contemporaries.

Journal de Paris. Review of *La Gaule poétique,* signed "N." March 27, 1815.

Lamennais, Félicité Robert de, *Essai sur l'indifférence en matière de religion.* 4th ed. 4 vols. Paris, 1828.

Lavallée, Joseph, "Discours préliminaire," *Mémoires de l'Académie celtique,* I, 1–20. Paris, 1807.

Montaigne, Michel de, *Essais,* ed. Maurice Rat. Vol. I. Paris, 1967.

Staël, Madame de, *De l'Allemagne.* 2 vols. Vol. X of *Œuvres complètes, publiées par son fils.* Brussels, 1830.

Voltaire, *Dictionnaire philosophique.* 4 vols. Vols. XVII–XX of *Œuvres complètes.* New ed. Paris, 1878.

———, *Essai sur les mœurs.* 3 vols. Vols. XI–XIII of *Œuvres complètes.* New ed. Paris, 1878.

II. FOLKLORE STUDIES

A. Secondary

Chase, Richard V., *Quest for Myth.* Baton Rouge, 1949. A brief "selective handbook" of theories and uses of myth from antiquity to the present.

Cocchiara, Giuseppe, *Storia del folklore in Europa.* Turin, 1952. The best general history of the subject, with an excellent bibliography.

Dorson, Richard M., ed., "Folklore Research Around the World," *Journal of American Folklore,* LXXIV (Oct. 1961), 287–460. Although France is omitted, the brief articles on research in other countries provide helpful bases for comparison with France.

———, Foreword to *Folktales of France,* ed. Geneviève Massignon. Chicago, 1968. An important essay on leading French folklorists from the late nineteenth century to our own time.

———, "The Question of Folklore in a New Nation," *Journal of the Folklore Institute,* III (Dec. 1966), 277–89. Ably demonstrates the role of folklore in the emerging national consciousness of the U.S., Norway, Ireland, China, and Finland.

Durocher, Léon, "La légende de Jacques Bonhomme," *La Tradition,* I (1887), 84–88. Quite inadequate.

Feldman, Burton and Robert D. Richardson, *The Rise of Modern Mythology (1680–1860).* Bloomington, 1972. This important contribution, which appeared after the present work was written, should prove to be extraordinarily helpful to students of myth historiography. A history through texts and critical commentaries with a lengthy bibliography.

Gaidoz, Henri, "De l'influence de l'Académie celtique sur les études de folk-lore," *Centenaire (1804–1904), Société nationale des Antiquaires de France: Recueil des mémoires,* pp. 135–43. Paris, 1904. This essay dwells particularly on the influence of the Academy on Jacob Grimm.

Gourvil, Francis, *Théodore-Claude-Henri Hersart de La Villemarqué (1815–1895) et le "Barzaz-Breiz."* Rennes, 1960. A solid study of a pioneering folklorist and his place in the Breton folklore movement.

Hilton, R. H., "The Origins of Robin Hood," *Past and Present,* No. 14

(Nov. 1958), pp. 30–44. Argues the traditional view of the popular origins of the Robin Hood legend.

Holt, J. C., "The Origins and Audience of the Ballads of Robin Hood," *Past and Present*, No. 18 (Nov. 1960), pp. 89–110. Argues that the ballads originated among the gentry.

La Villemarqué, Théodore Hersart de, "Les précurseurs de nos études—Chateaubriand," *Revue des traditions populaires*, III (Aug. 1888), 418–20. A sketchy discussion of Chateaubriand's interest in folklore.

Paris, Gaston, "De l'étude de la poésie populaire en France, *Mélusine* I (Paris, 1878), 2–3.

Saintyves, P. [E. Nourry], *Manuel de folklore*. Paris, 1936. Articles and unpublished essays brought together in book form by the author's widow. Included are several thoughtful chapters on the historical development of folklore studies.

Sébillot, Paul, "L'imagerie populaire," *Revue des traditions populaires*, III (June 1888), 305–16.

———, *La littérature orale en France*. Paris, 1891. An extremely brief but informative historical sketch of French folklore studies.

———, "Notes pour servir à l'histoire du folklore en France," *Revue des traditions populaires*, XXVIII (1913), 49–62, 171–82.

Tiersot, Julien, *La chanson populaire et les écrivains romantiques*. Paris, 1931. A brief survey.

Tronchon, Henri, "Quelques notes sur le premier mouvement folkloriste en France: Voix françaises, voix étrangères," *Mélanges d'histoire littéraire générale et comparée offerts à Fernard Baldensperger*, II, 296–311. Paris, 1930. A valuable essay, filled with specific references.

Van Gennep, Arnold, *Le folklore*. Paris, 1924. A brief introductory discussion of the history, methods, and objectives of folklore studies.

———, *Manuel de folklore français contemporain*. 4 vols. Paris, 1937–58.

B. Primary

Byron, Martial, "Sobriquets et superstitions militaires," *Revue des traditions populaires*, III (Jan. 1888), 53–54.

Demesmay, Auguste, *Traditions populaires de Franche Comté, poésies suivies de notes*. Paris, 1838.

Dessaix, Antony, *Légendes et traditions populaires de la Haute-Savoie*. Annecy, 1875.

Grazier, A., "Lettres à Gregoire sur les patois de France," *Revue des Langues romanes*, V (1874), 418–34; VI (1875), 575–89; VII (1875) 107–33; VIII (1875), 71–113; IX (1876), 274–87; X (1876), 28–37; XI (1877), 178–93, 230–40; XII (1877), 213–34; XIII (1878), 9–26, 237–61; XIV (1878), 51–72, 169–83; XV (1879), 53–78, 183–250.

Laisnel de La Salle, Germain, *Croyances et légendes du centre de la France*. Paris, 1875.

La Villemarqué, Théodore Hersart de, *Barzas-Breiz: Chants populaires de la Bretagne*, 2 vols. Paris, 1839.

————, *La légende celtique en Irelande, en Cambrie et en Bretagne.* New ed. Paris and Saint Brieuc, n.d.

Marchangy, Louis-Antoine-François de, "Dictionnaire de mythologie française et de fables nationales," Archives nationales, 233 AP 1, Marchangy MSS, n.d.

Marmier, Xavier, *Chants populaires du Nord.* Paris, 1842.

Monnier, Desiré, *Du culte des esprits dans la Séquanie.* Lons-le-Saunier, 1834.

————, *Mœurs et usages singuliers du peuple dans le Jura.* Lons-le-Saunier, 1823.

Paris, Paulin, *Etudes sur les chansons de geste et sur le "Garin le Loherain" de Jean de Flagy.* Paris, 1863.

Percy, Thomas, *Reliques of Ancient English Poetry,* consisting of old Heroic Ballads, Songs, and Other Pieces of our Earlier Poets, chiefly of the Lyric Kind, Together with Some Few of Later Date. 3 vols. London, 1765.

Puymaigre, Th., *Chants populaires recueillis dans le pays Messin.* Paris, 1865.

Quellien, Narcisse, *Chansons et danses des Bretons.* Paris, 1889.

Rivarès, Frédéric, *Chansons et airs populaires de Béarn.* Paris, 1844.

Souvestre, Emile, *Causeries historiques et littéraires,* 2 vols.

————, *Le foyer breton, contes et récits populaires.* New ed. 2 vols. Paris, 1853.

Veaugeois, Gabriel, "Notice abrégée d'un journal d'un voyage archéologique et géologique," *Mémoires de la Société royale des Antiquaires de France,* III, 370–90. Paris, 1821.

Vico, Giambattista, *The New Science.* Translated and edited by Thomas Goddard Bergin and Max Harold Fisch. Abridged and revised. Garden City, New York, 1961.

III. HISTORIOGRAPHY

A. General Studies

Barzun, Jacques, "Romantic Historiography as a Political Force in France," *Journal of the History of Ideas,* II (June 1941), 318–29.

Engel-Jánosi, Friedrich, *Four Studies in French Romantic Historical Writing.* The Johns Hopkins University Studies in Historical and Political Science, Ser. LXXI, No. 2. Baltimore, 1955. An introduction and essays on Chateaubriand, Barante, Thierry, and Tocqueville.

Fueter, Eduard, *Geschichte der neueren Historiographie.* Munich and Berlin, 1911.

Gooch, G. P., *History and Historians in the Nineteenth Century.* Boston, 1962.

Halphen, Louis, *L'histoire en France depuis cent ans.* Paris, 1914. A good, brief survey of nineteenth-century French historiography. This work, more than any other on the subject, deserves to be called a history, for it is more than a chronicle or a series of essays.

Jullian, Camille, "Augustin Thierry et le mouvement historique sous la restauration," *Revue de synthèse historique,* XIII (Oct. 1906), 129–42.

————, ed., *Extraits des historiens français du XIXe siècle.* Paris, 1897. Jullian's introduction is outstanding.

Levrault, Léon, *L'histoire: Evolution du genre.* Paris, 1915. Brief, sketchy, popular.

Meinecke, Friedrich, *Die Entstehung des Historismus.* 2nd ed. Munich, 1946. Most useful here for background on eighteenth-century French historiography.

Mellon, Stanley, *The Political Uses of History: A Study of Historians in the French Restoration.* Stanford, 1958.

Momigliano, Arnaldo, *Studies in Historiography.* New York, 1966.

Monod, Gabriel, "Du progrès des études historiques en France depuis le XVIe siècle," *Revue historique,* I (1876), 5–38. A short survey leading to a statement of purpose for the new *Revue.*

Moreau, Pierre, *L'histoire en France au XIXe siècle.* Vol. 35 of *Etudes françaises.* Paris, 1935.

Neff, Emery, *The Poetry of History: The Contribution of Literature and Literary Scholarship to the Writing of History Since Voltaire.* New York, 1947. Brief, urbane essays on Thierry, Michelet, and Renan, among others.

Réizov, Boris Georgievich, *L'historiographie romantique française, 1815–1830.* "Authorized translation" from the Russian. Moscow, 1962. The best general study of historical writing during the Restoration, despite the curious or mistaken interpretations dictated by the author's ideology.

Tronchon, Henri, "Les études historiques et la philosophie de l'histoire aux alentours de 1830," *Revue de synthèse historique,* XXXIV (Jan. 1922), 35–71.

B. Selected Historians and Their Works

1. Primary

Ballanche, Pierre Simon, *Essais de palingénésie sociale.* 2 vols. Vols. III–IV of *Œuvres de M. Ballanche de l'Académie de Lyon.* Paris, 1830.

————, *Essai sur les institutions sociales dans leur rapport avec les idées nouvelles.* Vol. II of *Œuvres de M. Ballanche de l'Académie de Lyon.* Paris, 1830.

Barante, Prosper de, *Etudes historiques et biographiques.* 2 vols. Paris, 1857.

————, *Histoire des ducs de Bourgogne et de la maison de Valois, 1364–1477.* 12 vols. Vols. I–III: 6th ed.; Vols. IV–IX, XII, "new ed."; Vols. X–XI: 5th ed. Paris, 1839.

————, *Mélanges historiques et littéraires.* 3 vols. Paris, 1835.

————, *Souvenirs du baron de Barante, 1782–1866,* publiés par son petit-fils C. de Barante. 8 vols. Paris, 1890–91.

Fauriel, Claude, editor and translator, *Chants populaires de la Grèce moderne,* recueillis et publiés, avec une traduction française, des éclaircissements et des notes. 2 vols. Paris, 1824–25.

————, *Histoire de la Gaule méridionale sous la domination des conquérants germains.* 4 vols. Paris, 1836.

————, *Histoire de la poésie provençale.* 3 vols. Paris, 1846.

Fauriel's Correspondence and Notes:

Galpin, Alfred, ed., *Fauriel in Italy: Unpublished Correspondence, 1822–1824.* Rome, 1962.

Glachant, Paul and Victor, editors. *Lettres à Fauriel.* Paris, 1902.

Mohl, Ottmar de, ed., *Correspondance de Fauriel et Mary Clarke,* Paris, 1911.

Tosi, E., ed., "Vico en France: Analyse inédite, par Fauriel," *La Revue de Littérature comparée,* XI (1931), 763–77.

Fortoul, Hippolyte, "De la littérature provençale," *Revue des Deux Mondes,* XIV (1846), 549–88.

Magnin, Charles, "Examen des systèmes de Vico et de Wolf sur la formation des poèmes homériques," *Causeries et méditations historiques et littéraires,* II, 12–49. Paris, 1843.

Martin, Henri, *De la France, de son génie, et de ses destinées.* Paris, 1847.

————, *Etudes d'archéologie celtique; notes de voyages dans les pays celtiques et scandinaves.* Paris, 1872.

————, *Histoire de France depuis les temps les plus reculés jusqu'en 1789.* 4th ed. 17 vols. Paris, 1855–60.

————, *Histoire de France depuis les temps les plus reculés jusqu'en juillet 1830, par les principaux historiens.* Paris, 1833.

————, *Jean Reynaud,* Paris, 1863.

Michelet, Jules, *Bible de l'humanité.* 3rd ed. Paris, 1864.

————, *Ecrits de jeunesse: Journal (1820–1823), Mémorial, Journal des idées:* Texte intégral, établi sur les manuscrits autographes et publié pour la première fois. Edited by Paul Viallaneix. Paris [1959].

————, *Histoire de France.* Edited by Claude Mettra. 15 vols. Lausanne, 1965–67.

————, *Histoire de la Révolution française.* Edited by Gérard Walter. 2 vols. Paris, 1952.

————, *Histoire romaine.* 3rd ed. 2 vols. Paris, 1843.

————, *Introduction à l'histoire universelle suivi du Discours d'ouverture prononcé a la faculté des lettres le 9 janvier 1834.* 2nd ed. Paris, 1834.

————, *Journal: Texte intégral,* établi sur les manuscrits autographes et publié pour la première fois. Edited by Paul Viallaneix. 2 vols. Paris [1959].

————, *Légendes démocratiques du Nord; la France devant l'Europe.* Edited by Michel Bréal. Paris, 1899.

————, *Lettres inédites à Alfred Dumesnil et à Eugène Noël (1841–1871).* Edited by Paul Sirven. Paris, 1924.

————, *Origines du droit français cherchées dans les symboles et formules du droit universel.* Paris, 1837.

————, *Le peuple.* 3rd ed. Paris, 1846.

————, *La sorcière.* New ed. Paris, 1878.

Manuscript letters to Michelet now in the Bibliothèque historique de la Ville de Paris: X. Marmier, 1833, No. 4775.1; 1840, No. 4875.48; La Villemarqué, 1836? No. 4881.34; J. J. Ampère, 1838, No. 4755.4; E. Souvestre, 1847, No. 4872.46; F. Baudry, 1862, No. 4758.4.

Montalembert, Charles de, *Histoire de Sainte Elisabeth de Hongrie.* 9th ed. 2 vols. Paris, 1861.

Ozanam, Frédéric, *La civilisation au cinquième siècle*. 2nd ed. 2 vols. Vols. I–II of *Oeuvres complètes*. 2nd ed. Paris, 1862.

————, *La civilisation chrétienne chez les Francs*. 3rd ed. Vol. IV of *Oeuvres complètes*. 2nd ed.

————, "Les dangers de Rome et ses espérances," *Le correspondant*, XXI (Feb. 10, 1848), 412–35.

————, *Dante et la philosophie catholique au treizième siècle*. Vol. VI of *Oeuvres complètes*. 4th ed. Paris, 1859.

————, "Des *Nibelungen* et de la poésie épique," *Mélanges*, Vol. II. *Oeuvres complètes*, VIII, 181–206. 2nd ed. Paris, 1859.

————, "Du progrès par le christianisme," *Mélanges*, Vol I. *Oeuvres complètes*, VII, 93–126. 2nd ed. Paris, 1859.

————, *Les Germains avant le christianisme*. 3rd ed. Vol. III of *Oeuvres complètes*. 2nd ed. Paris, 1861.

————, *Lettres de Frédéric Ozanam, 1831–1853*. 5th ed. 2 vols. Paris, 1881.

————, "La littérature allemande au moyen âge," *Mélanges*, Vol. II. *Oeuvres complètes*, VIII, 151–78. 2nd ed. Paris, 1859.

————, *Un pèlerinage au pays du Cid*, *Mélanges*, Vol. I. *Oeuvres complètes*, VII, 1–90. 2nd ed. Paris, 1859.

————, *Les poètes franciscains en Italie au treizième siècle;* avec un choix des *Petites fleurs de Saint François* traduites de l'italien; Suivis de recherches nouvelles sur les sources poétiques de la *Divine Comédie*. 3rd ed. Vol. V of *Oeuvres complètes*. 2nd ed. Paris, 1859.

————, "Réflexions sur la doctrine de Saint-Simon," *Mélanges*, Vol. I. *Oeuvres complètes*, VII, 271–357. 2nd ed. Paris, 1859.

Quinet, Edgar, *Le christianisme et la Révolution française*. 4th ed. *Oeuvres complètes*, III, 9–275. Paris, n.d.

————, *Correspondance: Lettres à sa mère*. 2 vols. Vols. XIX–XX of *Oeuvres complètes*. Paris, n.d.

————, *La création*. 3rd ed. 2 vols. Vols. XXI–XXII of *Oeuvres complètes*. Paris [1879].

————, *De l'avenir des religions*. 3rd ed. *Oeuvres complètes*, VI, 394–403. Paris, n.d.

————, *De l'histoire de la poésie*, 3rd ed. *Oeuvres complètes*, XXVII, 296–476. Paris, n.d.

————, *De l'origine des dieux*. 3rd ed. *Oeuvres complètes*, I, 415–37, Paris, n.d.

————, *L'enseignement du peuple*. 5th ed. *Oeuvres complètes*, XI, 1–136. Paris, n.d.

————, *Epopées françaises inédites du douzième siècle*. 3rd ed. *Oeuvres complètes*, XXVII, 479–505. Paris, n.d.

————, *L'esprit nouveau*. 4th ed. Vol. XXIII of *Oeuvres complètes*. Paris [1880].

————, *Essai sur les œuvres de Herder*, 4th ed. *Oeuvres complètes*, II, 393–439. Paris, n.d.

————, *Examen de la Vie de Jésus*. 4th ed. *Oeuvres complètes*, III, 285–352. Paris, n.d.

————, *Génie des religions*. 5th ed. *Oeuvres complètes*, I, 9–395. Paris, n.d.

————, *Histoire de mes idées.* 2nd ed. Vol. X of *Œuvres complètes.* Paris [1880].

————, *L'introduction à la philosophie de l'histoire de l'humanité.* 4th ed. *Œuvres complètes,* II, 345–90. Paris, n.d.

————, *Les Jésuites.* 10th ed. *Œuvres complètes,* II, 1–126. Paris, n.d.

————, *Napoléon. Œuvres complètes,* VIII, 137–326. Paris, 1857.

————, *Philosophie de l'histoire de France.* 4th ed. *Œuvres complètes,* III, 355–422. Paris, n.d.

————, *La Révolution,* précédée de *La critique de la Révolution.* 8th ed. 3 vols. Vols. XII–XIV of *Œuvres complètes.* Paris, n.d.

————, *L'ultramontanisme ou l'église romaine et la société moderne.* 5th ed. *Œuvres complètes,* II, 129–304. Paris, n.d.

Renan, Ernest, *Essais de morale et critique.* 2nd ed. Paris, 1860.

————, *Vie de Jésus.* 5th ed. Vol. I of *Histoire des origines du christianisme.* Paris, 1863.

————, *Cahiers de jeunesse, 1845–46.* 2nd ed. 2 vols. Paris, 1906.

————, *Dialogues et fragments philosophiques.* Paris, 1886.

Thierry, Augustin, *Dix ans d'études historiques.* 4th ed. Paris, 1842.

————, *Histoire de la conquête de l'Angleterre par les Normands.* 7th ed. 4 vols. Paris, 1846.

————, *Lettres sur l'histoire de France,* pour servir d'introduction à l'étude de cette histoire. Paris, 1827; and "new ed.," 1866.

————, *Récits des temps mérovingiens, précédés de "Considérations sur l'histoire de France."* New ed. 2 vols. Paris, 1867.

2. Secondary

Albouy, Pierre, *Mythes et mythologies dans la littérature française.* Paris, 1969. Contains sympathetic treatment of Michelet as mythmaker.

Cornuz, Jeanlouis, *Jules Michelet: Un aspect de la pensée religieuse du XIXᵉ siècle.* Geneva, 1955. A thoughtful study of Michelet's ideas analyzed through close textual comparison; not limited to religious ideas in the strict sense.

Egger, Emile, "Cours de littérature étrangère—M. Fauriel," *Journal général de l'instruction publique,* V (1836). 12 articles.

Febvre, Lucien, ed., *Michelet, 1798–1874. Les Classiques de la liberté.* Geneva, 1946. The highly sympathetic introduction is a noteworthy effort to rehabilitate Michelet, whose vision of eternal France and French liberty helped to sustain Febvre during the Second World War.

Galley, J. B., *Claude Fauriel, membre de l'Institut, 1772–1843.* Saint-Etienne, 1909. As far as this biography goes, it is satisfactory, but there is a need for a new biographer who could more knowledgeably assess Fauriel's thought and writing.

Galopin, Eugène, *Essai de bibliographie chronologique sur Antoine-Frédéric Ozanam, 1813–1853.* Paris, 1933.

George, Albert Joseph, *Pierre-Simon Ballanche, Precursor of Romanticism.* Syracuse, New York, 1945.

Geyl, Pieter, *Debates With Historians.* Cleveland, 1964. Included is a hostile essay on Michelet as a nationalist, "revolutionary imperialist," and "absolutist thinker."

Goyau, Georges, *Ozanam.* New ed. Paris, 1931.

Guéhenno, Jean, *L'évangile éternel: Etude sur Michelet.* Paris, 1927.

Guizot, François, "M. de Barante, ses souvenirs de famille, sa vie et ses œuvres," *Revue des Deux Mondes,* LXX (July 1, 1867), 5–66. This article is most useful as a review of Barante's public career, though it also contains some personal memories and correspondence.

Haac, Oscar Alfred, *Les principes inspirateurs de Michelet.* Paris, 1951. An analytical discussion of Michelet's basic, constant "principles."

Hanotaux, Gabriel, *Henri Martin: Sa vie—ses œuvres—son temps.* Paris, 1885. A highly sympathetic treatment by a French historian who shared many of Martin's attitudes and values. It lacks the personal details and insights that give life to a biography, but it develops at length the historical context in which Martin lived and worked.

Huit, Charles, *La vie et les œuvres de Ballanche.* Lyons, 1904.

Ibrovac, Miodrag, *Claude Fauriel et la fortune européenne des poésies populaires grecque et serbe.* Paris, 1966. A long, solid study containing a review of Fauriel's work, an assessment of its influence, and Fauriel's lectures on Greek and Serbian popular poetry, thitherto unpublished.

Kaegi, Werner, *Michelet und Deutschland.* Basel, 1936. Contains Michelet-Grimm correspondence.

Kohn, Hans, *Prophets and Peoples: Studies in Nineteenth Century Nationalism.* New York, 1952. Chapter 2 is a lively essay on Michelet and his "messianic nationalism," tending to oversimplify Michelet's faith in France's mission.

Méjecaze, Abbé F., *Essai de synthèse des idées et des jugements littéraires de Frédéric Ozanam.* Lyons, 1932. A sympathetic, scholarly study piecing together from Ozanam's various works his ideas on topics in literary history.

———, *Frédéric Ozanam et l'église catholique.* Paris and Lyons, 1932.

Monin, H., "La rupture de Michelet et de Quinet," *Revue d'histoire littéraire de la France,* XIX (1912), 818–41.

Monod, Gabriel, *Jules Michelet.* Paris, 1875. A personal and sympathetic brief account of Michelet's life and works.

———, *Jules Michelet: Etudes sur sa vie et ses œuvres, avec des fragments inédits.* Paris, 1905.

———, *La vie et la pensée de Jules Michelet, 1798–1852;* cours professé au Collège de France. Paris, 1923. Detailed and digressive. Though Monod knew Michelet and warmly acknowledged the latter's influence on him, this book treats its subject with cool reserve, focusing on the external Michelet: intellectual influences, formal thought, friends, and travels.

Pommier, Jean, *Renan, d'après des documents inédits.* Paris, 1923. A concise authoritative biography.

Powers, Richard H., "Edgar Quinet and the First French Translation of Herder's *Ideen zur Geschichte der Menschheit,*" *Romantic Review,* XLV (April 1954), 109–114.

———, *Edgar Quinet: A Study in French Patriotism*. Dallas, 1957.

Renan, Ernest, "Dante et les origines de la langue et de la littérature italiennes," *Revue des Deux Mondes*, XII (Dec. 15, 1855), 1389–90. A respectful short review and general estimate of Fauriel as a scholar.

Renker, Fritz, *Niebuhr und die Romantik*. Leipzig, 1935.

Sainte-Beuve, C.A., "M. Fauriel," *Portraits contemporains*, IV, 124–268. New ed. Paris, 1870.

Teuteberg, René, *Prosper de Barante (1782–1866): Ein romantischer Historiker des französischen Liberalismus*. Basel, 1945. This is the most complete recent study of Barante, but it adds little that is new.

Thierry, Augustin (b. 1870), *Augustin Thierry, d'après sa correspondance et ses papiers de famille*. Paris, 1922. This work by the historian's namesake is far from thorough or objective, yet it is useful.

Van Tieghem, Philippe, *Renan*. Paris, 1948. A satisfactory biography, particularly good in its treatment of Renan's literary accomplishments.

Viallaneix, Paul, *La voie royale: Essai sur l'idée de peuple dans l'œuvre de Michelet*. Paris, 1959.

Wardman, H. W., *Ernest Renan: A Critical Biography*. London, 1964.

Wilson, Edmund, *To the Finland Station*. Garden City, New York, n.d. The first five chapters present a sympathetic and perceptive analysis of Michelet's style in relation to his life and political ideas.

Notes

CHAPTER 1

1. Gabriel Veaugeois, "Notice abrégée d'un journal d'un voyage archéologique et géologique," *Mémoires de la Société royale des Antiquaires de France*, III (Paris, 1821), 370–90.

2. These examples are taken from the first five volumes. For the best account of folklore research in other European countries, see Giuseppe Cocchiara, *Storia del folklore in Europa* (Turin, 1952).

3. For a discussion of the early Academy, see Henri Gaidoz, "De l'influence de l'Académie celtique sur les études de folklore," *Centenaire (1804–1904), Société nationale des Antiquaires de France: Recueil des mémoires* (Paris, 1904), 135–43.

4. Paul Sébillot, *La littérature orale en France* (Paris, 1891), 5–6; A. Grazier, "Lettres à Grégoire sur les patois de France," *Revue des Langues Romanes*, V (1874), 418–34; for the numerous succeeding articles in this series, see the bibliography.

5. Sébillot, *La Littérature orale*, 6.

6. Desiré Monnier, *Mœurs et usages singuliers du peuple dans le Jura* (Lons-le-Saunier, 1823), 3, 59.

7. "De la propagation des livres irreligieux depuis la Restauration," *Le Mémorial catholique*, II (May 1825), 270, 274.

8. *Journal de Paris*, March 27, 1814, 1–2.

9. Madame de Staël, *De l'Allemagne* in *Œuvres complètes*, Vol. X (Brussels, 1830), I, 17, 72, II, 281 et passim.

10. Joseph Lavallée, "Discours préliminaire," *Mémoires de l'Académie celtique* (Paris, 1807), I, 5–6. Folklorists in France long continued to complain of the prejudices fostered by classical studies. The scholar Puymaigre, for example, observed in 1864: "In France we are more classicist than we believe. In spite of the romantic revolution which has made the end of the Restoration the '89 of literature, we have kept many prejudices, we have not freed ourselves of our college memories, in taste we have preserved aristocratic penchants that have long made us consider with disdain the trivialities, the crude locutions of the old rustic Muse. . . ."; see Th. Puymaigre, *Chants populaires recueillis dans le pays Messin* (Paris, 1865), 1.

11. Voltaire, *Essai sur les mœurs*, in *Œuvres complètes*, XI (Paris, 1878), 15: "Volumes could be written on this subject [the origins of religion], but all these volumes can be reduced to a few words: the bulk of the human race has been and long will be senseless and stupid; and perhaps the most senseless of all have been those people who have wanted to find some sense

in these absurd fables and to introduce reason into folly."

12. Frank E. Manuel's *The Eighteenth Century Confronts the Gods* (Cambridge, Mass., 1959) brilliantly treats the leading mythographers. Both this book and Peter Gay's *The Enlightenment, An Interpretation* (New York, 1966, esp. pp. 89, 239, 399) discuss the philosophes' fundamental opposition to myth.

13. *The New Science of Giambattista Vico*, trans. Thomas Goddard Bergin and Max Harold Fisch, abridged and revised (Garden City, New York, 1961), 74, 79.

14. Madame de Staël, *Lettres sur les écrits de Rousseau*, in *Œuvres*, I (1820), 15, quoted in Arthur O. Lovejoy, *Essays in the History of Ideas* (New York, 1960), 25; Auguste Viatte, *Les sources occultes du romantisme* (2nd ed.; Paris, 1965), I, 284, II, 168.

15. Jean-René Derré, *Le renouvellement de la pensée religieuse en France de 1824 à 1834* (Paris, 1962), 14 et passim. Félicité Robert de Lamennais, *Essai sur l'indifférence en matière de religion* (4th ed.; Paris, 1828), II, 5–6. George Cogordan, *Joseph de Maistre* (Paris, 1894), 136, 194.

16. Desiré Monnier, *Du culte des esprits dans la Séquanie* (Lons-le-Saunier, 1834), 10.

17. This subject has been treated fully by Raymond Schwab in his *La Renaissance orientale* (Paris, 1950).

18. Paul Van Tieghem, "La notion de vraie poésie dans le préromantisme européen," *Revue de Littérature comparée*, I (1921), 215–51. See also George Boas, *Vox Populi: Essays in the History of an Idea* (Baltimore, 1969), 122–42.

19. Michel de Montaigne, *Essais*, ed. Maurice Rat (Paris, 1967), I, 347. This often-cited passage appears in Book I, Chap. 54, "Des vaines subtilitez."

20. For a long chronicle of the slow, small steps by which Herder's name came to be known in France, see Henri Tronchon, *La fortune intellectuelle de Herder en France* (Paris, 1920).

21. Paul Van Tieghem, *Ossian en France* (Paris, 1917), II, 20.

22. Paul Van Tieghem, *Le préromantisme* (Paris, 1924), I, 222.

23. X. Marmier, *Chants populaires du Nord* (Paris, 1842), xvii.

24. Henri Tronchon, "Quelques notes sur le premier mouvement folkloriste en France," *Mélanges d'histoire littéraire générale et comparée offerts à Fernand Baldensperger* (Paris, 1930), II, 302–303.

25. See the recent study of Lionel Gossman, *Medievalism and the Ideologies of the Enlightenment: The World and Work of La Curne de Sainte-Palaye* (Baltimore, 1968). Gossman shows not only the importance of the eighteenth-century scholar's literary researches, but also his pioneering advocacy and use of medieval literature as a source for historical study.

26. See the *Mémoires de la Société royale des Antiquaires de France*, V (Paris, 1823), cxii.

27. *Mémoires de l'Académie celtique*, I (Paris, 1807), 64.

28. *Mémoires de la Société royale des Antiquaires de France*, II (Paris, 1820), 6.

29. Louis-Antoine François de Marchangy, Archives Nationales, 233

AP 1, Marchangy MSS, n.d. The correct title of Noël's work was *Abrégé de la mythologie universelle, ou Dictionnaire de la fable.*

30. Gaston Paris, "De l'étude de la poésie populaire en France," *Mélusine* (Paris, 1878), I, 2. Paris' article first appeared in the *Revue critique* (May 22, 1866).

31. L. Kérardven [Louis Antoine Dufilhol], *Guionvac'h, études sur la Bretagne* (Paris, 1835); Emile Souvestre, *Les derniers Bretons* (4 vols., Paris, 1835–37).

32. Frédéric Rivarès, *Chansons et airs populaires de Béarn* (Paris, 1844), viii; Auguste Demesmay, *Traditions populaires de Franche Comté, poésies suivies de notes* (Paris, 1838), vii.

33. Thomas Percy, *Reliques of Ancient English Poetry* (London, 1765), I, vi–vii.

34. The *Gazette* is quoted in Van Tieghem, *Le préromantisme*, I, 258.

35. Christopher Morrill Greene, "Historical Consciousness and Historical Monuments in France after 1789" (unpublished Ph.D. thesis, Harvard University, 1964).

36. François Auguste René, Vicomte de Chateaubriand, *Etudes historiques* (New ed.; Paris, 1872), 109: "The serious century into which we have come has difficulty conceiving that frivolity of judgment, those superficial views of the age which preceded us."

37. See Friedrich Meinecke, *Die Entstehung des Historismus* (2nd ed.; Munich, 1946), 192–94 (on Mallet); Cocchiara, *Storia del folklore*, 182–87 (on Müller); Fritz Renker, *Niebuhr und die Romantik* (Leipzig, 1935), chapter 2.

CHAPTER 2

1. Thierry's New History

1. Augustin Thierry, *Récits des temps mérovingiens* (New ed.; Paris, 1867), xii–xiii. Chateaubriand, who was fond of French popular poetry, modeled his Frankish war song on songs recorded in medieval manuscripts. See Théodore Hersart de la Villemarqué, "Les précurseurs de nos études—Chateaubriand," *Revue des traditions populaires*, III (Aug. 1888), 419. For some compelling doubts about the credibility of Thierry's story, see Louis Maigron, *Le roman historique à l'époque romantique* (New ed.; Paris, 1912), 213–217.

2. On Thierry and Rousseau, one has to rely on the sketchy information found in A. Augustin-Thierry, *Augustin Thierry d'après sa correspondance et ses papiers de famille* (Paris, 1922), 17. See also Friedrich Engel-Jánosi, *Four Studies in French Romantic Historical Writing* (Baltimore, 1955), 91.

3. For a discussion of the intellectual relationship of Thierry and Saint-Simon, see Frank E. Manuel, *The New World of Henri Saint-Simon* (Cambridge, Mass., 1956), 151–53, 156, 194–95.

4. Thierry's articles appeared in the *Censeur européen;* some of the historical essays were reprinted in his *Lettres sur l'histoire de France* (Paris, 1827); more of them in his *Dix ans d'études historiques* (Paris, 1834); the fourth edition, dated 1842, is used here.

5. A detailed study of this period may be found in Engel-Jánosi's *Four Studies*, 88–120.

6. Thierry, "Sur l'esprit national des Irlandais à propos des *Mélodies irlandaises* de Thomas Moore," *Dix ans*, 165. This review originally appeared in the *Censeur européen* of Feb. 28, 1820. Thierry's article on *Ivanhoe* ("Sur la conquête de l'Angleterre par les Normands à propos du roman d'*Ivanhoe*," *Dix ans*, 180) first appeared in the *Censeur européen* of May 27, 1820.

7. The first letter is the most important one for the purposes of this study. Published first in the *Courrier français* of July 23, 1820, it was reprinted in *Dix ans*, 345–52. Thierry's retrospective summary of his program appeared in the preface to his *Dix ans*, 20, 21.

8. Pierre Moreau, *L'histoire en France au XIXᵉ siècle, Etudes françaises*, Vol. 35 (Paris, 1935), 21–22.

9. Thierry, "Première lettre," *Dix ans*, 347.

10. Thierry, "Sur l'affranchissement des communes," *Dix ans*, 369–70; first printed in the *Courrier français*, Oct. 13, 1820.

11. Thierry, "Sur l'affranchissement des communes," 369.

12. Thierry, "Première lettre," 347. "In this truly national history, if it found a pen worthy of writing it, France would figure with its cities and its diverse populations, which would be presented to us as so many collective beings, gifted with will and action." See also the extract from the *Courrier français* of 1820 reprinted in *Dix ans*, 354, and entitled "Sur la classification de l'histoire de France par races royales."

13. Thierry, "Sur l'esprit national des Irlandais," 166.

14. Thierry, "Histoire véritable de Jacques Bonhomme," *Dix ans*, 326–35. On the background of this name, see—*faute de mieux*—the inadequate essay by Léon Durocher, "La légende de Jacques Bonhomme," *La Tradition*, I (1887), 84–88.

15. Stanley Mellon, *The Political Uses of History; a Study of Historians in the French Restoration* (Stanford, 1958). Boris Georgievich Réizov, *L'historiographie romantique française, 1815–1830* (Moscow, 1962); see also Jacques Barzun's article, "Romantic Historiography as a Political Force in France," *Journal of the History of Ideas*, II (June 1941), 318–29.

16. Thierry, *Lettres sur l'histoire*, 3.

17. D. G. Charlton, *Secular Religions in France, 1815–1870* (London, 1963), 2.

18. Thierry, *Lettres sur l'histoire*, 5.

2. Barante's History: Public Opinion and Tradition

1. Augustin Thierry, *Lettres sur l'histoire de France* (Paris, 1827), viii.

2. There is no satisfactory biography of Barante. The most recent full-length study is René Teuteberg's *Prosper de Barante: ein romantischer Historiker des französischen Liberalismus* (Basel, 1945), but it adds little that is not found in writings of a century ago. The basic primary work is *Souvenirs de Baron de Barante, 1782–1866* (Paris, 1890–91), 8 vols.

3. He translated Schiller's dramas, frequently contributed essays and reviews, and wrote *De la Littérature française pendant le dix-huitième siècle*

(1807), which "was an almost popular book, . . . often given as a prize for the competitive examinations of lycées and schools," recalled François Guizot in his article, "M. de Barante, ses souvenirs de famille, sa vie et ses œuvres," *Revue des Deux Mondes*, LXX (July 1, 1867), 17.

4. Prosper de Barante, *Histoire des ducs de Bourgogne et de la maison de Valois* (6th ed.; Paris, 1839), I, xvi–xxiii, xxxv.

5. Ibid., xxxi.

6. Barante, *Souvenirs*, I, 269, 271. The Vendean narrative was M. L. V. Du Vergier de la Rochejacquelin's *Mémoires* (n.p., 1816).

7. Barante, *Histoire des ducs*, I, ii.

8. "*Le Jouvencel*, roman du XVe siècle," (1829) *Mélanges historiques et littéraires* (Brussels, 1835), II, 149, 151; *Histoire des ducs*, I, xxxviii. See also Barante's articles on Gregory of Tours, Froissart, Commines, and others in *Mélanges historiques et littéraires*, Vol. I.

9. Barante, *Histoire des ducs*, I, xxvii–xxxi.

10. Ibid., xxvi–xxvii.

11. Ibid. See also Barante's article, "De l'histoire," *Mélanges*, II, 7–8. "The *Iliad* and other epics are histories, but cast in the poetic molds of cosmogonic narratives. The imagination is mixed with memory, but in all sincerity, without any literary calculation."

12. Barante, "*Le Jouvencel*," pp. 151–52. Scott's imagination, Barante held, inevitably reflected something of its surroundings, and consequently, fiction actually written in the period depicted was probably truer history than a later novel.

13. See, for example, Voltaire's *Dictionnaire philosophique*, in *Œuvres* (Paris, 1879), XIX, 430, where Voltaire disapproved of a familiar kind of free-wheeling imagination. He described this "passive imagination," independent of reflection, as "the source of our passions and errors."

14. Barante, "De l'histoire," 50. Barante, however, felt that narrative alone would persuasively convey his own beliefs without the need for any dissertations. See *Histoire des ducs*, I, lxxviii–lxxix.

15. Barante, *Histoire des ducs*, I, lii; "*Histoire des Français aux XIVe siècle* par M. Monteil" (1830), *Etudes historiques et biographiques* (Paris, 1857), II, 383; "De l'histoire," 5.

16. Barante, "*Le Jouvencel*," 152–55.

17. Barante, "De *La mort de Henri III*, par M. Vitet, et des drames historiques" (1829), *Mélanges*, II, 194–95.

18. Barante, "De *La mort de Henri III*," 194–95.

19. Barante, *Histoire des ducs*, I, xl.

20. Voltaire, "Histoire," *Dictionnaire philosophique*, in *Œuvres*, XIX (Paris, 1879), 346–47.

21. Barante, *Histoire des ducs*, I, xl. His study of public opinion, he declared, "introduces into history its most powerful motive force, and, if one can so speak, its principal personage."

22. Ibid., xii.

23. Barante, "*Histoire des Français*," 397.

24. Barante, "Jacques Bonhomme" (1832) *Mélanges*, II, 298–326.

25. Barante, *Histoire des ducs*, I, xlvi–xlvii.

26. Ibid., v–vii.

27. Barante, *"Sur les tableaux de genre et d'histoire* publiés par M. Barrière, et sur l'histoire de France au XVIIIe siècle" (1828), *Mélanges*, II, 271–72; "De *La mort de Henri III*," 189.

3. Ballanche: The Truth of Primitive Traditions

1. Pierre-Simon Ballanche, *Essais de palingénésie sociale,* in *Œuvres de M. Ballanche de l'Académie de Lyon,* Vols. III–IV (Paris, 1830, I, 26–27).

2. The same rather limited biographical information may be found in Albert Joseph George's *Pierre-Simon Ballanche, Precursor of Romanticism* (Syracuse, 1945) or Charles Huit's *La vie et les œuvres de Ballanche* (Lyons, 1904).

3. See Léon Cellier, *L'épopée romantique: Ballanche, Quinet, Lamartine, Soumet, Constant, Hugo* (Paris, 1954).

4. Ballanche, *Essai sur les institutions sociales dans leur rapport avec les idées nouvelles,* in *Œuvres,* Vol. II (Paris, 1830), 31, 319, 324, 354–58.

5. Ballanche, *Palingénésie,* I, 201–202.

6. Ibid., 25, 256.

7. Ibid., 25.

8. *The Autobiography of Giambattista Vico,* trans. Max Harold Fisch and Thomas Goddard Bergin (Ithaca, New York, 1963). See esp. the fourth section of the introduction, "Vico's Reputation and Influence," 61–107, written by Fisch.

9. Ballanche, *Palingénésie,* II, 532.

10. Ballanche, *Institutions,* 209.

11. Ballanche, *Palingénésie,* II, 533–534.

12. Ballanche, *Institutions,* 46.

13. Ibid., 20, 49.

14. Ibid., 42, 51; Ballanche, *Palingénésie,* I, 16, 71–72.

15. Ballanche, *Palingénésie,* I, 13.

16. Ballanche, *Institutions,* 242–76.

17. Ibid., 276–77, 305–306, 312.

18. Ibid., 296.

19. Ballanche, *Palingénésie,* I, 40–44, 71, 190; see also *Institutions,* 332.

20. Ballanche, *Institutions,* 97–98.

21. Ballanche, *Palingénésie,* I, 49, 158.

22. Ibid., 232–33.

23. Ibid., 48–80.

24. Ibid., 99.

25. Ibid., II, 6.

26. Ibid., I, 254, 352.

27. Ibid., 234.

28. In this case at least, Ballanche's remarks on Vico's fate are true: "What a singular destiny [Vico had]! He who was so intuitive, emerges from the tomb when he no longer has anything to teach; he who had so much the faculty of prevision, and who consumed it all in the study of the past, reappears only when he no longer has anything to predict." Ibid., 338.

29. Ibid., 83–85, 201; II, 530–31.

30. Ibid., II, 518–19.

31. Ballanche, *Institutions*, 291.

32. Ballanche, *Palingénésie*, II, 351.

33. Ibid., I, 145–81.

34. Ibid., II, 524. Roger Henry Soltau, for one, identifies Ballanche with Maistre and Bonald; see Soltau's *French Political Thought in the Nineteenth Century* (New Haven, 1931), 15–16. Soltau's opinion of Ballanche, with which I strongly disagree, seems to be based on less than thorough knowledge: "The works of Ballanche may be allowed to fall into oblivion: his *Palingénésie* is not only unreadable but contains nothing that cannot be found in the writings of his better-known fellow-schoolmen Maistre and Bonald."

35. Ballanche, *Institutions*, 314, 362.

36. Fernand Denis, *Journal*, 1829–48 (Fribourg, 1932), 56; Entry for Oct. 30, 1832.

CHAPTER 3

1. Fauriel and Thierry: The Folklore of the Vanquished

1. Claude Fauriel (ed. and trans.), *Chants populaires de la Grèce moderne*, recueillis et publiés, avec une traduction française, des éclaircissements et des notes (2 vols., Paris, 1824–25).

2. E. Tosi, "Vico en France: Analyse inédite, par Fauriel," *La Revue de Littérature comparée*, XI (1931), 763–77.

3. J.-B. Galley, *Claude Fauriel, membre de l'Institut 1772–1843* (Saint-Etienne, 1909), 10–12, 190–91.

4. Ibid., 21, 48–49.

5. Fauriel, *Chants populaires*, I, cxxvi. See also Fauriel's lectures of 1831 on Serbian and Greek popular poetry in Miodrag Ibrovac, *Claude Fauriel et la fortune européenne des poésies populaires grecque et serbe* (Paris, 1966), 413–14.

6. Claude Fauriel, *Histoire de la Gaule méridionale sous la domination des conquérants Germains* (3 vols.; Paris, 1836).

7. C. A. Sainte-Beuve, *Portraits contemporains* (New ed.; Paris, 1870), IV, 126.

8. Ernest Renan, "Dante et les origines de langue et de la littérature italiennes," *Revue des Deux Mondes*, XII (Dec. 15, 1855), 1389–90.

9. Letter from Augustin Thierry to Fauriel, written in 1829, quoted in Galley, *Fauriel*, xviii.

10. Letter from Fauriel to Arnaud, dated *24 ventôse, an IX* (March 11, 1801), quoted in Galley, *Fauriel*, 83.

11. See letters of 1793 quoted in Galley, *Fauriel*, 23, and *Correspondance de Fauriel et Mary Clarke*, ed. Ottmar de Mohl (Paris, 1911), 25 (letter of August 15, 1822 to Mary Clarke); 271 (letter of Sept. 20 or 21, 1821 to Mary Clarke); 309 (letter of Oct. 4, 1829 to Mary Clarke); 399 (letter of Sept. 21,

1834 to Julius Mohl). Physical ailments (headaches, gout) added to Fauriel's melancholy.

12. Paul and Victor Glachant (eds.), *Lettres à Fauriel* (Paris, 1902), 12–13.

13. Letter from Augustin Thierry to Fauriel, dated Oct. 25, 1821, quoted in Galley, *Fauriel*, 243.

14. For a bibliography of Fauriel's writing, see Galley, *Fauriel*, 490–94.

15. Ibid., 20–22, 24, 35, 37–39, 51, 185–89. Fauriel bought a biography of Penn in 1793.

16. Fauriel, *Chants populaires*, I, ii, vii–viii.

17. Galley, *Fauriel*, 81–82.

18. Fauriel, *Poésie provençale*, I, 428–29, III, 387.

19. See ibid., I, passim, esp. 171–81, 419–48; II, 84 ff., 311, 323–27.

20. Ibid., I, 15–16; II, 84, 276–77.

21. Ibid., I, 16, 424 passim.

22. Ibid., 17, 28–54.

23. See Emile Ripert, *La renaissance provençale, 1800–1860* (Paris, 1917), 84 passim.

24. H. Fortoul, "De la littérature provençale," *Revue des Deux Mondes*, XIV (1846), 551.

25. Paulin Paris, *Etudes sur les chansons de geste et sur le "Garin le Loherain"* (Paris, 1863), 7. There is general agreement that Fauriel was largely responsible for acquainting French scholars with the *cantilène* theory, though Charles Magnin also played a part, perhaps reaching a larger audience than Fauriel with his article "Examen des systèmes de Vico et de Wolf sur la formation des poèmes homériques," *Causeries et méditations historiques et littéraires* (Paris, 1843), 12–49, an article which first appeared in the *Globe*, June 24 and July 23, 1830.

26. Fauriel, *Chants populaires*, I, xxv.

27. Fauriel, *Gaule méridionale*, II, 503–04, III, 35; *Poésie provençal*, II, 267.

28. See Fauriel, *Chants populaires*, I, xxv, cxiv–cxv, cxxxix, cxli, and Fauriel's course on Serbian and Greek poetry (1831), in Ibrovac, *Claude Fauriel*, 426.

29. Fauriel, *Poésie provençale*, I, 478–547. Contrast Fauriel's views with those of the staunch Catholic Montalembert, whose *Histoire de Sainte Elisabeth de Hongrie* appeared in 1836: "We will say nothing of the Provençal literature of the troubadours, although modern criticism has deigned to leave it its reputation, and although it was still in all its éclat in the thirteenth century, because we believe that it contained no Catholic element, that it very rarely rose above the cult of material beauty, and that it presents, except for several exceptions, the materialist and immoral tendency of the Southern heresies of this epoch." Le comte de Montalembert, *Histoire de Sainte Elisabeth de Hongrie*, (New ed.; Paris, 1861), I, 100.

30. Ibrovac, *Fauriel*, 590–92 (Fauriel's course of 1831 on Greek and Serbian popular poetry); Fauriel, *Chants populaires*, I, lxxx ff.

31. See the series of articles summarizing Fauriel's lectures on the Homeric epics in the *Journal général de l'instruction publique*, V (1836), 372, 507, 587, 708–709.

32. Alfred Galpin, *Fauriel in Italy: Unpublished Correspondence, 1822–1825* (Rome, 1962), 43–44. Letter from Fauriel at Paris to Mary Clarke at Edinburgh, dated August 15, 1822.

33. Galley, *Fauriel*, 242.

34. Augustin Thierry, *Dix ans d'études historiques* (4th ed.; Paris, 1842), 29.

35. Ibid., 37–38.

36. Augustin Thierry, *Histoire de la conquête de l'Angleterre par les Normands* (7th ed.; Paris, 1846), I, 5.

37. Thierry, *Dix ans*, 14.

38. Thierry, *Conquête*, I, x.

39. Ibid., xiv.

40. Ibid., 93. Thierry's view of Robin Hood as an Anglo-Saxon hero fighting Normans has not found acceptance since his time. For a survey of the relevant historiography and recent conclusions on the question, see R. H. Hilton, "The Origins of Robin Hood," *Past and Present*, No. 14 (Nov. 1958), 30–77, and J. C. Holt, "The Origins and Audience of the Ballads of Robin Hood," *Past and Present*, No. 18 (Nov. 1960), 89–110.

41. Thierry, *Conquête*, I, 94.

42. Augustin Thierry, *Récits des temps mérovingiens, précédés de "Considérations sur l'histoire de France"* (New ed.; Paris, 1867), I, 329–30. Similarly, in his *Lettres sur l'histoire de France* (Paris, 1866), 94–98, he remarked that the saint's miracles were of interest to him because of the information they yielded concerning popular attitudes and beliefs. See also *Conquête*, I, 95, 270; III, 57. Camille Jullian, I think, unjustly criticized Thierry along with other Restoration historians for failing to understand the "religious and superstitious" side of Jacques Bonhomme; see Camille Jullian, "Augustin Thierry et le mouvement historique sous la Restauration," *Revue de Synthèse historique*, XIII (Oct. 1906), 138–39.

43. Thierry, *Dix ans*, 32.

44. Thierry, *Histoire de la conquête*, 11.

45. Thierry, *Dix ans*, 25.

46. Thierry, "Considérations sur l'histoire de France," *Récits*, I, 5.

47. Thierry, *Dix ans*, 41.

48. Ibid., 32.

49. Thierry, "Considérations sur l'histoire de France," 200–201.

2. Michelet: Between History and Legend

1. Jules Michelet, "Journal des idées," *Ecrits de jeunesse*, ed. Paul Viallaneix (Paris, 1959), 242; entry for March 16, 1828. In a note on page 419 Viallaneix states that Michelet was inspired to plan this project by the example of "Charles [sic] Fauriel" and the latter's anthology of Greek songs. Fauriel's work was published in 1824–25, three and four years before Michelet's entry. It seems as likely that Michelet was inspired by Herder's example, which was brought to his attention in 1828 by an essay on the German written by Michelet's closest friend, Edgar Quinet.

2. "Journal de mes lectures," *Ecrits de jeunesse*, 329. The translation was entitled *Chants populaires de Midi de l'Ecosse*.

3. Jules Michelet, *Journal: Texte intégral*, établi sur les manuscrits autographes et publié pour la première fois, ed. Paul Viallaneix (Paris, 1959), I, 51.

4. Michelet, "Journal de mes lectures," 329–31; "Journal des idées," 243, 247.

5. Michelet, "Journal des idées," 247–48. The "Ecole Préparatoire" was the name under which Mgr. Frayssinous reestablished the Ecole Normale Supérieure in 1826.

6. Michelet, "Journal des idées," 247.

7. See Gabriel Monod, *La vie et la pensée de Jules Michelet, 1798–1852* (Paris, 1923), I, 1–2, 5; Jules Michelet, "Preface of 1869," *Histoire de France*, ed. Claude Mettra (Lausanne, 1965), I, 52.

8. Jules Michelet, *Le Peuple* (3rd ed., Paris, 1846), 6.

9. Michelet, *Journal*, I, 291; entry for February 1839.

10. Giambattista Vico, *The New Science*, trans. and ed. by Thomas Goddard Bergin and Max Harold Fisch, abridged and revised (Garden City, New York, 1961), 29.

11. Michelet, "Preface of 1869," *Histoire de France*, I, 45.

12. Michelet, "Journal des idées," 224, 227, 234.

13. See Michelet, *Journal*, I, 45, for a letter written to Quinet on July 21, 1828, summarizing the reasons for the journey.

14. Jules Michelet, *Histoire romaine* (3rd ed.; Paris, 1843), I, 378–79.

15. Michelet, *Journal*, I, 75, 91, 134, 165. This interest is also apparent in Michelet's correspondence with folklorists of the period; brief exchanges of ideas on traditional songs, legends, and myths may be found in the following letters to Michelet—all in the Bibliothèque historique de la Ville de Paris: X. Marmier, 1833, No. 4775.1; 1840, No. 4875.48; La Villemarqué, 1836?, No. 4881.34; J. J. Ampère, 1838, No. 4755.4; E. Souvestre, 1847, No. 4872.46; F. Baudry, 1862, No. 4758.4.

16. *Histoire de France*, I, 323–91.

17. Jules Michelet, *L'introduction à l'histoire universelle* (2nd ed.; Paris, 1834), 100.

18. Jules Michelet, *Origines du droit français cherchées dans les symboles et formules du droit universel* (Paris, 1837), viii. For the correspondence, see Werner Kaegi, *Michelet und Deutschland* (Basel, 1936). See also Michelet's tribute to Grimm in *Légendes démocratiques du Nord; La France devant l'Europe* (Paris, 1899), 401.

19. Michelet, *Droit français*, iii.

20. Ibid., cvii–cix.

21. Ibid., cv.

22. Ibid., cxxii.

23. Ibid., cx–cxi, cxviii.

24. Ibid., cxx. His conclusion was, as he himself remarked, based on the paucity of French symbolic laws in comparison to the abundance of German examples, but it was doubtless based also on the reputation of his nation for reason and criticism, and perhaps on the fact that his own knowledge of symbolic interpretation derived largely from non-French thinkers—chiefly Vico, Creuzer, Schelling and Hegel via Cousin.

25. Ibid., cxvii–cxviii.

26. Michelet, *Le Peuple,* 346.

27. Ibid., 211.

28. Ibid., 258.

29. Ibid., 262–63. "This prejudice [against instinct] had been murderous for all the poor sons of instinct. It has made the cultivated classes disdainful, full of hatred for the non-cultivated classes. It has inflicted on children the hell of our education. To the misfortune of the infant peoples, it has authorized a thousand absurd and malevolent fables which have contributed much to reassure our so-called Christians in the extermination of these peoples." Michelet referred specifically to the killing of the highlanders of Scotland, North American Indians, peoples of Northern India, and Africans.

30. Jules Michelet, *La Sorcière* (New ed.; Paris, 1878), 73, n. 1.

31. Ibid., 3–4, 12, 78, 146.

32. Ibid., 412. The idea that science is an outgrowth of magic has been extensively developed, notably by James Frazer and Lynn Thorndike—see the latter's *History of Magic and Experimental Science,* 8 vols. (New York, 1958). This idea is in direct opposition to Voltaire's view of magic as the foe of science. See Margaret Sherwood Libby, *The Attitude of Voltaire to Magic and the Sciences* (New York, 1935), 236.

33. Michelet, Journal (1820–23), *Ecrits de jeunesse,* 88 (June 20, 1820).

34. See *Le peuple,* 332–58; *L'étudiant* (1848); *Nos fils* (1870); *Histoire de la Révolution,* I, 5; *Journal,* I, 693, entry for June 27, 1848; *Journal* (1849–1860), ed. Paul Viallaneix (Paris, 1962), II, esp. 33–111.

35. Michelet, *Journal,* I, 691 (June 16, 1848).

36. See Michelet, *Le peuple,* 161, 347–48; Jules Michelet, *Lettres inédites à Alfred Dumesnil et à Eugene Noël* (1841–47), ed. Paul Sirven (Paris, 1924), 207, letter of Oct. 17, 1853, to Eugene Noël.

37. Michelet, *Lettres,* 219; letter of May 17, 1854, to Noël.

38. Michelet, *Journal,* I, 680; entry for Dec. 3, 1847.

39. Ibid., 491; entry undated, made in 1843.

40. Michelet, *Le peuple,* 8–9.

41. Jules Michelet, *Histoire de la Révolution française,* ed. Gérard Walter (Angers, 1952), I, 282.

42. Ibid.

43. Ibid., 283–87.

44. In addition to sections of *Le peuple*—chiefly chapter 6, "France supérieure, comme dogme, et comme légende"—and other works discussed below, note Michelet's letter to M. Accrusi, dated May 15, 1851; "Mazzini, who has done me the honor of writing to me, would prefer that I create [*fisse*] history rather than legend. For the moment, I could not do it. I must limit myself to legends; I will do even very little of that. The sixth volume of the French Revolution weighs upon me horribly." Letter published in Gabriel Monod, *Jules Michelet, Etudes sur sa vie et ses œuvres* (Paris, 1905), 39–40.

45. Michelet, *Le peuple,* 356–57.

46. Ibid., 328–30, and footnote 1 on 330.

47. Michelet, *Légendes démocratiques du Nord; La France devant l'Europe,* ed. Michel Bréal (Paris, 1899), 29, 126, 334. Michelet also introduced into his book some examples of Rumanian popular songs. For a recent scholarly edition, see Michel Cadot, ed., *Légendes démocratiques du Nord* (Paris, 1968).

48. Jules Michelet, *Bible de l'humanité* (3rd ed.; Paris, 1864), 484.

49. Gordon Wright has called Michelet "France's favorite historian" —see Wright's textbook *France in Modern Times: 1760 to the Present* (Chicago, 1960), 23. For an estimate of the influence of Michelet's *Histoire de la Révolution,* see Pieter Geyl, *Debates with Historians* (Cleveland, 1964), 78. For a brief discussion of Michelet's general influence on his successors, see Camille Jullian, ed., *Extraits des historiens français du XIXᵉ siècle* (Paris, 1897), lxxxiii, and Pierre Moreau, *L'histoire en France au XIXᵉ siècle, Etudes françaises,* Vol. 35 (Paris, 1935), 109–10.

In the opinion of Pierre Albouy, Michelet was the "greatest creator" of "national myths" in the nineteenth century *(myth* here meaning symbolic stories or images with universal and religious significance). See Albouy's *Mythes et mythologies dans la littérature française* (Paris, 1969) for a discussion of such myths as Joan of Arc, *Le Peuple,* and Hercules in Michelet's writing.

50. Hans Kohn, *Prophets and Peoples: Studies in Nineteenth Century Nationalism* (New York, 1952), 65; Geyl, *Debates,* 83–84, 98–99.

51. Edmund Wilson, *To the Finland Station* (Garden City, New York, n.d.), chapters 1–5; Lucien Febvre, ed., *Michelet, 1798–1874.*

52. Oscar A. Haac, *Les principes inspirateurs de Michelet* (Paris, 1951), esp. chapter 7; Jeanlouis Cornuz, *Jules Michelet: un aspect de la pensée religieuse au XIXᵉ siècle* (Paris, 1955); Paul Viallaneix, *La Voie royale: Essai sur l'idée de peuple dans l'œuvre de Michelet* (Paris, 1959), see esp. 288–92; 392–419.

3. Henri Martin and Druidic Wisdom

1. Gabriel Hanotaux, *Henri Martin* (Paris, 1885), 281.

2. Ibid., 15, 29–34.

3. Henri Martin, *Histoire de France depuis les temps les plus reculés jusqu'en juillet 1830, par les principaux historiens* (Paris, 1833).

4. The Prospectus was reprinted on p. 4 of Martin's *Histoire de France* of 1833.

5. Martin, *Histoire de France* (1833), 13.

6. The Académie des Inscriptions et Belles-Lettres awarded the first Gobert prize to volumes 10 and 11 in 1844, the Académie Française gave the second Gobert prize to volumes 15 and 16 in 1851, and the Instiut gave Martin a prize for the whole work in 1869.

7. The phrase *incorrigible Celt* is quoted from one of Martin's letters in Hanotaux, *Martin,* 235.

An interesting friend of Martin's and an equally enthusiastic *celtisant* was one Charles de Gaulle, uncle of a rather well-known general of the same name. De Gaulle, like Martin, was not Breton; he was born in Paris in 1837. But he became an ardent student of Celtic culture and secretary of the Breton organization Breuriez-Breiz, wrote Gaelic poems under the

Breton name Barz Bro-C'hall, and took a leading part in efforts to preserve and to study Breton culture in the nineteenth century. See Francis Gourvil, *Théodore-Claude-Henri Hersart de la Villemarqué (1815–1895) et le "Barzaz-Breiz"* (Rennes, 1960), 163–65; Charles de Gaulle's *Celtes au XIXᵉ siècle* (New ed.; Paris, 1903), first published in the *Revue de Bretagne et de Vendée* (1863); and Paul Marie de la Gorce, *De Gaulle entre deux mondes* (Paris, 1964), 18.

8. Henri Martin, *Histoire de France depuis les temps les plus reculés jusqu'en 1789* (4th ed.; Paris, 1855), I, xix. The quotation appears in his "Divertissement de 1854." This edition is used hereafter, unless otherwise noted.

9. Martin, *De la France, de son génie, et de ses destinées* (Paris, 1847), 18–19, 23–24, 35–37, 269 ff., 288; Henri Martin, *Jean Reynaud* (Paris, 1863), 20–21.

10. Martin, *Histoire de France* (1833), 3.

11. Martin, *Histoire de France*, I, 51–79.

12. Ibid., 59–62.

13. Martin, *De la France*, 127–30.

14. Hanotaux, *Martin*, 76–77.

15. Martin, *Histoire de France*, I, 85–87.

16. Ibid., 82–84, 88–89; III, 356.

17. Ibid., I, 203; III, 351–55; *De la France*, 126, 147.

18. Martin, *De la France*, 148.

19. Ibid.

20. Martin, *Histoire de France*, V, 45.

21. Ibid., I, 69–70, 80.

22. For a discussion of Martin's travels, see Hanotaux, *Martin*, 223–26.

23. Henri Martin, *Etudes d'archéologie celtique* (Paris, 1872), i–ii. This volume contains reports of Martin's folklore activities and controversies.

24. Hanotaux, *Martin*, 280.

CHAPTER 4

1. Quinet: Merlin and His Disenchantment

1. Edgar Quinet, *La Révolution* (8th ed.), in *Œuvres complètes*, XII–XIV (Paris, n.d.), I, 10. The quoted phrases are from the preface dated Nov. 2, 1865, and from the *Critique de la Révolution*, dated 1867.

The collected works of Quinet used here (except for *Napoléon* cited in n. 3) are not dated; they were all published by Germer-Baillère between 1879 and 1882.

On the personal relationship between Michelet and Quinet see H. Monin, "La rupture de Michelet et Quinet," *Revue d'histoire littéraire de France*, XIX (1912), 818–41.

2. Quinet, *La Révolution*, I, 60.

3. Edgar Quinet, *Napoléon*, in *Œuvres complètes*, VIII (Paris, 1857), 152.

4. See Richard H. Powers, *Edgar Quinet: A Study in French Patriotism* (Dallas, 1957), 36, and the same writer's "Edgar Quinet and the First French Translation of Herder's *Ideen zur Geschichte der Menschheit*," *Romantic Review*, XLV (April 1954), 109–14.

5. Edgar Quinet, "L'introduction à la philosophie de l'histoire de

l'humanité" (4th ed.), in *Œuvres complètes*, II (Paris, n.d.), 345–90, and "Essai sur les œuvres de Herder," in the same volume, 393–439.

6. See the letter of April 1828 written from Heidelberg in Quinet's *Correspondance: Lettres à sa mère*, in *Œuvres complètes*, vols. XIX–XX (Paris, n.d.), II, 71.

7. Jules Michelet, *Le peuple* (3rd ed.; Paris, 1846), 5.

8. For Quinet's comments on these men, his friends, see Quinet, *Correspondance*, II, 94, 139, 237, 284.

9. It was in his letter of Oct. 18, 1827, that Quinet told of meeting Niebuhr and Schlegel; see *Correspondance*, II, 59. For his comments on Niebuhr, see the letter of Jan. 5, 1828, ibid., 67.

10. See the letter of Feb. 23, 1827, ibid., 29, and the letter of July 8, 1827, in the same volume, 42.

11. Ibid., 22 (letter of Dec. 20, 1826); 25–26 (letter of Jan. 4, 1827); 29 (letter of Feb. 23, 1827); 32 (letter of March 17, 1827); 39–40 (letter of May 28, 1827); 81 (letter of July 7, 1828).

12. See Quinet's "Introduction à la philosophie de l'histoire de l'humanité" (4th ed.), in *Œuvres complètes*, II (Paris, n.d.), esp. 380–82, 389–90.

13. Quinet, *Histoire de mes idées* (2nd ed.), in *Œuvres complètes*, X (Paris, 1880), 132.

14. Quinet, *Correspondance*, II, 270–71. Letter to his mother, written from Heidelberg, July 1827.

15. Quinet, "Essai sur les œuvres de Herder," 401–403.

16. Edgar Quinet, *De l'origines des dieux* (3rd ed.), in *Œuvres complètes*, I (Paris, n.d.), 418.

17. Ibid., 431. For the following, see pp. 427–428, 431.

18. Ibid., 424.

19. Ibid., 419 ff., 429–32.

20. For an excellent full discussion of Quinet's *Ahasvérus* treated in relation to his life and other works, see Georgette Vabre Pradal, *La dimension historique de l'homme, ou Le mythe du Juif Errant dans la pensée d'Edgar Quinet* (Paris, 1961).

21. In a letter to his mother (May 27, 1831) Quinet with typical immodesty remarked that his work was analogous to that done abroad already by "Goethe, Tieck, Schlegel, Walter Scott, etc. . . . ," *Correspondance*, II, 196. For his official report on the old epics, see "Epopées françaises inédites du douzième siècle" (3rd ed.) in *Œuvres complètes*, XXVII (Paris, n.d.). The importance of his "discoveries" was sharply challenged by Paulin Paris.

22. Quinet, *Correspondance*, II, 66.

23. Edgar Quinet, *De l'histoire de la poésie* (3rd ed.), in *Œuvres complètes*, XXVII (Paris, n.d.), 301.

24. Ibid., 330–34.

25. Edgar Quinet, "Examen de la vie de Jésus" (4th ed.), in *Œuvres complètes*, III (Paris, n.d.), 287–352.

26. See Quinet's "Introduction à la philosophie de l'histoire de l'humanité," 364–66. "History, in its beginning as in its end, is the spectacle of liberty, the protest of mankind against the world that enchains it, the

triumph of the infinite over the finite, the liberation of the spirit, the reign of the soul." (p. 366.)

27. Edgar Quinet, "De l'avenir des religions," *Revue des Deux Mondes*, III (1831), 213–20; reprinted (3rd ed.) in *Œuvres complètes*, VI (Paris, n.d.), 394–403. Quinet's epic *Abasvérus* also presented Catholicism as but one stage in a succession of faiths—indeed one stage located well back in the past.

28. Quinet, *Histoire de poésie*, 423.

29. Ibid., 419–20.

30. Ibid., 405–407.

31. Ibid., 421.

32. Edgar Quinet, *Génie des religions* (5th ed.), in *Œuvres complètes*, I (Paris, n.d.), 27–30.

33. Ibid., 32.

34. Ibid., 12.

35. See Quinet, *Les Jésuites* (10th ed.) in *Œuvres complètes*, II (Paris, n.d.), 67. *L'ultramontanisme ou l'église romaine et la société moderne* (5th ed.) in the same volume, pp. 209–210.

36. See Quinet, *Les Jésuites*, 1–126; *L'ultramontanisme*, 129–304; and *Le christianisme et la Révolution française*, in *Œuvres complètes*, III (4th ed.; Paris, n.d.), 9–275.

37. Edgar Quinet, "L'enseignement du peuple" (5th ed.), *Œuvres complètes*, XI (Paris, n.d.), 125.

38. Quinet, *Napoléon*, 139.

39. Edgar Quinet, "Philosophie de l'histoire de France" (4th ed.), in *Œuvres complètes*, III (Paris, n.d.), 355–422.

2. Ozanam: Christianity and Folklore

1. There are numerous biographies of Ozanam, many of them resembling hagiography. The following scholarly works are outstanding: Abbé F. Méjecaze, *Frédéric Ozanam et l'église catholique* (Paris and Lyons, 1932), the same author's *Essai des idées et des jugements littéraires de Frédéric Ozanam* (Paris and Lyons, 1932), and Georges Goyau, *Ozanam* (Paris, 1931). For a listing of Ozanam's manuscripts and publications, see Eugène Galopin, *Essai de bibliographie chronologique sur Antoine Frédéric Ozanam, 1813–1853* (Paris, 1933).

2. *Lettres de Frédéric Ozanam, 1831–1853* (5th ed.; Paris, 1881), I, 4, 6–7. The letter is dated Jan. 15, 1831, and was written to H. Fortoul, a law student in Paris. See also Ozanam's letter of March 25, 1832, p. 59, for further comment on Ballanche's work.

3. For a list of titles and notes on these early works, some of them never published, see Galopin, *Essai de Bibliographie*, and *Lettres de Ozanam*, I, 48 passim.

4. *Lettres de Ozanam*, I, 35. Letter to his father, written Nov. 12, 1831.

5. "Réflexions sur la doctrine de Saint-Simon," *Mélanges*, in *Œuvres complètes*, VII (2nd ed.; Paris, 1859), 271–357. The "Réflexions" appeared in the Lyons newspaper, *Le Précurseur*, May 11 and 14, 1831. It was first published as an incomplete "Exposition sommaire de la doctrine de Saint-

Simon," in *L'Organisateur*, No. 1, August 15, 1829; No. 19, Dec. 20, 1829.

6. "Du progrès par le christianisme," *Mélanges*, in *Œuvres complètes*, VII (2nd ed.; Paris, 1859), 93–126. It first appeared in the *Revue européenne*, 2nd series, I (April 1835), 1–24.

7. Frédéric Ozanam, "La littérature allemande au moyen âge," *Mélanges*, in *Œuvres complètes*, VIII (Paris, 1859), 151–78; it first appeared in the *Journal général de l'instruction publique* (1841). "Des *Nibelungen* et de la poésie épique," in the same volume, 181–206; first printed in *L'université catholique* (1842).

8. Ozanam, *"Nibelungen,"* 190.

9. Ibid., 188, 191 ff.

10. Ibid., 191.

11. Ozanam, "Littérature allemande," 169, 177.

12. Frédéric Ozanam, *Les Germains avant le christianisme*, in *Œuvres complètes*, III (3rd ed.; Paris, 1861), 225, 270–75.

13. Ibid., 217.

14. Ibid., 56–58, 76, 96, 233 ff.

15. Ibid., 240.

16. To the subject of barbarian and pagan religion Ozanam returned again and again in his histories. See esp. *Germains*, 56–58, 98–100, 236; *La civilisation au cinquième siècle*, in *Œuvres complètes*, Vols. I–II (2nd ed.; Paris, 1862), I, 6, 112–18, 147 ff., 175–76; *Civilisation chrétienne chez les Francs*, in *Œuvres complètes*, IV (3rd ed.; Paris, 1861), 303–304.

17. Ozanam, *Germains*, 267, 274.

18. Ibid., 259, 266–67.

19. See Ozanam, *Cinquième siècle*, I, 16–17, 69–70.

20. Ozanam's letters are full of self-reproaches of this kind. The examples mentioned above recur especially in his letters to Lyons in the years 1831–32. See *Lettres de Ozanam*, I, 40 et passim. Even after Ozanam's health broke in 1846 and he was ordered to rest for a year, his conscience permitted him little leisure; after several years of poor health, he died at the age of 40.

21. See "Les dangers de Rome et ses espérances," *Le Correspondant*, XXI (Feb. 10, 1848), 412–35. The phrase *passons aux barbares* appeared on p. 435.

22. On the socialists, see Ozanam's "Origines du socialisme," *Mélanges*, in *Œuvres complètes*, VII (Paris, 1859), 185–250.

23. Ozanam, *Cinquième siècle*, I, 283, 343; II, 192, 226, 232; *Civilisation chrétienne*, 305–308.

24. Ozanam, *Cinquième siècle*, II, 141–43; *Des sources poétiques de la "Divine Comédie,"* V (2nd ed.; Paris, 1859), 353; *Les poètes franciscains en Italie au treizième siècle*, in *Œuvres complètes*, V (3rd ed.; Paris, 1859), 39; *Civilisation chrétienne*, 15–16.

25. Frédéric Ozanam, *Poètes franciscains en Italie au treizième siècle*, in *Œuvres complètes*, V (2nd ed.; Paris, 1859).

26. Frédéric Ozanam, "Un pèlerinage au pays de Cid," in *Œuvres complètes*, VII (Paris, 1859), 16–19, 25, 50.

27. Ozanam, *Cinquième siècle*, II, 202–206.

28. Ozanam, *Poètes franciscains*, 5, 228.

29. Ozanam, *Dante et la philosophie catholique au treizième siècle*, in *Œuvres complètes*, VI (4th ed.; Paris, 1859), 324 ff.; 339 ff.

CHAPTER 5

1. Ernest Renan, *La réforme intellectuelle et morale*, in *Œuvres complètes*, Vol. I (Paris, 1947), 334–35.

2. Ernest Renan, "Les sciences de la nature et les sciences historiques: Lettre à M. Marcellin Berthelot," *Dialogues et fragments philosophiques* (Paris, 1886), 153–54.

3. Philippe Van Tieghem, *Renan* (Paris, 1848), 89; Jean Pommier, *Renan d'après des documents inédits* (Paris, 1923), 154 and n. 1. According to Adrien Dansette—in his *Histoire religieuse de la France contemporaine* (Paris, 1943), I, 426—100,000 copies were sold in two years.

4. Ernest Renan, *Cahiers de jeunesse, 1845–1846* (2nd ed.; Paris, 1906), I, 120–21. For Renan's comments on Celtic folklore, see his *Essais de morale et critique* (2nd ed.; Paris, 1860), xviii–xix and the essay "La poésie des races celtiques," 375–456.

5. Ernest Renan, *Vie de Jésus* (5th ed.; Paris, 1863), Vol. I of *Histoire des origines du Christianisme*, lii–liii.

6. Ibid., xxii.

7. Ibid., xlviii.

8. Ibid., 448.

9. Jules Michelet, *Histoire romaine* (3rd ed.; Paris, 1843), I, 6.

10. Edgar Quinet, *La création* (3rd ed.), in *Œuvres complètes*, XXI–XXII (Paris, n.d.), I, 318–23.

11. Edgar Quinet, *L'esprit nouveau* (4th ed.), in *Œuvres complètes*, XXIII (Paris, 1880), 151.

12. Ibid., 150.

13. Ibid., 153–158.

14. Ibid., 151–52.

15. Ibid., 162–65.

16. Ibid., 160–62.

17. Ibid., 250–59.

18. Quinet, *La création*, I, 253–54.

19. Quinet, *L'esprit nouveau*, 242.

20. Ibid., 24 passim, 51, 79, 85–88.

21. Gabriel Monod, "Introduction: Du progrès des études historiques en France depuis le XVIᵉ siècle," *Revue historique*, I (1876), 26.

22. Louis Halphen, *L'histoire en France depuis cent ans* (Paris, 1914), 143. The phrase *reign of criticism* is the title of chap. 6.

23. For a pedagogical statement of these characteristics, see Charles Victor Langlois' and Charles Seignobos' *Introduction aux études historiques* (Paris, 1898).

24. See Francis Gourvil, *Théodore-Claude-Henri Hersart de La Villemarqué (1815–1895) et le "Barzaz-Breiz"* (Rennes, 1959), 179 et passim, 210–11.

25. Julien Tiersot, *La chanson populaire et les écrivains romantiques* (Paris, 1931), 320–22.

26. Xavier Charmes, ed., *Le Comité des travaux historiques et scientifiques, Actes officiels, 1833–1885*, Vol. II (Paris, 1886), 157–58.

27. On the contributions of this generation, see Richard M. Dorson's Foreword to *Folktales of France*, ed. Geneviève Massignon (Chicago, 1968), x–xxxvi.

28. Gaston Paris, "De l'étude de la poésie populaire en France," *Mélusine*, I (1878), 2.

29. Th. Puymaigre, *Le folklore* (Paris, 1885), 9–10.

30. Antony Dessaix, *Légendes et traditions populaires de la Haute-Savoie* (Annecy, 1875), v–vi.

31. Arnold Van Gennep, *Le folklore* (Paris, 1924), 32; see also his introduction to his *Manuel de folklore français contemporain*, Vol. I (Paris, 1943). In practice, however, Van Gennep himself was far from a-historical. See Giuseppe Cocchiara, *Storia del folklore*, chap. 27.

32. Damase Arbaud, *Chants populaires de Provence* (Aix, 1862), ix.

CHAPTER 6

1. P. Saintyves [E. Nourry], *Manuel de folklore* (Paris, 1936), 140.

2. Théodore Hersart de La Villemarqué, *La légende celtique en Irelande, en Cambrie et en Bretagne* (New ed.; Paris and Saint Brieuc, n.d.), xiv–xv. "The example of Ozanam has borne fruit and found imitators. Those who read the book that I offer to the public will see there a reflection of the light abundantly cast on popular legend by him: however pale it may be, this reflection comes from him, and must go back to him as a homage" (p. xv).

3. Théodore Hersart de La Villemarqué, *Barzas-Breiz* (Paris, 1839), I, vi. François-Adolphe Loève-Veimars, editor of *Ballades, Légendes et chants populaires de l'Angleterre et de l'Ecosse* (Paris, 1825) expressed similar admiration for Thierry's work, observing that "recent works have made us realize what great value for the history of a nation and for the knowledge of a people's *mœurs* national romances, legends, and popular traditions can become." He went on to acknowledge his use of "some of the documents so skillfully elaborated by M. Thierry in his great historical work on the conquest of England."

4. Emile Souvestre, *Le foyer breton, contes et récits populaires* (New ed.; Paris, 1853), I, 9 ff.

5. Emile Souvestre, *Causeries historiques et littéraires* (Paris, 1854), I, 13.

6. Narcisse Quellien, *Chansons et danses des Bretons* (Paris, 1889), 4. In 1880 Quellien was charged by the Ministry of Public Instruction to make the first thorough collection of the melodies and words of Breton folk songs.

7. On philosophy of history, see Henri Tronchon, *Romantisme et préromantisme* (Paris, 1930), 23–27. See the same book, 1–22, for a discussion of the "*crise d'âmes.*" Herbert James Hunt gives an authoritative account of the new flowering of epic poetry in his book *The Epic in Nineteenth-Century France: A Study in Heroic and Humanitarian Poetry from "Les Martyrs" to "Les Siècles morts"* (Oxford, 1941). Léon Cellier goes over much of the same

material, but adds enough of the new to make his *L'épopée romantique* (Paris, 1954) worth consulting.

8. Not that the historians were consistently optimistic. Their discouragement during the last years of the July Monarchy, after the Revolution of 1848, and during the Second Empire has already been discussed. One should also note the pessimism of Michelet in his last years, especially after 1870. Still, the men figuring in this study were—during most of their lives and with regard to most of history—believers in a general historical progress. For an admirable study of pessimism in French thought, see Koenraad W. Swart, *The Sense of Decadence in Nineteenth-Century France* (The Hague, 1964), esp. chapters 3–5.

9. See Laisnel de La Salle, *Croyances et légendes du centre de la France* (Paris, 1875), xviii–xix. This writer was particularly embittered about the railroad and "the demon of skepticism."

10. See Paul Sébillot, "L'imagerie populaire," *Revue des traditions populaires*, III (June 1889), esp. p. 306.

11. Victor Brunet, *Contes populaires du Bocage*, 133, cited by Martial Byron, "Sobriquets et superstitions militaires," *Revue des traditions populaires*, III (January 1888), 53.

12. Arnaldo Momigliano, *Studies in Historiography* (New York, 1966), 234.

Index